Becoming Pro-Palestinian

Becoming Pro-Palestinian:

Testimonies from the Global Solidarity Movement

Edited by Rosemary Sayigh

I.B. TAURIS

LONDON • NEW YORK • OXFORD • NEW DELHI • SYDNEY

I.B. TAURIS
Bloomsbury Publishing Plc
50 Bedford Square, London, WC1B 3DP, UK
1385 Broadway, New York, NY 10018, USA

BLOOMSBURY, I.B. TAURIS and the I.B. Tauris logo are trademarks
of Bloomsbury Publishing Plc

First published in Great Britain 2024

Cover design by Adriana Brioso
Cover image © The Canadian Press / Alamy Stock Photo

A catalogue record for this book is available from the British Library.

A catalog record for this book is available from the Library of Congress.

ISBN: HB: 978-0-7556-9208-8
        PB: 978-0-7556-9209-5
        ePDF: 978-0-7556-9210-1
        eBook: 978-0-7556-9211-8

Typeset by RefineCatch Limited, Bungay, Suffolk
Printed and bound in Great Britain

To find out more about our authors and books visit www.bloomsbury.com
and sign up for our newsletters.

Contents

EUROPE

AUSTRALIA, NEW ZEALAND

LATIN AMERICA

Acknowledgements

I wish first to thank all the contributors to this book. They wrote without remuneration or any hope of recompense other than receiving an eventual copy. I hope they will find reading these testimonies as rewarding as I have.

I would like to give special thanks to Raja Khalidi and Francesca Albinese, who encouraged me to embark on the project, and helped me find writers. Also to Dr Aseel Sawalha, who put me in touch with writers in Latin America where I had no contacts.

Preface

I learned the word "Sumud" from Raja Shehadeh's eloquent account of life in occupied Palestine. It provided a framework for understanding what I had seen years earlier in visits to Palestinian villages under military occupation, a framework for appreciating the dignity and dedication of people who could not cross the road to visit friends without first travelling to Haifa to receive authorization from some bureaucrat. The purpose of the cruel regulations was not security but rather humiliation, to convey the message that this is our land, not yours. You are here on sufferance, temporarily. We might decide to remove you to establish a park or a firing range – and when that has been forgotten by the world, though not by us, to establish a new settlement as we proceed to take over the land that was promised to us millennia ago according to our founding lore.

Later, I was privileged to witness first-hand some of the signs of a richer and more complex version of *Sumud* during the first Intifada. With Palestinian and Israeli friends, I was able to travel through the West Bank, to Nablus, where a new society was being built under constant cruel attack, to Hebron where we could watch crazed settlers carry out their depredations with impunity while the IDF defended them from retaliation. We were able to find our way over back roads with the assistance of al-Haq to break military curfew to enter villages that had been smashed by Israeli violence, and to visit a hospital in Ramallah where the entire staff had been forced to flee from Israeli threats but the patients, victims of IDF and settler violence, remained defiant and even optimistic: we will not be removed, we will emerge victorious. And much more. And throughout, we could observe the incredible courage and persistence of people determined not only to remain where they belonged but also to carry out a social revolution and create a new and better society.

In later years, I was able to see much the same in Gaza, attending an international conference sandwiched between two of Israel's vicious assaults on its defenceless shooting range. And in the miserable refugee camps in Lebanon, where the same spirit prevails under awful conditions.

It is, truly, an inspiration.

Israel, the Palestinians, and the United States have formed a structure unique in modern history. This structure took shape in its current form in 1967, when Israel performed a major service to US power, and US-Israeli relations radically changed. A war was then underway between two major forces in the Arab world, radical Islam based in Saudi Arabia and secular nationalism with its home in Nasser's Egypt. Like Britain before it, the US has tended to support radical Islam, regarding secular nationalism as a greater threat to imperial domination. Israel smashed secular nationalism, delivering a major victory to radical Islam. It at once became a close US ally, a base for US power in the Middle East along with Saudi Arabia and Iran, then under the brutal rule of the Shah. These three "pillars" of imperial power were technically at war with one another, but under the surface were allies, a relationship that became very clear when the Shah was overthrown and the record was revealed.

As far back as 1948, the US military was impressed with Israeli military power and regarded Israel as a potential base for US power. Relations however remained limited. All changed in 1967, rapidly and dramatically.

The intellectual world and information system tend to hew closely to official state policy. Accordingly, this sharp turn in US policy was reflected very quickly in the world of opinion-making and public reactions. Previously, Israel had been largely a matter of indifference, even in the Jewish community. In 1967, all changed. It became a Holy State. Questioning of its magnificence was vilified and often just suppressed.

The Holocaust suddenly became a huge issue. Holocaust museums and courses sprang up everywhere. That had not been true in the late '40s, when it would have been possible to rescue survivors. Many remained in Nazi camps that had hardly changed apart from an end to literal extermination, as official US government investigations revealed. It is hardly in doubt that they would have welcomed the chance to go to the one country that had been untouched by the war, and was rich and flourishing. That was not to be. They were still barred by the racist 1924 immigration laws, directed mostly against Jews and Italians, which sent many Jews to extermination camps. Apart from some anti-Zionist groups, the Jewish community did not press for their exemption from these laws. They were to be sent to Palestine; not wanted in the US.

In the years following the '67 war, the victors faced a choice. It soon became quite clear that peace with the Arab states was achievable with some arrangement for Palestinian self-determination in the occupied territories, perhaps the two-state solution called for in UN Security Council resolutions backed by the major Arab states and vetoed by the US – and pretty much vetoed from history, as is the norm when the US stands apart from the world. Another option was rejection of security in favour of settlement and annexation in violation of orders of the Security Council and the World Court.

The latter option was adopted, setting the stage for what has followed: harsh and brutal takeover of the occupied territories, a sharp shift to the right in Israeli public opinion, greater reliance on the US for protection, and gradual estrangement from liberal opinion worldwide – a fact that has been recognized for some time by Israeli strategic analysts and that has considerable significance in the emerging world order. A natural development is closer association with the most reactionary elements of global society.

One illustration is the Abraham Accords, Trump's sole diplomatic achievement. Celebrated in the US, the Accords formalize what had previously been tacit: an alliance of the most brutal and oppressive states of the Middle East-North Africa region, closely linked to some of most extreme of them, Saudi Arabia and Egypt, now under the rule of the harshest dictatorship of its ugly history. Elsewhere Israel is aligning more closely with reactionary regimes worldwide. One is Orban's "illiberal democracy" in Hungary, a racist Christian nationalist regime that has suppressed media, universities, and independent thought. India is a natural partner under the Modi regime that is dismantling Indian secular democracy and instituting a racist Hindu ethnocracy. The convoluted India-Israel relation goes back many years, but is now rapidly solidifying as Modi's project progresses.

One of the most striking examples is Myanmar. The media harshly condemn Russia and other authoritarian states for maintaining relations with the military dictatorship despite its horrendous crimes.[1] They scrupulously avoid Israel's central role in expediting these crimes for many years by constructing and arming the dictatorship's military machine and intelligence system, one of many services to Israel's crimes.[2]

What is plainly happening cannot be suppressed forever. Some elements of it are leaking through, even in mainstream discussion. Public opinion in the US has shifted substantially. After 1967, books critical of Israel policies were banned, meetings broken up, torrents of vilification flowed, police protection was necessary for talks on Israel-Palestine, and much more. Israel was untouchable even through the worst crimes, like the murderous 1982 invasion of Lebanon and other major crimes in Lebanon that followed.

That has changed dramatically, particularly since Operation Cast Lead in 2008–9. Those crimes broke the dam. They were too much to accept. By now support for Palestinian rights is very broad, particularly among the young, including American Jews. The political base for support for Israel used to be the liberal core of the Democratic Party. Now it has shifted to the far right of the Republican Party: Evangelical Christians, the security establishment, ultranationalist elements generally. The Israel lobby has been working overtime to try to slow the erosion of support among Democrats, even backing far-right Republicans to block liberal Democrats who do not show sufficient loyalty to Israel. Cracks in the Democratic Party have reached as far as resolutions calling on banning US aid to Israel, adhering to US law that bans aid to military forces engaged in systematic human rights violations. Such moves were unthinkable a few years ago.

There are major changes underway in the structure of global order. How they will develop is uncertain, but Israel's status will not remain untouched.

Meanwhile, as the essays collected here reveal with great clarity, the Samidin and their supporters continue their struggles in new ways, determined, confident that in the end Palestinians will win the rights they have long deserved.

Noam Chomsky

---

[1] https://www.nytimes.com/2022/10/26/world/asia/russia-myanmar-junta.html

[2] https://www.haaretz.com/israel-news/2022-10-06/ty-article-magazine/.highlight/israel-saw-brutal-myanmar-regimes-as-a-business-opportunity-documents-reveal/00000183-adbd-d5eb-a3af-fdbfb0c30000?utm_source=mailchimp&utm_medium=Content&utm_campaign=daily-brief&utm_content=9b3663197e

Foreword

When Israel attacked Gaza in May 2021, world public opinion reacted with pro-Palestinian demonstrations on a scale not witnessed before. Starting on May 9, protests erupted in Amman, Istanbul, Cape Town, Stockholm, Gothenburg, Paris, Chicago, Milwaukee, Madrid, Brussels, Nairobi, Tokyo, Berlin, and in various cities in India, the UK, USA, Canada, and Kyrgistan. On May 22 an estimated 180,000 people demonstrated for Palestine in Hyde Park, London, probably the largest demonstration for Palestine in British history. Demonstrations continued until the war against Gaza ended in a cease-fire on August 7.

The global spread and scale of support for Palestinians amazed me. As someone who had supported the Palestinians since the 1950s, and contested the pro-Israeli bias of mainstream US/European media, I strove to understand what historic changes or activist engagements had raised support for the Palestinians from barely above zero in 1948, when the state of Israel was established, to a level where it has become a factor that Israel has to reckon with. To help explain this shift, this book gathers the personal perspectives of around forty individuals of different nationalities who "became pro-Palestinian" through engagement with the Palestinian people, whether as scholars, health workers, film-makers, lawyers, NGO personnel, advocates, journalists, witnesses, and dockworkers such as those who, in June 2021, refused to unload an Israeli cargo at the US port of Oakland.[1]

This Foreword's main aim is to thank the contributors to this book who wrote in generous response to an invitation without financial recompense and, further, to give readers some description of their backgrounds, skills, and connection to Palestine and Palestinians. Many are friends made through my long life spent researching and writing about Palestinians: Dr Swee Chai Ang, Dr Philomena McKenna, and Dr Chris Giannou have all worked with Palestinian medical services in Lebanon.[2] David McDowall was the first person to publish a report on the Palestinians with the Minority Rights Group, London [1987]. Luisa Morgantini is former Vice President of the EU Parliament [1999–2009], founder of AssopacePalestina Italy, and lifetime supporter of human and Palestinian rights. Birgitte Rahbek is a cultural sociologist, one of the earliest to write reports about Palestinians in Lebanon. Bertus Hendrix and Elisabetta Donnini were members of an early European solidarity group. Klaudia Wieser is an activist and researcher based in Vienna, who is currently finishing her Ph.D. thesis on "Epistemologies of Liberation: Palestinian affairs in Revolutionary Beirut". Helga

---

[1] See *Law for Palestine*, June 5, 2021.
[2] Swee Chai Ang [1989] *From Beirut to Jerusalem*, first published by Grafton Books & Times Books International, republished by The Other Press, Kuala Lumpur, 2002. Chris Giannou [1991] *Besieged: A Doctor's Story of Life and Death in Beirut*, Ithaca, Olive Branch Press.

Baumgarten is a German academic who taught for many years at Birzeit University. She has been living with her husband Mustafa al-Kurd, Palestinian composer, songwriter, and singer of political songs, in Mustafa's hometown Jerusalem since 1985.

Among social scientists, anthropologists are those most experienced in crossing cultural barriers and interpreting "the Other", of whom refugees and migrants are often viewed as an extreme example. Hence the inclusion in this volume of Lori Allen, Helena Manfrinato, and Hugo Benvenides. Lori Allen first became interested in the Palestinian issue as a student, writing her first book about human rights in Palestine, while her latest book about investigative commissions sent to Palestine over the past century is an acute critique of liberalism and international law.[3] Helena Manfrinato was engaged at the time of writing for this volume in studying relations between Palestinian refugees from Syria and poor Brazilians living together in cheap housing in Sao Paolo. Hugo Benvenides from Ecuador was sensitized to the Palestinian struggle through viewing "Julia" as a young child, a film about the Nazi Holocaust that resonated with his own experience as a child of poor immigrants to the US.

Anni Kanafani is well-known for the model kindergartens she has established in Palestinian camps in Lebanon in memory of her husband Ghassan Kanafani, assassinated by the Mossad in 1972. Penny Johnson is a human rights activist living in the West Bank, author of a charming book about Palestine's animals.[4] Toine van Teeffelen is a Dutch author and activist also living in the West Bank, from where he writes a regular "Column from Bethlehem".

Two of the contributors are lawyers: Dmitri Lascaris, lawyer, journalist, and political activist, has represented numerous activists for Palestine in Canada; Lex Takkenberg, a legal expert from the Netherlands, has occupied several posts within UNRWA since 1985, authored books on international law and the refugees,[5] and is now Senior Advisor with the Arab Renaissance for Democracy and Development [ARDD].

Rafi Silver once served with the Israeli army but left it to become a Canadian citizen; he writes from inside knowledge of how the IDF conducts the occupation. Bianca Marcossi is one member of a Jewish anti-Zionist collective in Brazil that demonstrates against the Israeli embassy and tries to "create a different kind of Jewishness".

As a fellow sufferer from British imperialism, India contains many supporters of the Palestinian struggle, in spite of prime minister Modi's militant Hinduism that has induced him to ally India with Israel. Vijay Prashad, a contributor to this book, is editor of the Tri-Continental Institute for Social Research and author of *The Darker Nations* [The New Press 2022]. Another Indian contributor, M. H. Ilias, is Dean of Social Sciences at the Mahatma Gandhi University, Kottayata, Kerala. Na'eem Jeenah, Surayya Dadoo, and Farid Esack[6] write from South Africa, clearly demonstrating along with

[3] Lori Allen, *A History of False Hope: Investigative Commissions in Palestine*, Stanford University Press, 2020.
[4] Penny Johnson, *Companions in Conflict: Animals in Occupied Palestine*, Melville House, Brooklyn, NY, 2019.
[5] Including with Francesca Albinese, *Palestinian Refugees in International Law*, Oxford University Press, 2020.
[6] Farid Esack famously wrote a letter "to my dear Palestinian brothers and sisters" on the Separation Wall: see Arjan El Fassed, *The Electronic Intifada*, April 20, 2009.

Zahid Rajan from Kenya and Ryantori from Indonesia that organized support for the Palestinian struggle reaches far beyond Europe. Australia has an eminent pro-Palestinian, Stuart Rees, professor emeritus at Sydney University, and founder of the Sydney Peace Foundation. Janfrie Wakim is an educator/activist in New Zealand who helped form the Palestine Human Rights Campaign [PHRC], which invites pro-Palestinian speakers to Wellington and organizes protests at Israeli events. Dr Swee Chai Ang, mentioned earlier as a medical doctor working for Palestinians, comes from Singapore. Japan was an early source of charity directed to Palestinian orphans through film-maker Ryuichi Hirokawa, and Japan is represented here by two distinguished scholars: Eisuke Naramoto, who teaches the modern history of the Middle East at Hosei and Dokkyo universities, and Hiroyuki Suzuki of Tokyo University, who did his Ph.D. on Palestinian political activities under Israeli rule.

Activists for Palestinian rights in the Middle East are represented here by Hadi Borhani, a professor at Tehran University and author of a critical study of western academic books on this region.[7] Representing Jews who support the Palestinians I thank two outstanding Israeli contributors: Ilan Pappe, director of the Centre for Palestine Studies at the University of Exeter, and Amira Hass, who reports on the Occupied West Bank for the Israeli newspaper *Haaretz*. Roger Heacock taught history and politics at Birzeit University until forced to leave Palestine by the Israeli Occupation through denial of a residence permit.[8] Sanem Ozturk is a Turkish sociologist/activist who was first influenced as a young child watching a TV news broadcast of Israeli violence in Palestine.

Among the contributors are several artists and film-makers: Jane Frere, an artist living in Scotland, created an installation called "Return of the Soul", hung with tiny wax figures representing Palestinians returning to Palestine.[9] Leena Saraste, Finnish photographer, visited Lebanon several times to take photos of people in the camps, and published a photo book "*For Palestine*".[10] Natalia Revale is an Argentinian artist who hangs her Palestinian posters in public places. Mats Grorud in his film *The Tower*, tells the stories of three generations of Palestinian refugees, introducing the Palestinian actor Muhammad Bakri. Monica Maurer made documentaries about the PLO in Lebanon and is now a film archivist in Berlin. Naomi Wallace's "The Fever Chart" is a trilogy of plays about the absurdity and violence of colonialism, and tells how she has suffered silencing in the US.

[7] Seyed Hadi Borhani, *Textbooks on Israel-Palestine: The Politics of Education and Knowledge*, London, I. B. Tauris, 2020.
[8] In March 2022, the Israeli Ministry of Defence imposed new limits on foreign teachers at Palestinian universities, governing who can be employed and what they can teach. *Middle East Eye*, March 8, 2022.
[9] "Return of the Soul" comprised more than 7,000 wax figures made by Palestinians whose families were forced to flee in the Nakba of 1948. Accompanying the figures were scrolls of personal handwritten testimonies, and audio and video presentations. The installation, commemorating the 60th anniversary of the Nakba in 2008, was first shown at Al Hoash in East Jerusalem, Edinburgh, Beirut, and Amman: Jane Frere, personal communication, May 5, 2023.
[10] Published in English by Zed Books, London, 1985.

Censorship is a constant factor when speaking or publishing on the Palestinians. Fear of German government retribution caused the withdrawal of a valuable contribution to this book. An American teacher withdrew her contribution for fear it might endanger her "Teach Palestine Project", aimed at increasing the coverage of Palestine in American school books. The silencing of Palestinian voices occurs in the many countries that have accepted the International Holocaust Remembrance Alliance [IHRA] definition of antisemitism as including criticism of Israel.

My own becoming pro-Palestinian followed a strange inversion. On leaving university, counting myself a socialist, I applied to join an Israeli kibbutz. I was not accepted and went instead to teach in Iraq. There, Iraqi friends corrected my ideas about a "progressive Israel", pointing to that country's ties to imperialist Britain and its expulsion of Palestine's indigenous population. The man I eventually married, a Palestinian, had been held as a prisoner of war by the Israelis from May 15, 1948, when he refused to flee from Jerusalem. His prison stories were part of our courtship and a re-viewing of my perception of Israel. Listening to the stories of Palestinians in refugee camps in Lebanon was an even more important stage in my historical revision. Every personal journey is unique, but as the personal testimonies for this book show, mine was far from exceptional.

MIDDLE EAST

Hadi Borhani

University teacher/author, Iran

I doubt that my fascination with the Israel-Palestine question can be an accident. I began life the same day that Israel completed its occupation of historic Palestine! I learnt this from my ID card, where June 10 1967 is registered as my birth date. Though I have no recollection of that day in the 1960s, I do remember my childhood in the 1970s when I started to read everything available about this question, mostly in newspapers. I was forbidden, then, to read them as my school grades began to decline due to this obsession. The only way to follow this "prohibited undertaking" was by secretly buying the cheap newspapers I could afford – like *Ayandegan* or *Rastakhiz*, and smuggling them into an isolated corner where I could read them far from my parents' watchful eyes.

For a long time, I managed to keep an extensive collection of news and articles about Palestine, Palestinians, and their struggle to liberate their homeland cut from those newspapers, but I have sadly lost them in a recent change of residence. Years after that loss, I still feel its pain, and am still hopeful to find them somewhere. If not, I have access to some of them by memory, for example, one about a guerrilla operation led by a Palestinian woman, Dalal Mughrabi. No way to lose the image of Dalal when she was killed by Israeli forces, or the image of Yasir Arafat on the paper's first page, showing the V-sign with his fingers.

It was during those days, in the '70s, that Iran began its transformation from a pro-Western monarchy to a pro-Palestinian republic. The very first event of that revolution took place only a few metres away from my primary school, Daryush, in Qom.

But it was my work in the Ministry of Foreign Affairs, much later in my life, that offered me the first opportunity to engage intellectually with the Israel-Palestine question. Early in my career at the ministry, I saw how everything that happens in the Middle East is affected by the Palestine question. Above all, what engaged me to the point of obsession was a perplexing paradox: how Western countries, the same countries that established the widest and most influential civilization in history in all its post-Renaissance magnificence – its modern education, knowledge, democracy, rule of law, and human rights in particular – could at the same time support such injustice in Palestine – a fundamental source of so much violence and misery in the Middle East.

The first chance to experience this issue directly was provided when I participated in the 40th Graduate Study Programme (GSP) of the United Nations Office in Geneva in 2002. Many young college graduates attended this programme, mostly from Western countries. The participants had to prepare a report on the main international issues, including human rights, as their assignment in the course. This was an opportunity to raise the Israel-Palestine question. I wrote a statement about the racist aspect of Zionism, in line with the NGOs' position in the Durban Conference to Combat Racism (2001), and followed the drafting procedure from the original version on human rights issues up to the level presented to the plenary session. The statement found its way finally into the concluding report of the programme, but the way it was treated there showed how different the West is when it comes to Israel from what I expected.

The same impression struck me when I made a contribution to the Fifth Annual Course on Arms Control and National Security in the Geneva Centre for Security Policy (2003). Several lecturers came to this course to encourage the participants, all of them from Arab countries and Iran, to support disarmament in the Middle East. The comments I made in the closing session about the dangers of such a unilateral policy in the absence of a similar policy in Israel was treated as if I was committing an unforgiveable sin. I am not sure if this is related to the fact that, belying all promises, I never received the course certificate. But for sure this was another event that made me aware how a critical view of Israel would be treated in the West.

These experiences, and similar ones such as at the International Annual Course of the United Nations University in Tokyo (2006), convinced me that conducting research on this topic, and contributing to a dialogue with Western societies about this anomaly, might be the best contribution I could make to a better relationship between the West and the Middle East.

One of several attempts I made to apply for a Ph.D. programme was accepted by the National University of Ireland, Galway (NUIG). I put forward an original proposal to conduct a comparative investigation into EU human rights policy towards certain Middle Eastern countries including Iran and Israel, to demonstrate how the West, the EU in this case, ignores its own values when it comes to Israel.

My path to further study didn't go according to expectation, and I had to sacrifice a lot to save my studies, including my job in the ministry. However, I learned one significant lesson while struggling with my Ph.D. project: the Western bias towards Israel is not limited to governments and politicians. Western knowledge, the most respected part of Western civilization to my mind, is corrupted as well. This became obvious when I consulted dominant textbooks in Western academia on the Israel-Palestine question, since I considered these to be the most significant subject for investigation regarding Western pro-Israeli bias. This realization coincided with my first encounter with Professor Ilan Pappé, who came to Dublin to speak about the Israeli invasion of Gaza in 2008–9. A link to this talk – which took place in Trinity College, Dublin – had been sent by Tommy Donnellan, a well-known pro-Palestinian activist in Galway on February 16 2009. I received it at night when I was alone in the quiet of the Ph.D. room at NUIG. I remained at my desk on campus till midnight to watch the video twice, and forwarded it to all my English-speaking contacts. This email provided me with an unprecedented moment because of the novel feeling I experienced, "I can love an Israeli, thank God!"

The days after this encounter were spent reading about this Israeli scholar and his studies on the Palestine question. In this process, I found his email address, enabling me to contact him, explain my ideas about my Ph.D. project, and ask for his supervision. His welcoming reply allowed me to conduct the project and become the first Iranian to receive a Ph.D. from the European Centre for Palestine Studies.

Professor Haim Bresheeth, a member of the examination board, suggested transforming the Ph.D. dissertation into a publishable monograph. Follow Haim's proposal, the first step was to communicate with those historians whom I had dared to analyze. My analysis in the dissertation not only criticized their historiography, but also scrutinized their background to assess their capacity to produce an unbiased history of the Israel-Palestine question. I sent a letter to the six historians I was able to contact. It explained briefly what I had done in my dissertation, and expressed my intention to convert the thesis into a book. I also requested any comment they might have about the work. I received four replies; the most encouraging came from Professor Tessler, a former president of the Association for Israel Studies. He described my work as a "very solid and useful contribution". Other replies were welcoming, polite, and professional.

Although I lost school grades, a job, and a course certificate, my engagement with Palestine had a happy ending, leading to further studies, a doctoral degree from the top university of Exeter, the chance to work with a world class scholar as my supervisor, and to have my dissertation published by I. B. Tauris, a first class publisher in the field. Moreover, the praise that the book has received from renowned scholars, some of them giants of the field, is a lifelong source of pride. This has been completed, just recently, by a national award, as the best book in the field of History, given by the 13th National Festival on Research and Technology.

I should like to end by acknowledging that many scholars, particularly Jews who have taken a critical stand towards Israel, have lost a lot from such an engagement. For them, this struggle has not only been against the "Other" but against their own friends and families. Because of this incredible sacrifice, I dedicated my award to all the wonderful free Jews, including my supervisor, who chose, against all odds, to tell the truth about the Israel-Palestine question.

Amira Hass

Journalist, Al-Bireh, Occupied Palestinian West Bank

'When did 'Israeli Landscape' Become for Me 'Palestinian Landscape'?[1]

It's tempting to say that I became pro-Palestinian at around the age of two, when my parents took me to a demonstration in Jerusalem protesting the Military Rule, which from 1948 until 1966 Israel imposed on the decimated Palestinian population, mourning its dead, traumatized by the expulsions and the loss of their homeland. I know I was taken to many such demonstrations but my infant memory did not hold on to them. As a two-year-old I could not grasp the meaning of Military Rule: absolute domination of people and their space, draconian restrictions of freedom of movement and the use of security excuses to grab and rob more and more land. But it is highly likely that at those non-registered protests I began to draw the line that made me separate "them" from "us". Emotion preceded facts, knowledge, analysis, and theory by many years. "They" included the regime, the General Security Service, the police, and policemen, people booing from the sidelines and all those who did not march with us. "We" were everyone whom the regime – any regime - tortures and oppresses, exploits and persecutes, and all those who oppose it. The demonstrations to which I was taken in my earlier years embodied the hope, no, the nearly-religious faith that injustice is doomed to end. In their worst nightmares, my communist parents could not have imagined that in thousands of texts since the 1990s to this day I would be reporting, describing, and analyzing another sophisticated, evil incarnation of that "Military Rule" policy: In the past three decades Israel, its army and Security Service – under the guise of what the world calls a peace process – continued and still continue to fragment and crush the remaining Palestinian territory (22% of historic Palestine), rob most of its lands with security and bureaucratic excuses, terrorize its indigenous inhabitants, kill them, restrict their freedom of movement, detain and arrest thousands of them every year, crowd them into disconnected enclaves, and enjoy impunity. The political and dissident environment into which I was born makes the question "how and why I became pro-Palestinian" irrelevant, by emphasizing "became". Even before they met,

---

[1]   Translated from the Hebrew by Tal Haran.

my parents had each refused the Jewish Agency's offer to settle in homes of Palestinian families who had been expelled from Jerusalem. Both immigrated, as refugees, from post-war East Europe to this country in late 1948 and early 1949. Even though they had not yet fully grasped the disastrous enormity of the Nakba they knew they could not live in the home of other refugees. Moreover, back then in 1949–1950, they were still sure that the Palestinian refugees would soon return to their homes. I learnt about this choice of theirs in my first years of elementary school. It was plain knowledge, devoid of any amazement or wonder. A simple fact, at the centre of which stood the absent Palestinians.

It was young, politicized me – at seven or eight – who asked my parents why they, who had never been Zionists, migrated to this country. The question reflected the unavoidable clash of the Zionist ideology that ruled outside, and the upbringing, discourse, and opinions expressed at home. Their response will be addressed below.

Not only the "became" part, the very definition "pro-Palestinian" is not quite adequate in my case. As a socialist leftist by choice (not merely channelled that way from childhood), my identification and my political, intellectual, and emotional support are a priori, and can't be established according to my national and ethnic belonging. The definition "pro-Palestinian" – even within a historical-political context – takes national identity as a frame of reference. Identification and support, like my journalistic writing, do not originate from the fact that Palestinians are Palestinian, but because the founding of the state of which I am a citizen, and my own people, have placed them in a situation of ongoing, structural injustice, still perpetrated to this day.

"Oh, so you love the Palestinians!", conclude especially Palestinian children – but at times even adults – whom I have met (and still meet) during typical circumstances of military domination and abuse: for example, waiting with Palestinian children on a summer night in 2021, near the Betunia checkpoint, for their father who was due to be released from the Ofer prison (built on Betunia lands, west of Ramallah) – he had been arrested for taking part in a Bethlehem demonstration; also in Rafah, southern Gaza Strip, in 2001, in a school to which families had fled after the Israeli army demolished their homes the night before, pretending to search for tunnels; during a three-week curfew in autumn 2001 in my neighborhood in Al-Bireh. And I answer, "I don't know every Palestinian, how can I love them all? That's not the issue. I hate the occupation." Born in a leftist home, my loathing of domination and one group's supremacy over another was and remains physical.

We could say that my first active, conscious expression of this repulsion happened at the age of five. My parents had gone abroad and I was staying for a few weeks with their friends, who – like them – were members of the Israeli Communist Party. They lived on Shmuel Hanavi Street, very close to the Sheikh Jarrah neighborhood where Israel is now – through right-wing associations and with the full approval of its judicial system – expelling and evicting Palestinian families. Jerusalem was then divided between the Jordanian/Palestinian and the Israeli sides, and my hosts lived west of the Mandelboim Gate border crossing. From my hosts' balcony I used to see the Palestinian children playing – back then we only knew them as Arabs. I remember the strange feeling: they were so close and yet untouchable. As if they were actors in a film I watched and I was an actor in a film they watched. Still, for the five-year-old this reality and its strangeness seemed normal. A part of the natural order of things.

One afternoon I was playing with some neighbour girls on the balcony of my hosts – Miriam and Nathan. Miriam came home from work and saw that one of the girls was sitting in the corner, sad, not playing with us. She approached her to find out what had happened and was told by the girl that "Amira does not let me play". Miriam, shocked, didn't even get to ask me why, for I jumped ahead and explained, "Sure I wouldn't let her play. She wanted us to play at killing Arabs." The truth is that I have no idea whether I remember the actual event or remember what I was told about it. Years ago, in my parents' papers, I found Miriam's letter to them in which she excitedly and proudly described that scene. Obviously, long before I became familiar with terms such as Palestine, Nakba, refugees, settler-colonialism, and before I realized the reality they reflect – I was brought up opposing it.

Still, I was living in Jewish-Israeli society. I could not completely escape the Zionist socialization that permeated our elementary school. I sang with the rest of my schoolmates de-sensitizing homeland songs and did not contest the key-term "pioneers".

I read children's stories about "infiltrators", and once came home with some stupid stereotype about Arabs that I had heard in school. One shocked glance from my father made me gather my wits. It is therefore more logical that I should be asked – and ask myself – questions such as: when did mountains, vegetation, ravines stop being "Israeli landscape" for me, and become Palestinian landscape; when did I begin to sense in depth the void that 1948 had created, feel its full weight? When did this begin to be unbearable? And if so, why didn't I emigrate?

The answer to the first two questions is that it was a gradual process – from the end of my elementary school (age thirteen to fourteen), growing stronger during my high school years. And still growing stronger, the more I age. After the 1967 occupation, appalled awareness of the construction going amok in the settler-colonies, and opposition to them became a natural part of our home menu. I was not yet formulating things this way ("void", "Palestinian landscape", "structural violence"), but the weight of that void and the helplessness vis-a-vis the situation became unbearable – the feeling that I did not belong, that I was a stranger in that landscape, I dreamt of leaving (although not only for political reasons). My attempts at leaving and settling abroad failed. I returned – with all that strangeness and alienation.

Then, in 1990, I got to know Gazans as a volunteer for *Kav LaOved* – the workers' hotline, an association working for the rights of Palestinian workers that was just then being founded. Typically, Palestinians from territory occupied in 1967 were (and are) exploited more than Israeli citizens, and the *Histadrut* (an absurd combination of employer and professional labour union) paid them no heed. In 1991, I began to visit Gaza and spend more and more time there, until I finally moved there in 1993. There, of all places, through friends I made in the refugee camps, many of them veteran political detainees and prisoners, and through their parents' memories of their villages and homes that were now gone, of exile, of Israeli massacres over the years, I felt linked to the entire country, a bond I had never felt before.

There is yet another reason for me not to embrace the definition "*pro*-Palestinian" – its binary nature, the assumption that whoever is pro-Palestinian must be *anti* the other people. Against Israel's policy? Sure. As written above. Against the institutions that exploit and settle the land, against the heritage of expulsion and dispossession? Definitely. Against the wars this state has initiated and the economic and bureaucratic warfare it wages? No question. But does anti-Israeli – the counter side of pro-Palestinian – also mean being against the Jewish-Israeli people?

Sociologically I am a part of the Jewish-Israeli people. My language is Hebrew. Emotionally – I am alienated, I feel repulsion, and over the years I have lost any expectation I had of that people, whose positions range from initiating dispossession and expulsion, through enthusiastic support, to apathy and standing aside. But from a political-leftist standpoint, and in my capacity as a journalist I am still motivated (like my friends in the tiny Israeli left) by the duty to act in order to generate change within the society, so that Israeli settler-colonialism will be checked, and a process of fundamental repair begin. How do these feelings live side by side? They do not, but inner contradictions are our daily bread …

This realization necessarily sends me back to the contradiction I discovered as a child between my parents' immigration to this country and the fact that they were not Zionists. Let me state this briefly: the Palestinian analysis of Zionism as a settler-colonialist movement from its onset, many years before the Nakba, proves to be exact time and time again: analysis, description, documentation, but not narrative. I do not use the term narrative because it invites tolerance of a multiplicity of subjective, contradictory "stories", equally correct and incorrect. The point of departure of leftist philosophy of history, as I understand it, is that of the dispossessed, the oppressed, the exploited, and the historical-economic-human phenomena that caused dispossession, exploitation, and change. But any historiographic analysis needs a complement (not a contrary narrative), addition, expansion – in order for us to understand reality better, and thus act to change it.

My completion, put very briefly, is that prior to the rise of Nazism in Europe, most Jews living in the diaspora did not support Zionism and its pretension to be a "liberation movement of the Jewish People". If they wished to emigrate – whether for reasons of ethnic-religious persecution, or economic distress, or both – it was to other countries. Not to Palestine, even when they felt religious longing for and belonging to the Holy Land. Others thought that the solution to ethnic persecution or economic distress was assimilation, cultural autonomy, or social struggle in the countries of their birth, without necessarily realizing that Zionism is an offspring of colonialist, colonizing Europe. Very few knew about the country in question, and much less about its indigenous people. The tens of thousands of Jews living in historic Palestine for generations were no reason for other Jews to move there. The essence of living in a diaspora was natural for the great majority of Jews, and the idea of national Jewish sovereignty did not appeal to them. But "Zionism had a winning card – Hitler", I heard my father say. He meant all those hundreds of thousands, like him and my mother, who survived the Nazi concentration and death camps and ghettos in their homes in the diaspora, and discovered that their family members and friends had been murdered because they were Jews, and then received a clear message from the society in which they had been born and raised, that they were not wanted, nor welcomed back. Expelled from the diaspora, they were looking for another home. Then hundreds of thousands of Jews came to Palestine/Israel from Arab and Muslim countries – as refugees from the antagonism created by founding a Jewish state at the expense of Arabs. This is no excuse nor justification, but a complementary historical explanation to the power and later demographic and political successes of the colonialist Zionist movement.

I fear that I will not get to see in my own lifetime the radical change that will put an end to the injustice that Israel inflicted and still inflicts on Palestinians, but I do persist in my belief that such an end and change will take place. This is no more a pro-Palestinian position than a pro-Jewish-Israeli one: Jewish Israelis should not expect to live well and safely forever as an occupying, dispossessing, and expelling society.

Sanem Ozturk

Sociologist, Turkey

"Activism as Crossing Borders"

Before I start this piece, I just want to put some of my feelings into words. First of all, it's an honour to take part in this beautiful collectivity created by Rosemary Sayigh, from whom I learnt a lot in my journey to become an activist for a free Palestine. And secondly, I had absolutely no idea how difficult and yet refreshing it would be to go back in my personal history and write about my own experiences and feelings. So yes, it will be a personal story rather than a political statement, but I believe that what is personal is political. And I sincerely appreciate this exceptional opportunity.

It is hard to remember exactly when my eyes and ears first encountered "Palestine" – it must have been the early 80s – but I surely remember where it happened: I was sitting on the floor in my aunt's living room, playing with a football set my grandmother had made for me from an old green carpet, wooden pegs, and a little ball. The TV was on, and there was the evening news. There was only one state channel in Turkey back then, and there was no limit to broadcasting very graphic images of violence. I won't describe here what I saw that day, but I remember I dropped my "goalkeeper" and sat in silence for a while.

Obviously, that moment was not when I became an activist, I was only five, or maybe six; but it was clearly a defining moment in my personal journey. A moment when you instinctively realize a direction for yourself, where to proceed to, and where not to go.

Politics was always important in the house I grew up in; it was really fun to grow up there. Leftism, nationalism, anarchism, socialism, religion had a part in all our discussions. I devoured all of them – discussions, arguments, TV panels, books, journals – since I had plans to become a journalist – I'm very glad I didn't become one, especially in Turkey today – and for that I needed all sources of information. But I think I didn't become politically active until I was 14. In fact, I was in high school in the mid '90s and it was impossible to stay away from politics in Turkey back then: the Kurdish issue, human rights violations, deaths, struggles springing out from attacks on the working class, the rise of the women's movement...It was an intensely political era, not only in my personal history, but also in Turkey's. I chose the left path, and stayed there. And in my political formation, people's right of self-determination has always had a central place.

I think that being in the Middle East Technical University in Ankara was a very important step for me. Until university, all I knew about Palestine or Palestinians was from books, political journals, and TV discussions. I had never met a Palestinian. At METU, being an international university, there were students from all around the world. The first day of English preparatory class, I was sitting in a classroom with Alaa, who corrected the lecturer after being introduced as an Israeli student: "No, I am Palestinian." I remember thinking that I had too many questions but very limited English. Today I'm grateful for my limited English, since I had the chance of his friendship before I stormed him with questions about what's going on in his country.

In the years I spent in METU, I had that chance with a lot of Palestinian friends. Studying, running between exams; eating falafel at the Sunshine Café (which opened the first falafel stand in Ankara through the initiative of a Palestinian student from the Business Department); cheering for the Palestinian team at the football tournament during spring festivals; and of course, talking about Palestine, about Turkey, about the whole world, and not only about struggles or politics, but also music, writers, history, people, and much more. Now when I look back, I feel so lucky we were in the same place in the same time.

The same day I got my diploma as a fresh sociologist, I also got my bus ticket to İstanbul. It was an impulsive decision, I had no plan, no idea about what to do next. I had a cousin in İstanbul I could stay with, yes. But that was it. I felt İstanbul was the place I needed to be. It was the heart of everything, including political activism. I was lucky enough to find a very low-paying job without security as a newly graduated sociologist – lucky compared to today's hopeless and precarious younger generations in Turkey. I was actually very happy, since I had a lot of time to meet new friends, read, and explore political circles in İstanbul. It was a time when exploitation had not yet reached the level of absorbing all the time and energy of working people under the slogan of "flexibility". I had my own time after work, I had a monthly bus pass, and I had my books, meetings, and demonstrations.

In 2004, I became a member of the Freedom and Solidarity Party, working directly in the monthly journal *Gelecek* (Future). Not confident enough at the beginning to write pieces, I translated some articles, and did some editing work. However, the team meetings were a school for me. And I was lucky again in working with Erhan Keleşoğlu, an academic (now one of the "peace academics" unjustly dismissed from university because he signed a petition) with a specific focus on Palestine. He had a lot to give, and I tried to absorb as much as I could. His support and that of other friends motivated me to start writing. My first piece was a critique of a new book about Arafat; then one about Naji Al Ali; then an interview with Mustafa Barghouti... I even started writing for other journals, as I kept reading whatever I could about Palestine, from history books to journalists' accounts, the history of Palestine, the history of Israel, politics, human rights and violations, struggles, old and new forms of activism. But I needed meaningful discussions with people who spent time and energy for the Palestinian cause. Once again, I was lucky.

The 2000s was a period when social forums were springing up all over the world. İstanbul hosted some of these meetings. The occupation in Palestine and in Iraq were major issues addressed in almost all the meetings. Personal encounters with people from the region and all over the world helped broaden my perspective, and created a collective energy that would later lead to very different forms of activism, such as Caravan Palestine in 2005. Ideas were being made into substance, which was the very definition of activism for me.

Here, let me share an observation about being a pro-Palestinian activist in Turkey. Most of the time, one is surrounded by two blocks of attitude: either a strong anti-Semitism from the right, or from the left a discourse of '70s nostalgia more related to Turkish revolutionaries than to the Palestinian struggle. And although the word "Palestine" places a smile on the faces of most, a very unique form of open or latent anti-Arabism can be felt from both left and right, especially in the last decade of influx of Syrian refugees. So, I don't know how it looks from the outside, but being a pro-Palestinian activist in Turkey today requires a great deal of debate, debate, and more debate with everyone, including the people with whom you share the same political path most of the time.

And as I mentioned before, Caravan Palestine 2005 was a very significant milestone in my personal history. I was thrilled when my beloved friend Özhan Önder called me: "Sanem, come quick! We have things to do." He – almost singlehandedly – designed and copied all the pamphlets, collaborated with the Chamber of Electrical Engineers to give us an office. It was in that room that we tried to organize the Turkey part of the journey. From Edirne to Antakya, there were a lot of stops for the Caravan, a demonstration to organize in each city, press to be contacted, places to be arranged for accommodation, food to be provided, and much to share. Hundreds of people from all over the world started a journey from Strasbourg to Quds, passing through the Balkans, Turkey, Syria, and Jordan, aimed at turning the eyes of international communities towards the Israeli occupation of Palestine, joining with Palestinians and Israeli activists in their demands for a free Palestine. People came from Italy, USA, Vietnam, Iraq, France, Bosnia, Brazil, Spain, Peru, Turkey, Argentina, Germany, Austria, Greece, Britain, and of course, Palestine. People between the ages of eight and eighty-two. I will never forget the face of the eighty-year-old French lady who had never left France before. And everything was organized with the support of local people, political groups, organizations, and trade unions. At Cilvegözü, I had to leave my companion Özhan in Turkey, and crossed an international border into Syria for the first time in my life.

And what a scene was there! Palestinians were waiting for us at the border, with coffee, music, and *dabkeh*, of course. After the welcoming party, our first destination was Nairab refugee camp near Aleppo for a short stop to refresh. The next stop was Yarmouk, which I visited many times after 2005, and where I met amazing people, and always remembered with a smile until I saw the ruins after the war in Syria. No, in fact, I still remember Yarmouk with a smile.

After our journey through Syria and Jordan, it was time to pass the Israeli-controlled border and meet with Palestinians and Israeli activists in al-Quds. However, this turned out to be impossible. Actually it was an hours-long physical and psychological battle until the Israeli forces threw us into a deserted zone in Jordan, without even a drop of water. We found our way to Madaba, where we were all hosted by a church, made a press conference, and then returned to Syria and then to Turkey. When I look back, even though we were not able to finish our journey as we wished, what we accomplished on the way through each other's company was not less valuable.

Two years after graduation, I had the urge to continue academic life, and started my masters in sociology at Mimar Sinan Fine Arts University in İstanbul. The Internet was emerging and spreading globally. My initial intention was to study this exceptional new public sphere, yet I felt a bit lost and confused about my focus. Meral Özbek, my advisor at the university, lit the first candle in my mind. Obviously The Internet, as a trans-border tool and public space, had a very specific role in Palestinians' daily lives, not only as a tool for communication and information, but also as a space to archive collective memory, spread the word in political forums, organize campaigns, find long-lost family members, reach people and places never reached before... it could also function as a sphere for income resources for families restricted by the borders of camps and countries. With this scope, I decided to start with the camps in Lebanon.

A land of many contradictions, Lebanon welcomed me even though, as usual, I didn't have any plans. I took my time there. From Tripoli to Saida, I tried to visit as many camps as possible, meet and talk with as many people as possible, though I didn't know a single word of Arabic. I had to wait until 2013 to start learning; I am still a beginner, but getting better thanks to Syrian and Palestinian women I have been working with for the last six years. In all my encounters in Lebanon, I had an amazing and very patient companion, Ara Seferian, who generously devoted his time and energy to me. Thanks to him, I also had the chance to be a resident in the Armenian district of Bourj Hammoud in Beirut. Without his help and support, and that of all those people who contributed their precious time to teaching me, I wouldn't have stood a chance of writing my thesis. What I could do in return, maybe, was to spread their words to others, especially to my students at Marmara University.

For the last six years, I have been working with refugee women in Turkey, most of whom are Syrian, with some Palestinians, since Turkey has become a "host country" (a concept I try to avoid since it inherently implies a hierarchy). Every single day, I learn from them. A couple of years ago, one of them expressed her feelings in this way: "We will go back to our country one day. When we go back, we will always remember you. I hope, actually I know, that we had an impact on you. I know that because I will not go back as the same person. Because we made contact, we changed each other." I think she has a strong point. And I think my activism was and still is being formed by all my encounters. I always believed in the power of "outside", despite the fact that I might find comfort in being "inside". To be clearer, sometimes the borders that define our comfort zone can also define our prison. And my way of activism is all about crossing borders, even within the land where I was born.

I'd like to stop here with a small detail from my journey, it's something I want to share. When we first arrived at Yarmouk camp in Damascus, we were all filthy from the hours-long road trip, hungry, and my sandals were literally split in two. After we were divided into groups and hosted by Palestinian families who fed us delicious meals, we wanted to make a tour of Yarmouk. When I opened the door to put on my sandals, I saw that they had been repaired. While we were eating and resting, Raha, the youngest daughter of the family, who studied literature at the university, noticed that my sandals were damaged and had them sewn at the shoe repair shop. When I think of Yarmouk camp, this is the story that, after years, first comes to mind. When I think of the people I had the chance to meet in Yarmouk and other camps of Syria, Lebanon, and Jordan, I always remember the sincerity with which they opened their doors, tables, and hearts to me. It may sound very personal, but as I said at the beginning, the personal is political.

Ilan Pappe

Scholar/director of the European Centre for Palestinian Studies, University of Exeter, UK; Israel

"Becoming an Ideological Palestinian"

Reaching the end of my seventh decade, I have a vantage point that helps to clarify the journey out of Zionism and the personal repercussions incurred by the substitution of an ideology that was taken for granted by an unconditional commitment to the Palestinian cause. I am glad that today there are many more Israeli Jews who undertook similar journeys (although we are all still a very small minority within the Israeli Jewish society). This common experience allows one to detect more clearly the similarities and dissimilarities between us, and has helped me to better understand my own motives, and the various stations on the way out of Zionism. I also benefit today from the emergence recently in the academia of fresh and constructive ideas about positionality; scholars now welcome the influence of one's identity and views on whatever we do professionally, and brush aside the old conventional academic fear that commitment to a cause such as Palestine undermines one's professionalism.

The last station in this journey is where I would like to begin this retrospective trip. In 2015, a group of my postgraduate students convened a conference at the University of Exeter on "Settler Colonialism in Palestine". Immediately after it was announced, all hell broke loose. Pro-Israeli and Zionist mouthpieces such as the *Jewish Chronicle* framed the intended conference as antisemitic. The pressure to jettison the conference altogether came from government offices as well. To the university's credit, at a time when the University of Southampton cancelled a scheduled academic conference on Palestine, Exeter did not cave in. However, there was a fear of violent opposition, and I was asked to meet the commander of the riot police in Exeter, who assured me he had at his disposal a fearsome force of mounted police (though inactive in the previous 300 years). He asked me if I was Palestinian and I got entangled in a long answer that I myself cut short by saying that it was a very complex question, and we did not have the time to discuss it. But it did trigger a new assessment of how to answer the question posed in this chapter. I am not a Palestinian but at times I do feel as if I am. We all probably have more than one identity, or for that matter history, and it reminded me of the wonderful passage in Elias Khoury's novel *The Gate of the Sun* when Khalil says to Yunis that he is "scared of a history that has only one version" and continues to say:

History has dozens of versions, and for it to ossify into only one leads only to death. We mustn't see ourselves only in their mirror, for they're prisoners of one story, as though that story had abbreviated and ossified them ... We mustn't become just one story ... I see you as a man who betrays and repents and loves and fears and dies. This is the only way if we're not to ossify and die.

Indeed part of my history is Palestinian, and part of the Palestinian history is my history.

It all began when I fell in love with Arabic and History – most of the other subjects in high school failed to attract me. Like all young Israeli Jews I was the object of intense indoctrination in school, at home, and in the army (at the age of eighteen I was still committed enough to Zionism not to consider refusing to serve in the army, as my children would do many years later).

Immediately after army service, I enrolled in the Hebrew University in Jerusalem and focused my studies on modern Middle Eastern history. I was about to continue postgraduate studies in Israel, but family connections in the UK and a sense that I needed to view realities and histories outside my comfort zone led me to St Antony's College in Oxford. There I joined a D. Phil program under the supervision of Albert Hourani and Roger Owen both now deceased.

The Middle East Centre at St Antony's College was a very different scholarly site from the Hebrew University. It was the first time I met Arab and Palestinian scholars in an egalitarian space, and with the help of my two supervisors I was exposed for the first time to a different historical narrative about Palestine. At that particular venue I was also fortunate enough to meet Edward Said, who became a mentor and a friend.

I think in hindsight that this different human environment turned a mundane doctoral dissertation into a more profound historiographical challenge to the hegemonic Zionist narrative in general, and that of the 1948 war in particular.

I decided to do my thesis on British policy towards the Nakba, naively believing that I would find a neutral perspective on both sides of the divide. Instead, the declassified documents I found in Britain, the UN, and mostly in Israel presented me with a powerful refutation of the Zionist narrative.

When I returned to Israel in 1984, my work together with that of few other Israeli historians was dubbed as "the new history of Israel" as our work challenged the Zionist narrative of the 1948 war on the basis of the newly declassified material, and substantiated important claims made by Palestinian historians.

The picture we jointly drew out of the archives was of a Zionist military capacity that was superior to that of the Palestinians and the troops the Arab states dispatched to Palestine – which debunked the Israeli myth that 1948 was a war of a David against Goliath (assisted by a secret understanding between Transjordan and the future Jewish state that neutralized the most capable Arab army at the time). More important, with various degrees of conviction among us, we refuted the Israeli myth that the Palestinians voluntarily left to become refugees under the orders of their leaders and those of the neighbouring Arab states.

But none of us, the "new historians", felt at the time that our findings undermined our belief in Zionism, even though for me serious doubt had already begun to surface about Israel as a whole when I watched from Britain, which I could not have easily done from Israel, the brutal Israeli assault on Lebanon in 1982. It was both clearly a massive war crime and a "political war" portrayed as a war of self-defence. I began to wonder whether other wars were also such acts, which led me eventually to view the Israeli military operations in 1948 as a means to an end – the ethnic cleansing of Palestine.

All this, I stress, did not yet salvage me from the Zionist camp. The Israel media was interested in those challenges put forward by the "new historians" and until 1992, I was part of the legitimate debate on such brutality in 1948 that did not question the legitimacy of the state, or the sanctity of the 1948 war in Israeli eyes.

And then came 1992 – I am still not sure why in that year, I took a huge leap out of the warm embrace of Zionist consensus. It could have been the impact of a sabbatical year in Oxford where I newly befriended Palestinian scholars and activists; and maybe it was also prodded by meetings I had after the first Intifada with the late Faysal Husayni, as part of a new book I had written on his family's history. At that point I discovered that what I already knew about past and present Israeli actions disabled me from having any proper conversation with my family and friends. We were worlds apart when discussing morality and politics. I had lost my reference group and still did not have a new one.

I found myself moving socially from a Jewish social milieu into a Palestinian one, in an apartheid state that encouraged segregation not integration. In 1992 I joined HADASH, "the Democratic Front for Peace and Equality", the former Communist party of Israel. I was not a communist, but at the time this was the only Palestinian party that included progressive Jews. I played for a while with the idea of a career in politics from above in the Palestinian minority in Israel, but it did not suit my capabilities or aspirations. But it was a very formative experience; my Arabic became more fluent, I understood much better the impossible reality of a 1948 Arab: an Israeli citizen and yet part of the Palestinian national movement. In those days we also had good contacts with the Left in the West Bank, and this also led to meetings with Yasser Arafat in Tunis. Each meeting expanded my understanding of the nature of the Israeli oppression in the past and present, and helped me to earn the confidence of many of my Palestinian friends: hopefully accepted as someone who genuinely believes that his comfort zone as an Israeli Jew should be an asset in the solidarity movement with the Palestinians. But more importantly, this was a stage where we interacted as human beings and we were bound by our humanity and not only by our political cause.

The Second Intifada triggered a rollercoaster of a journey out of, and more importantly, against Zionism. Watching the Israeli brutality in October 2000 coincided with the Tantura affair. I was defending an MA student at Haifa University who exposed in his dissertation, written in 2000, a relatively unknown massacre that took place during the Nakba in Tantura, a village south of Haifa. He was taken to court for his finding, and ended up without a degree, two strokes, and tough life as a pariah in Jewish society. My own role in it led to my expulsion from Haifa University, and I moved to the University of Exeter in 2007 after a few years of fruitless struggle for a different way of teaching and research on the Nakba in Haifa University.

I became involved with ADRID, the committee of the Palestinian refugees in Israel, and left the political world, and was totally impressed by the ever growing '48 Arab civil society, which since 1998 has re-located the Nakba as the signifier of its identity and orientation. This was manifested by annual processions, *masirat al-Nakba*, to villages destroyed in 1948, and by other activities which were part of our attempt to defend Nakba memory and fight against its denial. I organized with my late friend, Salman Natour, two conferences on the Right of Return – one in Haifa and one in Nazareth – trying to push forward the idea that without the implementation of such a right any attempts at reconciliation, such as the Oslo accord, were doomed to fail.

While engaged in all of this, I wrote the *Ethnic Cleansing of Palestine*, benefiting from a declassification of military documents in the Israeli archives in 1998, and from my own realization of the importance of Palestinian oral history in search of a more complete picture of what happened during the Nakba.

However, I needed the exile in Exeter, to have an even more lucid picture in my mind (and I am sure I still have a lot to learn). It was there that, in the footsteps of Palestinian scholars such as Fayez Sayigh and Jamil Hilal, anti-Zionist activists and Australian scholars such as Patrick Wolfe and Lorenzo Veracini, I changed my own vocabulary on Palestine (a search which culminated in 2010 in a dialogue on it with Noam Chomsky in a joint book titled *On Palestine*). Viewing Zionism as a settler colonial movement, informed by what Wolfe called the logic of the "elimination of the native", framing Israel as an Apartheid state (again not pretending to be the first one who did it), and describing Israeli policies against the Gaza Strip since 2006 as an incremental genocide was now part of my daily, professional, and activist, discourse.

It produced other understandings such as total disbelief in the validity and morality of a two states solution, full commitment to the BDS campaign, and above all a clear, and a very rewarding, stance towards the future that was not there before.

With the help of Palestinian colleagues such as Ghada Karmi and Nadia Naser-Najjab, I founded the first ever centre for Palestine studies as an integral part of a university in the west and opened a program called Palestine Studies. All these new entries in my vocabulary were now subject to a proper and professional analysis and research, as was done in many other parts of the world and in Palestinian universities and institutes of research. The academic validation of these framings recently persuaded Amnesty International to define Israel as an Apartheid state, not as a polemic political position, and on the basis of this academic research.

Palestinians do not need the fruits of my or others' research to know the truth about the past and present. But we have a sacred role, I believe, to try and rectify years of denial and fabrication, and give power to a truth, and be part of a struggle for the decolonization and liberation of Palestine in the twenty-first century, one which should be Palestinian led, but also intersect with a strong solidarity movement, co-resistance of anti-Zionist Jews such as myself, and in alliance with other current struggles for political and social justice around the world.

The final station for me in this journey is my dream of establishing a physical centre against Nakba denial in London. There are quite a few centres against Holocaust denial, and this is fine. But we need at least one against Nakba denial, and to locate it in the capital of the past Empire that enabled the 1948 ethnic cleansing of Palestinians and their subsequent oppression is surely appropriate. The centre will only be a small contribution to the struggle, but I believe it will thrive because there is a new assertive young Palestinian generation, many of them still in Palestine, that will make sure the liberation struggle continues. They will benefit from a global public opinion that singles out support for Palestine as its first priority, not because it is a place where the worst atrocities are committed or because they turn a blind eye to disasters in the Arab world since 2012. It is within a perspective of other human and natural catastrophes that Palestine is cited as one of the longest, most continuous, and most denied. The struggle for human and civil rights in the Arab world and beyond, and the call for world solidarity in the face of poverty, ecological disasters, and pandemics, cannot be fulfilled if the West continues to provide exceptional immunity to an oppression that is more than 100 years old. I have been a member of that global community for more than thirty years, and I do not regret for one moment being part of it, whatever so far has been the price, which pales in comparison to the one paid by my Palestinian friends.

SOUTH ASIA

M. H. Ilias

University professor, India

"An Indian Academic Activist's Engagement with the Question of Palestine"

I suggest that the nature of engagement I have with the question of Palestine is a triadic relationship between activism, academics, and attachment. For the sake of compactness and convenience, I start with the first one, activism. I grew up in an atmosphere where the question of Palestine was politically intimate not just to intellectual and activist circles but to ordinary people as well. This was towards the middle of the 1980s in the State of Kerala in South India. Imagine student organizations using pictures of Yasser Arafat in posters, and quoting the words of Mahmoud Darwish and Ghassan Kanafani in pamphlets wooing voters in college union elections! Imagine school assemblies passing unanimous resolutions demanding – sometimes even warning – Israel to stop attacking Palestine! Communist and socialist party offices in villages decorated their walls with photographs of Arafat along with those of their founder-leaders. Without exaggeration, in the late '70s and '80s, support for the Palestinian cause was a well-acknowledged gesture and much-valued political act in Kerala. Most of the parties and civil society movements, with the exception of the right-wing Hindu outfits, used Palestinian symbols to show their political correctness. The rest of India was never an exception, though the magnitude of response varied in different Indian states.

With the Intifada in the late '80s there was a sudden surge in Palestine solidarity groups. The Intifada was an unarmed mass insurrection of ordinary Palestinians, and television visuals showing them being brutally handled by the Israeli army had a great deal of resonance in Indian politics. People who watched the visuals of the Intifada became emotionally charged by seeing footage of Palestinian civilians being killed. I read, saw on TV, and heard from friends and relatives living in the Gulf countries about the sufferings of Palestinians. And there were many like me. The support movements on college campuses, film societies in rural and urban areas that screened movies of Palestinian resistance, as well as gestures of solidarity by the political parties on every occasion of Israeli aggression all played a key role in popularizing the issue. Not long ago, translations of resistance literature from Palestine constituted a considerable portion of translated works published in Malayalam, the language of Kerala. We knew Mahmoud Darwish as well as poets in Malayalam through his translated works.

My interest in Palestine as an activist grew with *Intifada*, when the leftist organization I was affiliated with in my early twenties launched a series of on-street demonstrations supporting the Palestinian cause. This was the case with most of the leftist organizations, since they viewed Western support for the suppression of Palestine as leading to further expansion of imperialist influence in West Asia. This period coincided with a series of anti-imperialist agitations in Kerala, and organizations across the left-liberal spectrum invoked the legacy of the anti-colonial national movement-era as usable history to help oppose settler colonialism in Palestine. This anti-colonial feeling, which functioned as the driving force for Palestinian solidarity movements in India in shaping their anti-Zionist ideology right from the beginning, traces its roots to the national movement in India. The feeling resonated first in the 1937 Calcutta session of the All India Congress Committee (AICC), which openly protested against the reign of terror as well as the proposal of partitioning Palestine. Mahatma Gandhi, though 'he appreciated the sufferings of the Jewish community in Europe in the context of the Holocaust, openly supported Palestinian Arab nationalism and kept a safe distance from Zionist nationalism because of its colonial nature. It is important to note that his statements in solidarity with the Palestinian Arabs came in the context of severe pressure on him from the Zionist quarters to issue a statement favouring the Jewish attempt to establish a national homeland in Palestine. Despite the pressure from Hermann Kallenbach, one of his close friends, assigned by the Zionist leaders to visit him to enlist his support, Gandhi opposed the move to create a Jewish state in a land occupied by another people.

Jawaharlal Nehru also endorsed Ghandi's anti-colonial position concerning the question of Palestine. He blamed British imperialist policy for creating the crisis and openly supported Palestinian self-determination. Under Indira Gandhi, support for the Palestinian cause became more politically intense. India was the first non-Arab country to recognize the Palestine Liberation Organization (PLO) "as the sole legitimate representative of the people of Palestine", and established full diplomatic ties with the PLO in 1980, though a PLO office had been set up in New Delhi as early as 1975. Support for the Palestinians has also been regarded as a gesture by the post-colonial Indian state to the political sensitivities of its largest minority, the Muslims.

The slogans of Palestinian solidarity that once echoed throughout the nation have now faded away, replaced by the right-wing political-religious parties' social media campaigns expressing support for Israel. The hope felt by pro-Palestine activists in the 1980s and '90s has dissipated, with an increasing number of takers for the "support for Israel" campaign. What went wrong over a period of thirty years? The reasons are more than one, but each invariably converges on two developments that India went through in the 1990s: i) a neo-liberal reconfiguration of the Indian economy; and ii) a phenomenal rise of Hindu nationalism in mainstream Indian politics.

The neoliberal turn in Indian policy was most overt in foreign policy in the 1990s, reflected in a partial or complete abandonment of anti-imperialism and a tilt towards the United States-dominated world order. This shift resulted, first and foremost, in a change in attitude towards the Palestinian cause. Since that time, support for the Palestinian struggle has been progressively diluted.

India officially recognized the State of Israel in 1950, but the formal relationship remained lukewarm, showing little enthusiasm due to public pressure and diplomatic considerations. At various times the Indian administration feared that ties with Israel would damage relations with the Arab world, and would eventually jeopardize the prospect for Indian labour migration to the Gulf countries, as well as the import of oil from the region. So India's move to open an embassy in Tel Aviv in 1992 marked not just a radical shift in the way the Indian administration viewed the Palestinian cause, but also created confusion among sections of the administration which had previously been "all-weather" supporters of the Palestinian cause.

This development coincided with the right-wing Hindu groups' propaganda portraying the Palestine issue as a Muslim issue. Perhaps more striking was a shift in the language of media reporting of resistance in Palestine, as this was influenced by the global media discourse equating resistance with "terrorism". Yet throughout this period the situation allowed the emergence of initiatives and movements in support of the Palestinian struggle, mostly among the students of the Indian universities. The reverberations of the Palestine solidarity movements across the country have been felt beyond activism. They probably played a part in the increasing popularity of the Palestine issue as a theme of research and writing, especially among the students of political science, area studies, and international relations, in the national institutions of higher learning such as Jawaharlal Nehru University, Jamia Millia Islamia, Hyderabad Central University, and provincial universities in South India like Mahatma Gandhi University, Kerala University, and Mysore University.

Given the unusual number of doctoral dissertations and other scholarly works on Palestine, it is feasible to see this newfound popularity of Palestine as a research theme partly as an academic response to the neo-liberal negligence of the issue. With major political parties failing to respond to Israeli aggression, many people began to explore the potential of academia for disseminating information, political messages, opinions, and views about the suffering of Palestinians. Many, including myself, turned academically to the question of Palestine as a form of political self-expression that we believed might overcome the post-liberalization stigma attached to support for the cause. My choice was to take the "process of de-Arabization of the Palestinian map" as the topic for my doctoral work at the Jawaharlal Nehru University.

Israel's longing to mobilize Indian public opinion in its favour had by then met some initial success with the right-wing groups' drive to weaken the political and moral foundations of civil society organizations engaged in popularizing the Palestinian cause in India by branding them "terrorists". Yet the Indian universities remained the major theatre of solidarity for Palestinians. I remember Jamia Millia Islamia, the university where I worked, named two of its conference halls after Yasser Arafat and Edward Said; and a garden after Mahmoud Darwish. Annual commemoration of the *Nakba* became a much valued political gesture among university students at a time when most of the world preferred to ignore the Palestinian struggle for justice. The presence of Palestinian students on the Jamia campus, and their weekly *dabke* classes, conveyed the feeling of their existence and struggle in the face of global attempts to negate both.

The present wave of Palestinian solidarity activities and research actually began in a small way in Indian academic circles almost two decades ago. The movement gained momentum in 2009 with the formation of the Palestinian Solidarity Committee in India, with representatives from political parties, civil society groups, and universities. The committee calls for boycott of Israeli products and services, organizes activities in solidarity with Palestine, and critiques the strategic relationship and growing military ties between India and Israel. The Indian Campaign for the Academic and Cultural Boycott of Israel (InCABI), a group of academics, activists, and artists, was set up the following year [2010] to extend support to the international campaign for the academic and cultural boycott of Israel (www.incacbi.in).

The emotional aspect of my engagement with Palestine was developed during my sojourn in the Gulf countries in the early 2000s. The first Arab I befriended from the region was a Palestinian, a citizen of Jordan working in a state-owned gas company in Qatar. The image of a typical Palestinian has been presented in popular narratives as being "short-tempered", "aggressive" and "stubborn". But, befriending a Palestinian in the diasporic setting would always be a favourite political gesture for a politically active Keralite in the Gulf Countries, in spite of the language hurdle. We made our weekend meetings a point to share our common concerns over the dwindling support for the Palestine cause by the rulers of the Gulf countries.

Such cross-cultural identification is common between Malayalee workers and Palestinians, creating a space not just for solidarity but for sharing criticism of the pro-Western policies and weak positions of the Gulf monarchies vis-à-vis US policies favouring Israel. These spaces operate through activities such as Palestine solidarity film festivals and not-so-open gatherings in support of the Palestinian cause, thereby creating an important form of popular politics in the Gulf. Since they exist outside formal institutions, and since most of their actions remain internal to the country, they attract no adverse reactions from the host state. I was a part of one such informal weekly gathering in Qatar, into which we used to introduce discussions with political undertones.

At a more personal level, belonging to such a group offered me an escape, since my personal political expressions as an expatriate were restricted by the government. I remember, towards the end of each meeting, we reiterated our hope that the world would one day realize Palestinian aspirations for justice and freedom.

Vijay Prashad

Historian, director of the Tri-Continental Institute for Social Research

"My Palestinian Life"

In 1982, the newspaper that came to my school carried a front-page story that captivated me. The picture that accompanied the story was of two women looking intently at dead bodies in a narrow roadway. The scene was sombre, the context unfamiliar to me. The story was written with great feeling, I remember, something unusual in the Indian papers. It is likely that the story had been reprinted from one of the international papers or drawn from a wire service, but I don't remember anything about that. I was fifteen years old. I learned about the Palestinian struggle through the massacre at Sabra and Shatila in Beirut.

I remember copying out most of the story into my notebook, which is what I often did with stories that moved me. It was a habit I developed very early, having been told about it from old-timer journalists whom I had interviewed for my school newspaper (*The Circle*). My immediate reaction to that news story went into my monthly column for the student newspaper. Years later, after my father died, I found a pile of these newspapers in a folder marked "Vijay's writings". I remember finding that particular column and being struck by the indignation of it. The following year, I wrote with similar outrage at the Nellie massacre in central Assam (February 1983), learning the skills that allowed me to shape the language to write about the Bhiwandi killings and the Delhi pogrom against the Sikhs of 1984. Disbelief at the hideousness of human action slowly morphed into a more precise sense of the power structure in our world and the way in which not all humans, but some humans – activated by specific histories and precise forms of power – acted in the world.

It moves me to acknowledge the role that the journalists played in Beirut in those years. When I lived in Beirut three decades later, I went in search of Arab journalists who could walk me through the days of 1982 and 1983. It is important to mention that many of the journalists either fled the city during the Israeli occupation, were killed during that period, or went underground. Nonetheless, those whom I met had many stories to tell, since even if they had left the city, when they returned, they went to the camps in Sabra and Shatila in a kind of pilgrimage to the atrocity perpetuated by a range of Western powers, Israeli, and of course the Lebanese fascists. Each year, in September, there is a gathering at the camps to honour the dead and to acknowledge that their struggle remains with us. I went with Robert Fisk to walk the road to the cemetery, his memories catapulting out about the terrible war crime that he had witnessed. I had listened to half a dozen other reporters from a range of different political opinions at different moments – people like Hanna Anbar and Maria Chakhtoura – talk about the great pain of that era, the Lebanese Civil War, but also the terrible atrocities during the Israeli occupation. There was a density of sorrow in their memories. What struck me was not that – which I had come to expect – but the fact that their writings in 1982 had reached out far and wide and found a generation of people like myself, disgusted by the actions of imperialism and Zionism and by the manufactured consent against the Palestinians.

I became two things at one time after what I had learned about Sabra and Shatila in 1982. I became a journalist, a writer who wanted to go into imperialism's wound, write about the damage as honestly as possible, and reach into the hearts of young people who *need* to know these stories. I became an adherent for the liberation of Palestinians, a struggle that sometimes appears impossible given the immense power of the Israeli state over the Palestinian people and through the Western capitals over the international narrative.

Writing Palestine

When I first went to Palestine, I was struck by how small everything seemed. I had imagined that the Jordan Valley would be vast, as infinite as the deserts of Arabia, as mythical as the Mayan ruins. The Jordan River was a trickle, the lands to its east a contested site filled with the aggression of the Israeli army and the brave resilience of the Palestinians. That's how I wrote my first stories, no nuance, no sense of the complexity, everything was black and white. Later, when I understood things a bit better, the nuance appeared – the surrender of parts of the Palestinian elite and the resistance of sections of Israeli society – but it was not important; the situation of the Zionist occupation of Palestine is almost entirely black and white, with nuance something that is an instinct of the writer and not a mirror of reality.

It is impossible to do a story about Palestine and ignore Nabi Saleh, the village that has fought to maintain its dignity for decades. But then there are other stories – the family that sells *knafeh* in old Jerusalem, whose son was killed by the Zionist police, who built a shrine to him in their shop; the mother in Hebron, who goes to every demonstration to remember her daughter, shot by an Israeli sniper; the sister and brother in Jenin who refuse to forget that their father sits in an Israeli cell, the administration detention extended year after year; the neighbourhoods in Gaza City, where it is impossible to meet a family that has not lost at least one person to the punctual bombing by the Israelis, their walls festooned with the names of political parties and their sorrow. These are familiar stories, written by journalist after journalist, accumulated by human rights report after human rights report. None of them seem to make a difference, but perhaps each of them makes its way to another young person who picks up a pen and echoes them to other people, a million readers who no longer want to believe the uncomfortable Zionist narrative.

Arms and Harm

I've been there before. Umm Majed of Gaza City is telling me about what the white phosphorus feels like when the cascading cloud descends onto her skin. "It burns and burns", she says, "burnt the skin off my hand". The words of Palestinians who talk about the impact of the Israeli attacks on their bodies are painful. These are words that are both familiar and disorienting: familiar because I've heard these stories in different parts of the world, from Afghanistan to Colombia; disorienting because these are words that simply should not be heard at all. The first time I covered a massacre – the pogrom against Muslims in Seelampur (India) in 1993 – I shuddered with the realization that these things actually happen and that we seem to continue to live as if they are not that important to our collective morality. Few deny that these things happen, that white phosphorus is used against the Palestinians (as it was used by the United States against the Iraqis) and that the impact of the white phosphorus – and such weapons – is horrendous for the people who are its victims.

When I read that story about Sabra and Shatila, the Indian government maintained its strong position of solidarity with the Palestinian struggle. The following year – 1983 – India hosted the Non-Aligned Movement summit, where Palestinian leader Yasir Arafat was feted by prime minister Indira Gandhi. It was normal for us to be intimate with the details of the Palestinian struggle, with the Indian media reporting on events in West Asia with a decidedly pro-Palestinian edge. Of course, there was complexity in any conflict, with violence terrible for all its victims; however, the asymmetry of the Zionist violence and the illegality of the occupation had to frame the picture. When the Intifada broke out in 1987, people in my circle understood the validity of the Palestinian cause.

By the time the Intifada died down in 1991, a great deal had changed. The Soviet Union and the socialist state system in eastern Europe had collapsed; the Third World Project had been weakened by the debt crisis; the United States had emerged as the unipolar power, illuminated by the crushing attack on Iraq (1991) and the formation of the World Trade Organisation (1994). These three elements led to a major reconsideration in the capitals of countries such as India, which had been close to the USSR and had certainly been close to the Palestinian cause. In these early years of the 1990s, the Indian administration opened talks with the United States to develop a new relationship with the major world power. A senior bureaucrat in the foreign ministry told me that the US diplomats were clear: the road to Washington had to go through Tel Aviv, meaning that India had to first recognize Israel before the US would allow it into the inner circle. So, that is what India did in 1992, recognize Israel for the first time since the Nakba of 1948.

Did I forget to mention that at least 3,000 Palestinians had been killed in Sabra and Shatila? I also forgot to mention that the operation had the sanction of Israel's Defence Minister Ariel Sharon, who – the Israeli Kahan Commission found – had personal responsibility for the massacre. In 2002, Sharon, as Israel's prime minister, came to India at the invitation of the right-wing government of India's prime minister Atal Behari Vajpayee. A decade of diplomatic connections and a longer history of covert military and intelligence sharing culminated in this visit, the first time a head of government from Israel came to India. We were furious. I hastily wrote a little book – *Namaste Sharon: Hindutva and Sharonism under US Hegemony* (LeftWord Books) – which traced the linkages between the right-wing in India (Hindutva) and Zionism that had been fostered by the tentacles of imperialism. We had wanted to go to the airport when Sharon arrived and throw copies of the book at his delegation, but – like many such theatrical plans – it did not work out. Nonetheless, the book circulated and made the point that India's ruling elite had been willing to pay the dowry of recognizing Israel to consummate the strategic marriage with the United States. It was a shameful disgrace the way that the Indian ruling elites, in such a short period, threw the Palestinian aspirations under the bus of venality.

The actual commercial links between India and Israel in 2002 were minimal: bilateral trade was at $1.27 billion, with two-thirds of it in diamonds. Now, twenty years later, the trade has reached over $4 billion, with a large portion of it in the import of arms (around $800 million) from Israel to India. After India tested nuclear weapons in 1998, it was not able to import the many weapons systems from the United States directly due to the Glenn Amendment (which allows the US president to block arms sales to non-nuclear Non-Proliferation states that explode a nuclear weapon). Instead, India turned to Israel's arms industry, which is in large part a joint-venture project with US arms manufacturers; Israel was able to sell weapons systems that India could not get directly from the US. India quickly became the largest purchaser of arms from Israel, which made it – in effect – an underwriter of the occupation of the Palestinians.

BDS in India

In January 2022, I spoke with Huda Ammori of Palestine Action, which had for over eighteen months fought against the Israeli arms manufacturer Elbit Systems and forced the company to close its plant in Oldham (UK). The brave activists of Palestine Action conducted an unrelenting campaign against Elbit, including breaking into the premises and pouring red paint on the factory's walls. Elbit – in close collaboration with the British military – makes a range of military equipment, a great deal of it used in Gaza; these punctual Israeli wars on the Palestinians of Gaza are used to erase the Palestinian political project and to test Israeli weapons for sale to other countries. It is brutality of settler-colonialism and of commerce.

Israel has established itself through two mechanisms. First, the US government makes it clear to any government that close relations with the US is premised on overt (preferably) or covert (at a minimum) ties with Israel. Second, the Israeli arms and technology industries have insinuated themselves into the essential development and production apparatus of the Western militaries and arms firms, so that any government that seeks to buy weapons systems from the Western companies ends up with an Israeli connection; linked to this is the intimate relationship between Western intelligence and Israeli intelligence, both of which operate together to provide governments in many parts of the world with intelligence and the equipment for intelligence (including systems such as the Pegasus software).

Nothing like Palestine Action exists in India nor does anything as direct as Elbit Systems. There are many Indian companies that have close links to Israel, but information about these linkages is neither easily available nor is there a cultural will to be bothered about them. As anti-Muslim sentiment has grown in India – egged by the right-wing political forces – disregard for the suffering and struggles of the Palestinians has developed. The right-wing makes the case that the Israelis are merely doing in Palestine what they would like to see done to the 120 million Indian Muslims. In this climate, it is not easy to make the case that Israel violates international law, since the right-wing forces routinely violate international human rights law and the Indian Constitution in its approach to Kashmir, the rights of Muslims in India, and the rights of Muslim migrants to India.

Nonetheless, there is a small, but vocal constituency that remains committed to the struggles for liberation by the Palestinians. Formed in 2010, the Indian Campaign for the Academic and Cultural Boycott of Israel (INCACBI) has moved several agendas that have drawn mass movements of the Left towards the BDS orientation. In 2017, the largest organization that represents farmers and agricultural workers – the All-India Kisan Sabha (AIKS) – joined the BDS movement. SFI has a membership of around five million, while the AIKS has a membership of sixteen million. Both are mass organizations of the Communist Party of India (Marxist). Their concrete acts of solidarity must be built upon in the years ahead.

Other Indian communists in the Jana Natya Manch (Janam), a theatre project based in New Delhi, travelled to Palestine in 2014 as guests of the Freedom Theatre (Jenin). They went by bus across the Occupied Palestinian Territory, from one end to the other. On that bus was Sudhanva Deshpande, who said at that time, "Theatre isn't pure art. It cannot be. As the Freedom Theatre people said to me, they're training freedom fighters. But the weapons used are tools of culture". The next year, actors from the Freedom Theatre travelled around India with Janam to perform a play about solidarity and struggle that they had both produced together. Faisal Abu Alhayjaa of the Freedom Theatre said during his time in India, "There's occupation, there's Fatah, there's Hamas, there are other political parties. There are killings, there are intifadas. There is no freedom. So, we have learnt to use art as a tool to resist the occupation". And art is a bridge between India and Palestine.

It has been forty years since the massacre at Sabra and Shatilla. Funny how it feels to look again at that photograph of the two women bending down over the dead bodies of Palestinians in Beirut. They are looking for loved ones. I wonder if they found them, or if they found someone they knew, and I wonder how they grieved for them. When I went to the neighbourhood with Robert Fisk, I was curious to see if we could find these two women, but we did not succeed. Perhaps they died of a broken heart. Or in the Israeli bombardment of Beirut in 2006.

EAST ASIA

Ang Swee Chai

Surgeon, United Kingdom/Singapore

"A Woman Surgeon with the Palestinians, Christian Zionist turned Palestinian Activist"

I was born in Penang, Malaysia and grew up in Singapore. My parents were Chinese-speaking atheists. They were imprisoned in 1941 for resisting the Japanese invasion and occupation of Malaya during the Second World War. Many prisoners died of torture and diseases in prison but my parents survived. They met after the Japanese surrendered, got married, and started a family of four children. Israel and Palestine did not feature in my childhood and teens.

When I was nineteen, I attended a Christian Evangelical Crusade and made the decision to follow Jesus. My parents saw Christianity as a form of colonialism: "First came the missionaries, and then came the traders and finally the armies which conquered and took our countries". Therefore, I had resisted Christianity until then. But I was totally attracted to Jesus Christ, who loved and died for all humanity.

Soon after, I was baptized in a fundamentalist, pro-Israeli church. I taught Sunday school, including the conquest of Canaan by Joshua, David and Goliath, and the victory of Elijah against the Philistines. For me, God had promised the land of Canaan to His chosen people, Israel. The creation of the State of Israel in 1948 transitioned neatly into a re-run of the Old Testament. My church and I saw it as the fulfilment of God's promise to Israel in the Old Testament. In 1967, we rejoiced with pride when Israel won the Six Day War, believing that Israel had decisively defeated the Arabs. My church even helped to raise money to help defend someone who had tried to blow up a mosque in Jerusalem, a mosque being an affront to Yahweh.

In 1973, I graduated from the University of Singapore as a medical doctor, and in 1977 I married a human rights lawyer. Two weeks after our wedding, he fled arrest by the security police. A month later I was arrested and imprisoned for questioning about him, and also signed a statement promising the security police that I would get him back to surrender to them. That was the first time I was put in prison, but I have been in prison a couple more times since then! The latest was in 2018 when I was medic on board the Freedom Flotilla Awda, loaded with antibiotics and dressings for Gaza. The boat was abducted in international waters by the Israeli Navy. All on board were taken to prison in Ashdod. The cargo and boat remain impounded to this day.

Upon release from Singapore prison, I joined my husband in London and we became political refugees. It was a great comedown. From being middle class professional Singaporeans we became homeless, jobless, stateless refugees. We struggled desperately to rebuild our lives.

By 1982, five years later, we were just about sorted out. I had become a Fellow of the Royal College of Surgeons of England and was working in St Thomas' Hospital. My husband found work as a journalist. We had a permanent place to live.

But God was about to change things.

Television ran nightly news on a war in Lebanon. The country was being relentlessly bombed. Its capital Beirut was under siege. Food, medicine, water, and electricity were blockaded. Although portrayed as a war against the terrorist PLO, it was clear that the bomb targets were civilians – hospitals, schools, homes, factories, shops – and not terrorists. The headlines were 14,000 killed and tens of thousands made homeless a couple of weeks into the war. There were pictures of wounded victims, many children, some dying, in partially bombed hospitals. Charred bodies were pulled out of bombed out buildings, including small children. My heart was torn apart watching the suffering. It was worse when I learnt that the offensive was by Israel. I became restless and anxious for the victims.

How could Israel do this? To compound matters, my Christian friends were celebrating the death and destruction, citing Biblical verses, calling this the work of God!

How should a Christian surgeon respond? What would Jesus say? I needed wisdom and guidance, but my immediate circle provided none. Finally God spoke. In his letter to the Corinthians, the Apostle Paul wrote about "seeing darkly as through a glass, but one day we will see face to face" and about how we "are children, and thought and spoke as children, but when we grow up we will put aside childish things". He went on: "Faith, hope and love endure forever, but the greatest of these is love." I began to ask God "How?"

A week later, an appeal came from Christian Aid for a volunteer orthopaedic surgeon to treat the wounded. God had answered my prayers. I resigned from St Thomas' Hospital, joined Christian Aid as a volunteer surgeon on their medical team, and left for Beirut. For the first time that summer my heart was at peace.

We had to get to Beirut by sea since the airport had been bombed. The ferry was not able to land. War planes pounded the city continuously around the time of our landing. We finally got in when there was a gap in the bombing.

The situation was hideous, blocks of high rise buildings reduced to heaps of rubble – just as on television – only this time life size and three dimensional. Homeless families were all over the pavements. Hundreds were buried under the rubble. There was no water or electricity. I started work in the converted car park basement of the Near East Theological College, treating horrendous war injuries – the young, the old, men, women, and babies.

Meanwhile, Israel had threatened to flatten the whole of Lebanon to destroy the PLO and its military forces. The indiscriminate bombardment by land, air, and sea continued. No one condemned Israel.

Ten weeks after the invasion started, the PLO agreed to leave Lebanon in exchange for a cease-fire under the US Habib Peace Plan. As part of the Habib plan, the US agreed that the civilians left behind would be protected by a multinational peacekeeping force.

With the evacuation, I left the basement operating theatre, and was seconded to work with the Palestine Red Crescent Society. Eight of their hospitals and thirteen clinics in Lebanon were totally destroyed. Their only hospital left standing was Gaza Hospital, which only lost the upper two floors and most of its windows. I was to set up an orthopaedic trauma department there.

Gaza Hospital overlooked Shatila refugee camp and neighbouring Sabra. For someone who grew up seeing Palestinians as terrorists, I was shocked to learn how the refugee camps of Lebanon came into existence. In 1948, more than half the population of Palestine – 750,000 persons – were driven out of their homes at gunpoint and by the threat of massacre. They fled into neighbouring Lebanon, Syria, and Jordan. Their country Palestine became Israel and the Palestinians were never allowed to return home. Over time tents gave way to buildings and the refugee camps became shanty-towns. Here children were born refugees, grew up refugees, and died refugees. The world moved on and they were forgotten. They remained stateless since Palestine no longer existed.

During the 1982 Israeli invasion of Lebanon every single home in Shatila camp was totally or partially destroyed. Re-assured by the guarantee of protection by the USA, women with young children and elderly relatives, many also wounded, carried their belongings back to these ruins. They had lost loved ones through the evacuation and the bombs, but they started to repair their damaged homes, clear the rubble, paint the walls, support each other, and pick up their broken lives.

These people had suffered so much yet remained so human, generous, kind, and dignified. I was overwhelmed by their hospitality in the midst of their poverty. Their story was not in any history textbook, but every Palestinian child knew the name of his/her village though many of these villages had been demolished. Gaza Hospital was named after the Gaza Strip in Palestine.

I sat in their bombed out homes while they served me Arabic coffee and shared their meagre UN rations with me. The women introduced me to their stunningly beautiful Palestinian embroidery. Motifs typical of their home villages were sewn onto black cloth with brilliantly coloured silk threads. Each stitch is a testimony to their history, cultural heritage, and resilience.

I fell in love with the Palestinians but was still wondering at the back of my mind how come they were labelled terrorists?

Three weeks later, the Multinational Peacekeeping Force protecting the Palestinian refugees abruptly withdrew and the Israeli invasion of West Beirut began. Israeli tanks overran West Beirut and some surrounded Shatila. They sealed the area so no one could escape and sent their allies, the right-wing Maronite Phalange, into the camps. What followed was the infamous massacre of more than 3,000 Palestinians and Lebanese.

Our surgical team worked seventy-two hours non-stop until we were forced out of Gaza Hospital at machine-gun point. We had worked in the basement operating theatre, mostly without food and water, to save many dozen lives – only to find that people had been killed by the thousands in the camp and around it. Many were tortured before death, women raped before being killed.

We were forced to march along the main road at machine-gun point. Lining both sides of the road were groups of civilians rounded up by armed men. Their terrified faces showed they knew they were going to be killed. A young mother tried to give me her baby – hoping I could take it to safety. The gunmen forced her to take her baby back. Both were killed along with the people rounded up by the roadside after we left that day.

The Sabra-Shatila massacre exploded the myth that Palestinians were terrorists. The heaps of bodies in the camp alleys finally convinced the world – and me – that they were the *victims* of terror. Robbed of their homeland, driven to live in poverty and insecurity in refugee camps, they were finally butchered on foreign soil. On each dead body was a refugee identity card stating their place of origin in Palestine.

Until then I had lived 33 years without knowing Palestinians existed. I bought into the lie that they were terrorists. I taught my Sunday school children that Israel must annihilate the PLO terrorists. I had blood on my hands. I felt crushed. I asked God to forgive me for my prejudice against them. They are children of God and my brothers and sisters. I asked God to allow me to be their friend and help them.

Palestinians only suffer and die daily because we fail to see them as human beings. I can no longer walk away. "God – take my life and use it for these people whom we have collectively wronged. Please give me a second chance to serve them."

This is my fortieth year journeying with the Palestinians. They have accepted me as their family.

That journey brought me to the Occupied Palestinian Territories where brutal abuses of human rights take place daily. In the West Bank arbitrary arrests, killings and house demolitions are the daily norm. In 2019 alone five and a half thousand Palestinians were arrested, of whom 889 were children and 128 were women.[1] The West Bank itself is imprisoned behind a 700 km separation wall cutting through Palestinian homes, schools, and farms.

Gaza has been blockaded for fifteen years, while being bombarded by air, sea, and land, leaving several thousands killed and many more homeless. Among the dead are more than 1,000 children. Electricity is scarce and safe drinking water non-existent. Since March 2018, more than 300 unarmed demonstrators asking for the right to return home have been killed by snipers, with 36,000 wounded, a third of them children and women. More than 1,300 will never walk normally again due to high velocity sniper wounds to their legs.[2] In May 2021, Gaza was bombarded again with massive destruction and the deaths of 256 Palestinians, 66 of them children.[3]

As we celebrated 2020, Gaza has become unliveable. My latest attempts to go and help Gaza resulted in my being imprisoned and deported.

I pray that God will give me courage to continue to be faithful to them in the face of persecution. I must have faith that after the crucifixion comes resurrection. I have often been asked by my Palestinian friends: "Swee – as Palestinians we are born to suffer and

---

[1] https://imemc.org/article/israel-detained-5500-palestinians-in-2019-including-889-children/
[2] https://www.ochaopt.org/content/least-1200-people-injured-gaza-demonstrations-will-require-limb-reconstruction
[3] https://www.ochaopt.org/poc/24-31-may-2021

have no choice. But why do you not walk away?" I recall Jesus asking His disciples the same question, "Will you also walk away?" Peter replied, "Lord – to whom shall we go?, You have the words of life." How can I walk away and stay human?

For me, being with the Palestinians is a great blessing from God. I always remember the broken woman surgeon emerging from the basement operating theatre of Gaza Hospital asking God to forgive her for her prejudice and bigotry, and asking Him to take her life and use it to serve the Palestinians. Now in deep gratitude forty years later, I thank Him for making that wish possible.

As a surgeon, I mend wounds. But as a human being, I must speak out about how they were caused. Since that time, I have a passion to speak out in obedience to God's command "to speak up for those who cannot speak for themselves, for the rights of all who are destitute". I must speak up for the Palestinians.

Speaking up invites persecution. Over the years, I have been vilified and threatened, subjected to smears and allegations of antisemitism because I speak out for the Palestinians. Even now, each time before I speak in public I pray Second Timothy 1:7 – "For God hath not given us the spirit of fear, but of power, and of love and a sound mind." I anticipate attacks but I am no longer afraid.

I still have with me my picture of destitute Palestinian children of Shatila camp standing amidst the ruin and rubble. They survived the massacre but lost their parents and homes. In the foreground of the picture were dead and decaying bodies; in the background their destroyed homes. The air was filled with the stench of decomposing bodies. But between death and destruction were the Palestinian children. As I focused my camera, they raised their hands in the victory sign and said to me: "We are not afraid, let Israel come". I have returned many times to Shatila looking for them but have never been able to find them. They may have perished since. Their wish was for me to show the picture of them standing courageously against this dark uncaring world to all my friends. I have honoured their wish.

They live forever in my heart. Whenever the situation becomes unbearable, I revisit this picture for strength. There will be no turning back from this journey towards humanity. And today I invite you to join us too.

Eisuke Naramoto

Professor Emeritus, Hosei University (Tokyo)/Retired News
Correspondent, Japan

"Meeting with Palestine: A Personal Story"

It was a few days after the two hijacked passenger airplanes crashed into the Twin Towers in Manhattan on September 11, 2001, causing almost a thousand deaths. Since the flight bound to Japan I had booked was cancelled, I had to stay in New York for a few more days. While drinking wine at a bar in Manhattan, I had an unexpected conversation with a man sitting next to me.

"Do you think they, ah. . . the Arab people hate America?", asked the middle-aged American.

"Well, I think so", I replied.

"Why?" he asked.

"Because they think the Americans are overly one-sided on the so-called Palestine Problem."

Then I tried to explain by mentioning part of UN resolution 181, i.e., the Palestine Partition Resolution.

"In 1947, that is some fifty years ago, the UN General Assembly passed a resolution to divide Palestine into two main sections – a Jewish state and an Arab state. At that time, the Jews there were about one third of the population and the Arabs were two thirds; the Jews possessed only some 7% of the land, the Arabs had most of the rest. But UNGA 181 gave almost 77% of Palestine to the Jewish minority while it gave only the remnant to the Arabs. It was clear that the resolution was unfair and unacceptable to the Arabs. But the USA strongly supported this one-sided resolution and put pressure on some UN member states to vote 'Yes' for it. The Soviet Union also supported the resolution; however, later it sided with the Arabs."

He said, "Well, I only wish that the conflict will be solved peacefully."

I didn't tell him about the Zionist movement, nor how the great powers were helping it for their own political interests, because that would have been a long story. However, he seemed to understand my explanation.

This was the first time I talked with a stranger abroad about the Palestine issue.

However, my curiosity about the Middle East itself goes back to 1956 when I was a junior high school student in Japan. An "Egypt Exhibition" was held in Kyoto to introduce modern Egypt after the 1952 Revolution. I went to the exhibition with a classmate and was deeply impressed by the photo panels displayed at the entrance, showing lively Egyptian girls with short pants jumping over hurdles, giving quite a different picture from the stereotyped image of silent veiled women. I thought I was looking at the birth of a new Middle East! In the same year, President Gamal Abdel Nasser nationalized the Suez Canal, which had been operated before by the French and British. That was really exciting news for an Asian boy like me. It was amazing that an Afro-Asian leader challenged the strong Western countries which had subjugated this poor nation before. At that time, I didn't know there was the Palestine problem, since the Japanese media reported almost nothing about it.

In 1962, when I was a university student, Algeria gained independence from France after a long and bitter struggle. Many Japanese students admired the brave Algerian people. Most of them – including me – had little knowledge about Palestine. But the Algerian independence war was the event that introduced many progressive young Japanese to the anti-imperialist struggles in the Middle East.

It wasn't until shortly before 1970 that progressive young Japanese became interested in the Palestinian struggle. At the time I was working for the newspaper *Mainichi Shinbun* as a correspondent for domestic news. Quite a few Japanese, not only journalists and youngsters, were surprised when in 1968 the PFLP hijacked an Israeli passenger plane to Algeria. A little after that incident a citizen in Japan started a plan to send a doctor and a nurse to a hospital in the Palestinian refugee camp, and I was asked to cover stories about them.

This opportunity made me start studying the Palestinian issue so as to write the news articles on the medical volunteers. At that time the Japanese media at large referred to it as "the Arab-Israeli conflict" and perceived it as basically a religious conflict.

I learned that the conflict was not between two races, nor between Jews and Muslims. In 1968, Fateh launched a program calling for a democratic, secular Palestine where Muslims, Christians, and Jews can live together peacefully with equal rights. Other Palestinian political groups also started discussions on "One Palestine". Fateh's first press briefing in January 1968 clearly distinguished between Jews and Zionists. It also said that the Palestinian struggle did not target "the Jews who have been living peacefully with us as neighbors", and did not aim "to throw them into the sea". Rather the Palestinians were against "the Zionist regime who have grabbed our land, expelled many of our brothers and are still now oppressing them". Similar documents and statements started to be issued by other Palestinian political factions.

At that time, many progressive Japanese youth presented themselves as "internationalists". They were attracted by those Palestinians who were trying to override narrow-minded national enmity and religious bigotry. I was no exception. Later I learned that there was much debate among the Palestinians and their supporters over how they would cooperate to form a united front; what a democratic Palestine would be like, an independent Palestine state or a Palestinian province federated with other Arab states? How would Jews be treated – as a religious minority? An ethnic minority? And so forth. Only a small number of progressive Japanese youth were conscious of these questions. But to me these were very interesting problems, though very complicated.

The first time I met with actual Palestinians was at the beginning of 1972. I took part in a Japanese tourist group of some ten people who went to Beirut. We stayed a week, visiting a refugee camp which had a clinic in it where there was a Japanese volunteer nurse whom I had interviewed in Japan before she came to Beirut. And then we made a call on a Palestinian elementary school and enjoyed watching the little children dancing the *dabkah*.

We also visited the offices of some of the Palestine guerrilla organizations. At the PFLP office, we met Ghassan Kanafani, a man with sharp sparkling black eyes. I didn't realize then that he was a famous novelist and well-known journalist. I remember that he gave us a briefing on the structure of the Palestinian refugee community and the political situation. He said, "it will take at least fifty years before Palestine is liberated". He was assassinated in July of the same year.

After returning from my tour of the Palestinian camps, I translated two books on the Palestine problem from English to Japanese: Sabri Jiryis, *The Arabs in Israel 1948–1966* (Institute for Palestine Studies, 1969) and G. H. Jansen, *Zionism, Israel and Asian Nationalism* (Institute for Palestine Studies, 1971). The first book was on the Palestinians who stayed in Palestine after the establishment of Israel and were subjugated under the harsh rule of the military government until 1966. The second discussed the differences between Zionism and other Asian nationalisms.

I thought that both these books would be useful for ordinary Japanese to understand the causes of the "Arab-Israeli Conflict". At the time most Japanese did not know that there were still native Palestinians in Israel besides the Jews who had emigrated there from Europe and other regions. Also, many Japanese believed the Zionists' story that the Jews won their national independence after a long struggle against British rule. Most Japanese have never realized the disaster that befell the native Palestinians expelled from their land that the Zionists claimed as their own.

Thanks to the opportunity that translating these books gave me, my interest in the modern history of the Middle East and Palestine grew so strong that I decided to quit my journalist job and to commit myself to Arab studies.

In 1982, American TV repeatedly transmitted images of brutality of the Israeli army as it besieged Palestinian refugee camps in Lebanon. The Israeli forces attacked the camps fiercely, using many kinds of weapons including phosphorous bombs, which give extreme pain when fragments touch human bodies. Later I learned that the Japanese volunteer doctor whom I had interviewed ten years before was staying in the camps and treating the many injured residents and fighters. At that time, I was in America studying the modern history of the Middle East as a graduate student. Every day, the ABC and the NBC reported the terrible reality of besieged Beirut, and this caused some change of American public opinion towards the Arab-Israeli conflict. Before the war in Lebanon, a great majority of Americans supported Israel as the "only democratic state in the region", and regarded the Palestinians as "terrorists" who intended to destroy Israel. But a considerable portion of the American public began to be critical of the Israelis during the siege of Beirut, though their number was not large enough to change the US's one-sided policy toward the Palestinians.

After going back to Japan in 1984, I started to teach Middle Eastern history, including the history of Palestine, at private universities in Tokyo. I also joined a small NGO called "Japan-Palestine Medical Association" based in Tokyo, which raised funds for the Palestinian Red Crescent Society [PRCS] and other medical institutions in Occupied Palestine. The Oslo Accords in 1993 enabled us to directly help humanitarian activities and organizations in the West Bank and Gaza.

Most Japanese people, like Americans and West Europeans, were so short-sighted as to think the Palestine problem would soon be solved through peaceful negotiations. But I was more cautious in my thinking about Oslo and its effects. It was obvious that the Israelis were the winners if one read the letters exchanged between Arafat and Rabin just before the Accord was signed, because Arafat promised many things including the amendment of the Palestinian National Covenant, while Rabin only said he would start negotiation with the PLO. It was my opinion that the Israelis' continued oppression of the Palestinians would make peace impossible. I hoped that the Israeli leaders would restrain themselves from constructing more settlements in the occupied territories. But it turned out as I feared; Israeli policies ruined that hope.

It was a few years before the Oslo Accords and a little after the start of the First Intifada that I wrote an introductory book for beginners, especially junior high school students, *Do You Know Palestine?* [Horupu Shuppan, 1990]. Luckily the book was read by as many as 100,000 readers, including adults, and ran into several print runs. I think the book helped attract curiosity about Palestine in many Japanese who had known little about it before. Around that time, a number of students and researchers in Japan started to specialize in Palestine and the modern Middle East.

Later, I wrote a book for adults, university students, and specialists, *A History of Palestine* (Akashi Shoten, 2015). It didn't sell so well, partly because ordinary Japanese had lost interest in Palestine when talks between Israel and the PLO stagnated after Oslo.

Before my retirement from the university in 2011, I used to visit the Middle East and other countries to read archives and to conduct interviews with people familiar with the modern history of the region: for example, I visited the US to read documents in the FDR Library, the Truman Library, the National Archives, and Jewish American archives. I was especially interested in US policy toward the Middle East after the First World War. There is no doubt that without strong support from the US and the USSR, the Zionists would not have been able to establish a Jewish state in Palestine.

Until the early 1930s, American Zionists were not so influential even among the Jewish American communities. Many were indifferent and some were even hostile to the Zionist idea, because the great majority of the Jewish Americans identified themselves first as "Americans". However, when the Evian Conference in 1938 failed to rescue Europeans persecuted by the Nazis, and especially after information about the genocide of Jews during the war reached America, the Zionist idea that the Jews needed a country of their own rapidly found support, first from Jewish Americans and then from the Christian majority.

The strategy adopted by American Zionists during the Second World War was extremely successful. They stressed that Jews needed a refuge from harsh persecution in Europe, a Jewish state in Palestine. They systematically lobbied local politicians, congress members of both Democrat and Republican parties, clergies of the Christian Churches, labour leaders and influential journalists, gaining support from an overwhelming majority of Jewish Americans. And because most Americans were reluctant to receive more immigrants to the US from war-torn Europe, they welcomed the idea of the Jewish state elsewhere.

When the hijacked airplanes crashed into the World Trade Center Buildings in September 2001, I was on my way to a Jewish American archive, a few kilometers from the WTC Building.

It might merely have been a chance that the American I met at the bar listened to my explanation of the UN Palestine Resolution and somehow understood it. Thirty years earlier, that kind of conversation wouldn't have happened because most Americans thought of Palestinians as unreasonable "terrorists".

About twenty years have passed since the 9/11 event, and more Americans seem to be trying to understand the root causes of the Palestine problem, and are becoming critical toward Israel's intransigent policy of clinging to the occupation, displacing Palestinians and expanding their settlements in the West Bank. In Congress, an increasing number of lawmakers are discussing the stopping or lessening of US political and military support for Israel.

In contrast to the US, Japan has become more and more accommodating to right-wing Israeli government policy, especially since 2014. That year Prime Minister Netanyahu visited Tokyo and signed a joint statement for coordination between both countries, especially in relation to security. Since then, military cooperation between the two parties has developed, and the exchange of visits of military personnel has increased. In October 2018, an Israeli security goods exhibition was held in a Japanese metropolitan area. Small groups of citizens are resisting these trends. I myself took part in the protest movement against the security exhibition. It may need a long time to rectify the right-wing Japanese government's policy toward the Middle East and Palestine.

Dr Ryantori

Aacademic-cum-activist, Indonesia

"The Palestinian Issue"

One of the international conflicts which has lasted for a long time is the Israeli-Palestinian one. It has caused many casualties, especially on the Palestinian side. This chapter is based in empathy and engagement with the Palestinian refugee issue. It attempts to explain its origins and also the support it receives from international actors, especially Indonesia. The Palestinian refugee is the topic that has attracted me academically, and I chose it for my thesis research.

The Palestinian issue is a very tragic issue, especially when we relate it to the Palestinian refugee problem. In·the Gaza Strip there are eight Palestinian refugee camps, while twenty-four others are spread across the West Bank and Jerusalem. There are as many as twelve official refugee camps in Lebanon, nine in Syria, and ten in Jordan. Meanwhile Palestinian refugees have gathered in a number of Arab countries such as Iraq.

The United Nations produced the UN General Assembly Resolution of November 29th, 1947 (No. 181) or better known as the Partition Resolution 1947, a resolution in the form of dividing the land of Palestine into three parts: a part for Israel, some for the Palestinians, and Jerusalem to be under UN control. The resolution was followed almost immediately by violence and conflict.

The conflict has given rise to two large waves of Palestinian refugees. The first wave resulted from the 1948 War with the number of refugees amounting to 726,000 people – two thirds of the entire Palestinian population of 1.2 million people. The second wave resulted from the 1967 War when 323,000 Palestinians lost their homes. Of that number, 113,000 of them have been refugees since 1948.[1]

The Zionist program to establish a Jewish state on Palestinian land has involved and continues to involve efforts to expel the indigenous Palestinian population. This raises an important question: do the expelled Palestinians have the right to return? For those

---

[1] Paul Findley, *They Dare to Speak Out: People and Institutions Confront Israel's Lobby*, Chicago, Lawrence Hill Books, 1989, p. 45.

expelled, the answer is, of course, yes. However, what about the international world? Count Folke Bernadotte, UN Mediator assassinated by the Zionist Stern Gang, stated (UN Doc Al 648, 1948):

> *It would be an offence against the principles of elemental justice if these innocent victims of the conflict were denied the right to return to their homes, while Jewish immigrants flow into Palestine.*

The Right of Return has a strong legal basis. The United Nations adopted Resolution 194 on December 11, 1948. Paragraph 11 of the resolution states:

> *... the refugees wishing to return to their homes and live at peace with their neighbours should be permitted to do so at the earliest practicable date... compensation should be paid for the property of those choosing not to return.*

Since then Resolution 194 has been continually reaffirmed in a universal consensus, with the exception of Israel and the United States. The resolution was further affirmed by UN General Assembly Resolution No. 3236 [1974], which asserts "the inalienable right of the Palestinians to return to their homes and property from which they have been displaced and uprooted, and calls for their return". The obstruction of this right is an act of aggression, which deserves a response from the UN Security Council. Israel's joining the UN was originally conditional on its adherence to relevant UN resolutions, including Resolution 194.

The validity of the Right to Return does not stem only from UN resolutions. Article 13 of the Universal Declaration of Human Rights has affirmed the right of every individual to leave and return to his/her homeland. Moreover, the Principle of Self Determination guarantees the ownership and domicile rights of an individual in his own homeland. The United Nations adopted this principle in 1947. From 1969 until now this principle has also been explicitly applied to the Palestinian people, including "the legality of the Peoples' struggle for Self-Determination and Liberation". International law has established that neither occupation nor dominion deprive people of their private property rights.

According to a report on the Amnesty International website, Israel has demolished thousands of Palestinian homes in the Gaza Strip, West Bank, and in the East Jerusalem area, whether on the pretext of security or because the homeowner does not have a permit. In addition, thousands of hectares of land belonging to Palestinians have been seized to establish settlements in the Occupied Territories. The construction of these settlements violates Article 49 of the Geneva Convention, which states that "an occupying power shall not transfer parts of its own civilian population into the territory it occupies".

However, an encouraging fact regarding the issue of repatriation of Palestinian refugees is that many elements of the international world support it, from organizations, countries, groups of countries, and the United Nations through UNHCR and UNRWA (the United Nations Relief and Works Agency). For example, UN Security Council Resolution 242 [November 1967] requires Israel to withdraw from Palestinian territories occupied in the 1967 war to allow Palestinians to return to their homes. Through the Oslo Accords [1993], refugees residing in the West Bank and the Gaza Strip obtained identity cards issued by the newly created Palestinian National Authority (PNA). Together with the inhabitants of these territories, they received assistance provided through the European Commission Humanitarian Office (ECHO).[2]

The Palestine Land Society, a body formed to document all property belonging to refugees in the territory currently occupied by Israel, has a plan called *From Refugees To Citizens At Home*,[3] based on a book written by Dr Salman Abu-Sitta. This plan for the refugees' return may be considered legal and necessary, but it remains theoretical, unless the force of international law is brought to bear on the responsible party. The victims must be rescued from the injustice visited upon them by a far superior military power. International law was implemented by the Great Powers in Kuwait, East Timor, Kosovo, and Bosnia. This could be done again in Palestine.

Though providing some information on the suffering of the refugees, some Arab countries do not treat them properly, under the pretext of economic and social problems. Yet these countries have stated their commitment to the Casablanca Protocol, issued at an Arab League meeting in 1965. The protocol essentially emphasizes that all Arab countries should protect the refugees living in their country.

Another form of support comes from the Organization of the Islamic Conference [OIC]. As an organization that focuses its programs on the Middle East, this is one of the organizations that cares for the Palestinian refugees. The "Islamabad Declaration" was the OIC's first declaration regarding refugee issues, especially Palestinian refugees. Article 9 of the declaration states:

> We reiterate that the establishment of an independent Palestinian state with Al-Quds Al Sharif as its capital, liberation of all occupied Arab territories of Palestine, Syria and Lebanon, return of Palestinian refugees and internally displaced persons to their homes and implementation of the Security Council resolutions 242, 338, 1397 and 1515 and General Assembly resolution 194 are vital for establishment of peace and security in the Middle East.[4]

The Boycott, Divestment and Sanctions movement (BDS) and the International Solidarity Movement (ISM) are relatively new but important initiatives, because they have maintained a global presence, uniting human and Palestinian values. The BDS

---

[2] Mick Dumper, "The Return of Palestinian Refugees and Displaced Persons: The Evolution of a European Union Policy on the Middle East Peace Process", in *Palestinian Refugees: Challenges of Repatriation and Development*, Rex Brynen and Roula El-Rifai, eds., New York, I. B. Tauris & Co Ltd, 2007, p. 70.

[3] Salman Abu-Sitta, "From Refugees to Citizens at Home: The Logistics of Return." *Plands*, accessed 11 Jan 2022, www.plands.org/en/books-reports/books/from-refugees-to-citizens-at-home/the-logistics-of-return

[4] "Islamabad Declaration Adopted by the Thirty Fourth Session of the Islamic Conference of Foreign Ministers (Session of Peace, Progress and Harmony) Islamabad, Islamic Republic of Pakistan 28 – 30 Rabi al-Thani 1428 H (15–17 May 2007)." *OIC-OCI*, 17 May 2007, www.oic-oci.org/docdown/?docID=435&refID=31

movement issued its first declaration in 2005, calling on the world's citizens to boycott Israel, and pressure governments to impose sanctions on it until Palestinian rights are recognized, the Israeli occupation ended, and the right of return and equality recognized. Based on a simulation of the anti-apartheid model in South Africa, this movement seeks transnational action towards an international siege of Israel, to pressure it to comply with Palestinian rights.

The International Solidarity Movement (ISM) is a Palestinian-led movement committed to resisting the long-entrenched oppression and dispossession of the Palestinian population, using non-violent, direct-action methods and principles. Founded in August 2001, ISM aims to support and strengthen Palestinian popular resistance by being beside Palestinians in olive groves, on school runs, at demonstrations, within villages under attack, beside houses being demolished, or where Palestinians are subject to attack by soldiers or settlers.

For Indonesia, supporting Palestine has always been a priority of its foreign policy. This is not based on religion, but rather on the Indonesian Constitution of 1945. The Preamble states: "Whereas independence is a genuine right of all nations and any form of alien occupation should thus be erased from the earth as not in conformity with humanity and justice. . ."

Indonesia is committed to full support for Palestinian independence, and to continue supporting Palestine through technical cooperation within the framework of South-South Cooperation and Triangular Cooperation. In addition, Palestine was one of the priority issues that Indonesia advocated in the UN Security Council after being selected as a non-permanent member of the UN Security Council from 1 January 2019 until 31 December 2020. Moreover, it has appealed to the international community to take steps to end the illegal Israeli occupation of the Palestinian territories to support the "two-state solution".

The Indonesian Minister of Defense, Prabowo Subianto, has emphasized that Indonesia is fully committed to supporting peace in Palestine: "Indonesia supports a peaceful resolution that includes a two-state solution for Palestine. Indonesia is very willing to do everything we can to increase the prospects for such a solution."

President Joko Widodo has reiterated Indonesia's commitment to continue supporting the Palestinian struggle to become a fully sovereign and independent state with East Jerusalem as its capital. This statement was made by the president during a bilateral meeting with Palestinian Prime Minister Muhammad Ibrahim Shtayyeh on the side-lines of the COP26 World Leaders Summit, in Glasgow, Scotland, November 2021.

On 19 May, 2021, in my capacity as Executive Director of the Indonesia Society for Middle East Studies (ISMES), I made a statement in a webinar held by the Indonesian Institute of Sciences (LIPI) entitled "Israel-Palestine Heats Up: How to Understand the Sustainability of the Crisis and Indonesia's Role?". I said that there are six main points in Indonesia's position on Palestine. The first is that Palestine must be independent and Indonesia must support its independence. Second, Indonesia must restore the centrality of the Palestinian issue in the international community during the current conflict in the Middle East. Third, Indonesia must continue to encourage member states of the United Nations and international organizations to recognize Palestinian sovereignty.

Fourth, it must support the initiative of the United Nations to revive Palestinian-Israeli peace negotiations based on the "two-state solution". Fifth, that Indonesia must mobilize the OIC countries to find a peaceful solution to the Palestinian-Israeli problem. Sixth, Indonesia must continue to advocate that Palestine, especially the Al-Aqsa Mosque Complex, should be placed under international protection.

Hiroyuki Suzuki

Scholar, the University of Tokyo, Japan

My interest in the Middle East, particularly the Israeli-Palestinian conflict, was sparked by TV coverage of 9/11. At that time, I was a fourteen-year-old boy in my second year of junior high school. A few years later, I started learning Arabic at Tokyo University of Foreign Studies, one of the hub universities for foreign studies in Japan. I completed my master's degree and doctoral research at the University of Tokyo, where I submitted a thesis on Palestinian political activities under Israeli rule since 1967.

Interest in Middle Eastern issues, including the Israeli-Palestinian conflict, is by no means common among Japanese people, likely due to Japan's geographical distance from the Middle East as well as limited opportunities for Japanese people to meet people from the Middle East in their daily lives. In fact, it was estimated that there are only 20,000 people of Middle Eastern and North African origin living in Japan as of December 2019, and approximately 10,000 Japanese nationals living in the Middle East and North Africa as of October 2020.[1] Therefore, political movements and public activities by Palestinian or Israeli groups, such as those seen in other parts of the world, have rarely occurred in Japan.

In this environment, why did I become interested in Middle Eastern issues and the Israeli-Palestinian conflict specifically? My interest originated with TV coverage of the Middle East. In 2001, a major Japanese TV station, NHK, broadcast an hour-long news program at 10 p.m. In that broadcast I, along with many other Japanese viewers, "witnessed" 9/11. At the beginning of the program that day, September 11, 2001, there were short news items about the first case of mad cow disease (BSE) in Japan, and an approaching big typhoon. The news anchor also mentioned a Japanese baseball player in the American Major Leagues who was absent from the game. Suddenly the announcer's tone became strained as an urgent report of a plane "crashing" into the World Trade Center building in New York City came in. At this point, it was

---

[1] Ministry of Foreign Affairs of Japan, "Statistics on Foreign Residents (formerly 'Statistics on Registered Foreigners')", https://www.moj.go.jp/isa/policies/statistics/toukei_ichiran_touroku.html (Accessed 9 Jul. 2022).

The number of Japanese residents in the Middle East was calculated from the data as of October 2020 as listed on the Japan Ministry of Foreign Affairs information pages for each country. In this chapter, the Middle East includes Turkey, Israel, Iran, and Afghanistan in addition to the Arab countries, in accordance with the Japanese Ministry of Foreign Affairs.

approximately 9:01 a.m. in New York City, a quarter hour after the first plane had crashed; several minutes later the second plane appeared. Many Japanese viewers, including me, witnessed the second attack during this live broadcast. The media coverage in Japan that followed became heated and interspersed with phrases such as "Al Qaeda", "Bin Laden", and the "Middle East". As a junior high school student, I followed the latest news.

While my interest in the Middle East grew, the US attacks on Afghanistan and Iraq began. Along with news coverage, I watched short documentaries and happened to see one that inspired my interest in the Palestinian cause. It was a short, 50-minute program broadcast only on the NHK satellite channel: "Said talks on the 'Iraq War': Cairo on the Eve of the Outbreak of the War." Edward W. Said was well-known in Japan; almost all of his books were translated into Japanese (there are just a few scholars and philosophers who have earned this glory, including Max Weber, Michel Foucault, and Hannah Arendt). Yet, TV coverage of Said was rare. The program contained Said's lecture at the American University in Cairo and his talk with Raji Sourani, a Palestinian lawyer. Their conversation covered not only 9/11 and the Iraq War, but also the Palestinian cause, including the al-Aqsa Intifada, the Israeli occupation, the wall, imperialism, and more. Honestly, I could not understand all that they said at first, but their conversation interested me. Regretfully, I did not record the program so I had to buy Said's translated essay. It was very difficult to understand, but I kept at it, reading it with the help of a dictionary, a guide to Palestinian history, and help from my father who was a history teacher. This was in the spring of 2003 when I was in my first year of high school. Three years later, I chose to study the Middle East at university.

When I became a university student in 2006, I realized that many of my classmates also had become interested in the Middle East based on TV coverage of 9/11, the war in Afghanistan, and the Iraq War. For my generation, people born in the late 1980s, TV broadcasts were the primary experiences that sparked our interest in this region. My interest in the Israeli-Palestinian conflict grew during my first year of college, after witnessing the Israeli invasion of Lebanon that summer, attending a graduate seminar, and participating in a public symposium on Middle Eastern issues. During that year, I also became acquainted with Toshikuni Doi, an independent journalist who was deeply involved in organizing the TV program on Said that inspired me in 2003. With Doi, I organized several public symposiums, especially after he filmed current conditions in Palestine and Israel that included daily life in the Gaza strip.

After I began to engage in academic and cultural activities, I realized that there was plentiful knowledge about the Palestinian cause in Japan, including translated books, handy guidebooks, academic writings, reportages, documentary movies, and public symposiums. In terms of Japanese interest in the Middle East generally, the tremendous impact of the 1973 oil crisis should be mentioned. This crisis was a catalyst for the entirety of Japanese society, including the government, business community, and academic community to become concerned with the Middle East. After the outbreak of the October War in 1973, the oil-producing Gulf countries took the lead in raising the official price of crude oil and announcing an oil embargo against pro-Israel countries. Japan's strong alliance with the United States raised fears within the Japanese government that Japan might be subject to this oil embargo.

The Japanese government's position on the Palestinian cause changed drastically during the 1970s. Susumu Nikaido, the Chief Cabinet Secretary at the time, stated that the Japanese government supported the "UN General Assembly resolution on the right of Palestinians to self-determination", even stating that the Japanese government "may have to reconsider its policy toward Israel depending on how the situation develops in the future", making clear Japan's pro-Arab stance.[2] The government also organized a diplomatic mission headed by Takeo Miki, Deputy Prime Minister [who later became Prime Minister], to Saudi Arabia and Egypt to explain its friendly stance toward Arab countries. This move was derided as "abura diplomacy" rather than "Arab diplomacy", using the word "abura", which means "oil" in Japanese. Relatedly, Japan's contribution to the United Nations Relief and Works Agency for Palestine Refugees in the Near East (UNRWA) increased substantially to $5 million in 1974, more than total Japanese contributions to UNRWA from 1953 to that time. The 1976 Annual Book of the Institute for Palestinian Studies (IPS) rightly noted that "Since the end of 1974, Japan has taken a position on Middle East affairs that is largely independent of Washington."[3]

These social challenges helped spread awareness of the Palestinian cause in Japanese society from the mid-1970s through the 1980s. It is important to note that even before the oil crisis, there was some sympathy for the Palestinian liberation movement in the "Third World", i.e. Asian, African, and Latin American countries, and solidarity with the Palestinians was expressed in the cultural context. The 1972 Lod Airport shooting by three young Japanese who belonged to the organization later called the Japanese Red Army was a radical and violent manifestation of this position. However, it was the oil crisis that brought critical change: the Palestine Liberation Organization (PLO) was allowed to open a representative office in Tokyo in 1977.

Academic efforts also multiplied. Along with academic papers, many guides to Middle Eastern topics were published. In particular, the handy pocketbook series, called *shinsho* in Japanese, could be purchased for approximately $6 and included several volumes that covered the Israeli-Palestinian conflict. This inexpensive book evoked interest in the Palestinian cause and helped younger generations acquire basic knowledge.

According to Yuzo Itagaki, a leading scholar of Middle Eastern studies in Japan, Japanese interest in the Palestinian cause, which in the 1970s was dominated by solidarity and support, changed in the 2000s to a position based on "neutral and moderate" values such as humanity and public interest.[4] When I organized public symposiums over a decade, I noted the same impression; younger generations tend to show their interest in the Palestinian cause in relation to human rights, international law, or human dignity. They are also attracted by NGO activities; some try to become

---

[2] Statement of the Chief Cabinet Secretary Susumu Nikaido, 22 Nov. 1973, https://worldjpn.grips. ac.jp/documents/texts/JPME/19731122.S1J.html (Accessed 18 Jul. 2022).

[3] The details of this history are described in *60 Chapters for Knowing Palestine* (Tokyo, Akashi-Shoten, 2016, in Japanese). The book was published as an introduction to the Palestinian cause and is often purchased on major online bookstores such as Amazon whenever there is major news on the Palestinian-Israeli conflict.

[4] Itagaki's insight and review of the Japan-Palestinian relationship is worth reading. Itagaki, Yuzo, ed. *Reprinted Edition, Considering the Palestinian Question*, Tokyo, Daisan-shokan, 2012, Appendix, p. 9.

involved in aid projects in Palestine, just as they are involved in other Asian or African countries. The Palestinian cause, once understood in a particular political context, is now addressed within the general context of humanity.

In turn, this evolution has led to the disappearance of a consciousness of the historical significance of the Palestinian cause. For example, it would be impossible to understand the Palestinian issue without contemporizing it with the process of decolonization that the Middle East has experienced and more broadly with independence movements in Asia and Africa. Indeed, I often hear talk that shows a crude understanding of history, including discussion that asserts that both sides, Israel and Palestine, should quickly make peace but ignores the political, economic, and military imbalance of power between the two. Some people even ask how the Jewish people who experienced the Holocaust, a tragedy in human history, could attack Palestinians (this is a typical question, often raised in public symposiums or lectures).

This challenge may weigh more heavily on younger generations. Learning history can be tedious, especially for a generation accustomed to getting information quickly from Wikipedia, YouTube, and other Internet sources. However, an overly dichotomous understanding of the Palestinian problem is likely if one fails to grasp the historical context. The current state of Middle Eastern studies in Japanese universities is far from sufficient in this regard. In Japan, where there are approximately 750 universities, an over-representation compared to other countries, only a few universities, including the University of Tokyo, Kyoto University, Kyushu University, Waseda University, Sophia University, Tokyo University of Foreign Studies, Osaka University, and Ritsumeikan University, offer courses on the Middle East.[5] It is much easier to find universities that do not offer a single class dealing with Middle Eastern topics, including the Palestinian cause, than ones that do. Japanese literacy on Middle Eastern topics requires further development.

My current concerns are that over the past decade economic ties between Japan and Israel have strengthened and that a discourse of unconditional support for Israel has emerged in recent years.[6] There has been a large increase in private investment by Japan in Israel, growing from approximately $2 million in 2012 to a record high of $2.9 billion in 2021. I have observed that the image and perception of Israel in Japanese society have improved significantly over the past twenty years, now reaching the stage where Israel is seen as a positive start-up state, a LGBT-friendly society with high-tech industry, and even as a Japanese-friendly country in the Middle East. The potential for this economic nexus to significantly change the approach to the Palestinian issue by the Japanese government, and even Japanese society, should not be underestimated.

---

[5] Based on the total number of universities in Japan in 2019. Ministry of Education, Culture, Sports, Science and Technology of Japan, "International Comparison of Number of Schools and Students" https://www.mext.go.jp/content/20210323-sigakugy-main5_a3_00003-014.pdf (Accessed 15 Jul. 2022).

[6] As an example, on May 12, 2021, while Israel's air strikes on the Gaza Strip were still ongoing, Deputy Minister of Defense Yasuhide Nakayama wrote on Twitter, "What would you do? When suddenly one day, in 24 hours, over 300 rockets were fired by terrorists, taking the lives of your loved ones and your home. Israel has the right to defend itself against terrorists. Who was it that fired the first rockets at civilians? Our hearts are with Israel." (This post was later deleted by Nakayama himself.)

AFRICA

Suraya Dadoo

Journalist/BDS activist, South Africa

"Repaying Our International Solidarity Debt:
South Africa and Palestine"

In 2001, the United Nations World Conference Against Racism (WCAR) was held in my hometown, the coastal city of Durban. I had just completed my postgraduate studies, and had returned home to cover the conference for a community newspaper. From 31 August to 8 September, the conference discussed racism, discrimination, xenophobia, and compensation for colonialism and slavery. In addition to the main conference that consisted of state actors, there was also a parallel NGO Forum representing 3,000 NGOs and attended by over 8,000 representatives from across the world.

It was at this NGO Forum that I heard – for the first time – the Palestinian issue being discussed in the same breath as the blockade of Cuba, China's occupation of Tibet, and racism against native Americans and Dalits [untouchables in India].

I was familiar with these injustices mainly because of my participation in student politics and involvement in the youth wings of the ANC and other mass democratic movements in South Africa. But on the question of Palestine it was the WCAR that really opened my eyes.

The NGO Forum adopted a Declaration that described Israel as a "racist, apartheid state" that was guilty of "war crimes, acts of genocide and ethnic cleansing" against the Palestinian people.

The NGO Forum Declaration wasn't an official document of the WCAR, but it was to be symbolically handed over to the Conference Secretary-General, Mary Robinson, at the conclusion of the Forum. Robinson, however, refused to accept the document, citing concerns over its language. Conference delegates voted to reject the language that implicitly accused Israel of racism. But the genie had been let out of the bottle as Israeli apartheid had been exposed on a global stage – in the country that had experienced apartheid and fought it.

At the WCAR, Israel was consistently described as an apartheid state by well-respected human rights activists. This was not a religious conflict. How had I missed it all those years?

From Al Aqsa to Apartheid

Growing up in Durban in the 1980s and 1990s, in my mind the issue of Palestine was a religious conflict centred on the call to "Free Al Aqsa". This was the slogan that I associated most closely with Palestine. I hadn't heard much about Palestinians being humiliated at Israeli military checkpoints; the theft of Palestinian land, or the multitude of laws that privilege Israelis over Palestinians. Palestine solidarity was largely concentrated within South Africa's Muslim community – which I was not a part of at that time.

In 1998, the secular Palestine Solidarity Committee (PSC) was formed in South Africa. The PSC tried to form a coalition with the Congress of South African Trade Unions (COSATU) and its affiliates, to further the Palestinian cause in South Africa. They failed to bring them on board, despite South African freedom fighters training alongside Palestinian fighters in Eastern Europe and Africa, and the PLO's support, arming and training of soldiers from the ANC's armed wing, Umkhonto weSizwe (MK).

While there were individual strong statements in support of Palestine from a freed Nelson Mandela and other ANC leaders in the 1990s, the ANC and its tripartite partners in the South African Communist Party (SACP) and COSATU had not joined the Palestine solidarity movement in South Africa.

The WCAR didn't just – as in my own case – change individual perceptions of Palestine, it fundamentally altered the nature of Palestine solidarity in South Africa. During the WCAR, the PSC launched its "Amandla Intifada!" campaign, and COSATU and its affiliates openly pledged their support for the Palestinian cause. It was a defining moment for Palestine solidarity in South Africa.

Post-WCAR, Palestine solidarity became formalized, louder, and an integral part of the foreign policy of the ruling ANC and its tripartite partners (COSATU and the SACP), as well as the South African government.

In October 2004 – before the formation of the BDS Movement in Palestine – South African solidarity groups had already called for a comprehensive boycott of Israel. The call was endorsed by major South African organizations and unions including COSATU, the Landless People's Movement, the South African NGO Coalition, the Anti-War Coalition, and Physicians for Human Rights.

Following Israel's invasion of Lebanon in 2006, several high-ranking COSATU officials visited the Occupied Palestinian Territories where they witnessed Israeli apartheid first-hand. COSATU and its affiliates became more vocal in their condemnation of Israel's apartheid practices and began to openly endorse the Palestinian-led Boycott, Divestment and Sanctions (BDS) movement against Israel.

So did I. These were groups and activists that had shaped my political consciousness. I took their accusation that Israel was practicing apartheid against the Palestinians seriously. As with South African apartheid, there was a need to act. Through my work with an NGO called Media Review Network, I soon became involved in the Palestine solidarity movement in South Africa.

Working at "Ground Zero"

The Israeli government calls South Africa the "ground zero" of the BDS Movement. From spying to lobbying, Tel Aviv has dedicated significant resources to countering the boycott movement here – with limited success. There is a massive outpouring and powerful shows of support for Palestine from the South African people and their political leadership. As much as I am proud of this, I also need to be honest about our shortcomings.

Although support for Palestine is incredibly strong (over 200,000 people attended a protest march against Israel's 2014 bombardment of Gaza), knowledge about what makes Israel an apartheid state, and why the Palestinian cause resonates with our own experience, is somewhat lacking among ordinary South Africans.

It is for this reason that I have chosen writing as my form of activism for Palestine. This stems from my father's influence. As I grew up, he would always remind me that the media, and newspapers in particular, were an incredibly important way to fight for what you believe in.

So, over the last fifteen years or so, I've been writing about the Palestinian issue, exposing Israeli apartheid and countering Israel's apologists in South African media. In my effort to educate people, I also co-authored a comprehensive reference book called *Why Israel?* [1] The title refers to the standard comment of Israel's apologists who ask, "Why Israel? Why is Israel being singled out?"

It's easy to focus on the ideology and politics of the occupation and overlook the human dimension. I did not want to be guilty of this in my writing, and so have tried to raise the voices of ordinary Palestinians.

When we speak, for example, about the impact of the occupation on education, I want people to know about students who must cross a checkpoint every day to get to school, or about someone who had to study repeatedly for an exam that eventually never took place, because the lecturers were not allowed through the checkpoint.

The human dimension is important for South Africans because we can relate to the experiences of Palestinians on an emotional level. Palestine's present is our past. We know what it is like to watch our home being demolished. We, too, have been forcibly relocated. Fietas is Sheikh Jarrah; Cator Manor is Silwan; District 6 is Umm el Hiran. The names of the towns in which home demolitions and forced removals took place have changed, the name of the regime has changed, but the policies and its motives are the same. And the feeling of dispossession is the same.

The fight against Israeli apartheid should be a natural next step for ordinary South Africans who experienced and opposed apartheid. However, Israel's well-oiled *hasbara* machine has been somewhat effective in making some South Africans believe that this is simply a real estate dispute between two equal sides – nothing to do with occupation, apartheid, and colonialism.

So the task is to reach out to justice-seeking South Africans and get them to see that the Palestinian present is our past. "Each one teach one" was a central message during South Africa's liberation struggle, particularly the trade union movement in which my

---

[1] Dadoo, S. and Osman, F., *Why Israel? The Anatomy of Zionist Apartheid: A South African Perspective*, Johannesburg, Porcupine Press, 2013.

father was active. It's more than just a slogan, and guides much of my own work in writing and educating people about the Palestinian cause.

There is also a tendency among South Africans, and indeed much of the world, to remember the Israeli occupation of Palestine only when the bombs are dropping on Gaza, or when Al-Aqsa mosque is being attacked. It is easy to focus on the physical violence of the occupation. After all, bombs, guns, tear gas, and arrests are perhaps "sexier" and more newsworthy than the structural violence of the permits, checkpoints, and the endless, humiliating Israeli bureaucracy that drives the occupation. To counter this tendency to focus on the violent aspects of the occupation, there is an urgent need for ongoing education and awareness.

Talking Left and Walking Right

It's no exaggeration to state that the South African ANC-led government remains one of the most outspoken critics of Israel, and consistently uses its presence at international forums to advance the cause of Palestine.

In her final address to the United Nations Security Council (UNSC) in October 2019, which brought to an end South Africa's tenure as a non-permanent member, Naledi Pandor, minister of international relations, slammed the UNSC for its inaction on Palestine, and called its failure to end Israel's occupation of Palestine, and secure Palestinian peace and freedom, "a profound stain" on the United Nations' mission.

"Clearly there is no intention to seek or achieve peace by those implementing these actions. How is it possible to believe in this Council, in peace and security in the face of such offending breaches of this Council's decisions?" Pandor asked in a fiery farewell address.

In his first address as the Chair of the African Union in February 2020, President Cyril Ramaphosa gave a stinging rebuke to Trump's Middle East plan, comparing it to the infamous Bantustan system in apartheid South Africa.

However, when it comes to Palestine and relations with Israel, the South African government "talks left" but "walks right". The ANC-led government has not *done* anything significant in solidarity with the Palestinians nor committed itself to do so. Let's not even talk about its support of the boycott movement against Israel. As I write this, President Cyril Ramaphosa has just accepted the credentials of the eighth Israeli ambassador to democratic South Africa.

I, along with everyone else in the South African Palestine solidarity movement, genuinely struggle to comprehend and understand why a regime that practises policies that many in the South African government have called "worse than South African apartheid" is still welcome in democratic South Africa. The South African government talks a good talk, but it refuses to *act* in any substantial way in solidarity with the Palestinian liberation struggle.

It's true that since 2018 South Africa hasn't had an ambassador in Israel. This followed a 2017 recommendation by the ANC Conference to downgrade our representation there. This is a significant step, but it is simply not enough. South Africans did not ask the world to downgrade ties with the apartheid regime. We asked for the complete boycott, divestment, sanctions, and isolation of Pretoria in order to compel the regime to abide by international law and human rights. Are Palestinians not deserving of the same solidarity?

Over the years, various Palestine solidarity groups have met with senior ANC and government officials to propose that they fully adopt BDS. This would isolate Israel politically and economically. Activists have also petitioned the government to stop using companies such as G4S, Caterpillar, and Cape Gate, which profit from the occupation and bolster Israel's repressive apparatus. South African companies are still free to trade with Israel. The ANC-led government has consistently ignored and refused these calls, leaving us all exasperated. When it comes to the Palestinians, the ANC-led government is struggling to repay its international solidarity debt.

Several years ago, during a holiday in Durban, my children asked me why I was so involved with Palestine – a place so far away from South Africa. They asked me that question while we were at a beach in uMhlanga. I wasn't allowed at that beach when I was growing up because of South Africa's racial segregation. "Part of the reason why you are now able to come here is because people thousands of kilometres away in Dar es Salaam, Lusaka, London, and New York fought for us," I explained. Now it's our turn to do the same for the Palestinians.

In some small way, I hope that my words in the media, in books, in articles, and in educational workshops contribute to the repayment of that debt.

Farid Esack

University professor/activist, South Africa

"Holding on to a Small Piece of Rubble – South African Reflections on Solidarity with the Palestinians"

I first visited Palestine during the first Intifada in 1988 when our South African liberation struggle was reaching new heights. I was deeply involved in that struggle and it was impossible to look at the State of Israel through benign eyes. Here was a country founded in response to and justified by many impulses – including to the savagery of Nazism. However, it was also a state that was now arming an unapologetically racist South African regime that had supported the Nazis to the hilt. Israel was a country that turned its unique preferential trade privileges with the United States and the European Economic Community into a springboard for world markets for South African goods. Much later I became aware that several of the neighbouring Arab countries had also been active in breaking sanctions against South Africa. Along with the US, Israel was one of the few countries that sided openly with Apartheid South Africa at the United Nations.

I have since undertaken about eight journeys to Palestine, and my memories of the first one have faded. However, I vividly remember the moment of my oath to support the Palestinian struggle for freedom and justice. Accompanied by the Reverend Naim Ateek, I visited the site of a Palestinian house that was demolished by the Israeli army the day before. They flattened the house, and the family was still roaming outside it in bewilderment and pain amidst the rubble. When the demolition started, an elderly matriarch had her grandchild – a young baby – with her. In rage and desperation, she thrust the baby at one of the soldiers, screaming: "Here; Take this child! Where will she sleep tonight? Where?" The soldiers charged her with the crime of assault. Her crime? "Pushing a soldier violently." The weapon listed on the charge sheet? "Baby."

I picked up a small piece of the cement rubble of the demolished home, held it tightly in my fist and committed myself to the Palestinian struggle. I was too small in 1960 when our house in Cape Town was demolished under Apartheid's Group Areas Act to pick up a souvenir. However, I do have clear memories of the truck journey to the middle of nowhere, to be dumped in an apartheid newly created "township" for "Coloured People". As I am writing this chapter, that thirty-five-year-old piece of rubble is now at my side in my office. Why do I hold on to it?

Well, first, it was impossible to ignore my own lifetime experience with and under Apartheid and not recognize it in Occupied Palestine. The idea of Israel as an Apartheid state is usually met with a sense of effrontery by Zionists, often including those committed to the so-called "peace process". They variously argue that this comparison is offensive, alienating, counterproductive; "It is an unhelpful analogy that does not admit to the complexity of the issues", their narrative goes. For them, the question is often not whether the comparison can be made but that it should not be made. Apartness is, of course, not unique to Palestine/Israel. When apartness is elevated to dogma and ideology and when it is enforced through the law and its agencies then we are dealing with something particularly horrific, regardless of how genuine the trauma that gave birth to it or the religious depth of the exclusivist beliefs underpinning it all. This is what is happening in Israel.

Second, I am astonished at how ordinary decent people whose "hearts are in the right place" equivocate when it comes to Israel and the dispossession and suffering of the Palestinians. And I wonder about the nature of "decency". Do "objectivity", "moderation", and "both sides" not have contexts? Is "moderation" in matters of manifest injustice a virtue? Do both parties deserve an "equal hearing" in a domestic violence situation where a woman gets beaten up by a male who was abused by his father years ago because "the perpetrator, too, is – or, more correctly, **was** – a victim"? Why must someone else suffer because the husband was abused by another male yesterday? Whose story are we tuned into, and whose interest do we serve by tuning in to the side that we do, or by opting for an illusionary neutrality?

Thus they do not see Palestine, and when others see it, they demand objectivity – an objectivity that is routinely scorned when it comes to race, gender, and sexuality. Postmodernist thinkers, feminists, liberation theologians, and other progressive scholars have long since debunked the myth of objectivity and insisted on "disclosure" as a precondition to dialogue; tell us about your class and gender interests? What are the lenses through which you view the world? In the words of David Tracy (1939–), the famous Catholic theologian, "There is no historyless, discourseless human being" (1987, 107). A denial of lenses is tantamount to accepting a dominant status quo. When I walk through the districts where sex is on sale, I can choose to see it through the eyes of the "sex tourist" or the eyes of the sex worker sold into the trade or driven there by poverty and exploitation. I choose to look at Palestine through the eyes of the marginalized and the exploited, and I decide to privilege this perspective over other perspectives. So is "sex tourism" "sexual exploitation"? Or, worse, is it a refusal to name it and a preference to speak about the seemingly neutral "just having some fun" or "relaxation"? It depends on where we are located in the power structure. Union Theological Seminary in New York is a bastion of progressive Christian theology in North America. As Marc Ellis so eloquently points out, it reflects a pattern in liberal thinking in much of the West, a willingness to locate oneself ideologically amongst the enlightened, but does so very carefully with an eye to not upsetting the applecart of power – particularly not the rotten and completely uncritiqued Zionist applecart.

Thirdly, I act because I live with that occupation myself. We **are** in the middle of it because we do business with the abusive husband (or we profit from his abuse of his wife), and we sustain his delusions that he is OK, a part of the civilized crowd. We seek refuge in "both sides have a story to tell" as a way of dodging our complicity. Rather than merely hallowing the abuser with the mantle of respectability, our silence draws us into a web of complicity. Talking about the "Jewish-German conflict", or the "Black-White situation", or "marital problems" in the face of the Holocaust, Apartheid, or domestic abuse respectively is no great virtue; it is the path initially of acquiescence and ultimately of complicity.

I speak because I have to live with myself. In some ways, this is born in a sense of self-righteousness, a kind of moral indignation, which assumes that you have the moral high ground. I am happy to assume all of those things, with the limitation that future generations may expose me as inadequate, as shallow, as inconsistent, as hypocritical – hopefully only inconsistent.

Why do I pick on Israel? Well, first, that is an untruth. Virtually all of us committed to Palestine solidarity do so as part of more extensive commitments to justice. However, human capacity forces me to pick my battles. In doing so, I constantly take a bow to the larger questions of injustice, such as xenophobia, homophobia, and environmental justice. While I focus on justice for the Palestinians, I weave in as many narratives of marginalization as possible.

When I see factory workers in the clothing industry, I recognize my mother immediately and identify with them. The factory floor is where she lived and died. I recognize her immediately when I see other women in abusive relationships, or when I see single mothers abandoned by abusive husbands. In the same way, I recognize the Palestinians immediately in the shadow of Zionism. I recognize my own life as a young Black person in Apartheid South Africa.

It is this that I tried to convey when I wrote my two kilometres long letter to Palestinians a decade ago, which is still inscribed on the Apartheid Wall on Highway 60, north of Jerusalem around Al Ramm, near the Qalandiyya checkpoint.

My dear Palestinian brothers and sisters, friends and comrades.

I have come to your land on eight occasions and I have recognized shades of my own.

My land was once one where some people imagined that they could build their security on the insecurity of others. They claimed that their lighter skin and European origins gave them the right to dispossess those of darker skin who lived in the land for thousands of years. I come from Apartheid South Africa. I have lived under South African Apartheid; I have fought against it peacefully and not so peacefully.

Arriving in your land, the land of Palestine, the sense of deja vu is inescapable. I am struck by the similarities. In some ways, all of us are the children of our histories. Yet, we may also choose to be struck by the stories of others. Perhaps this ability is what is called morality. We cannot always act upon what we see but we always have the freedom to see and to be moved.

I come from a land where people braved onslaughts of bulldozers, bullets, machine guns, and teargas for the sake of freedom. We resisted at a time when it was not fashionable. And now that we have been liberated, everyone declares that they were always on our side. It's a bit like Europe after the Second World War. During the war, only a few people resisted. After the war, not a single supporter of the Nazis could be found, and the vast majority claimed that they always supported the resistance to the Nazis.

And today, the world is witness to how you, the Palestinian people, are bravely resisting the onslaught of bullets, bulldozers and machine guns.

We pay homage to your resistance against your dispossession by the Zionist occupiers, your determination to remember where you, your parents and your grandparents come from. Memory has become your weapon – although not your only weapon.

We pay homage to your mobilization at a grassroots level through the formations of women's organizations, trade unions and various other kinds of civil society and political initiatives.

You resist despite the daily humiliation at checkpoints, the disgrace of an Apartheid Wall that cuts people off from their land, livelihood, and history, and against the torture, detention without trial, and targeted killings of those who dare to resist.

Many of you have committed extraordinary acts of bravery in this struggle against Apartheid and occupation. This is painfully visible in the scars of the bodies of so many young and some not so young Palestinians; This is visible in countless times that so many of you – armed only with stones – have faced the might of the fourth largest military force in the world. Your resistance is visible from a large number of fathers ageing in Israeli prisons and young men deprived of an opportunity to serve their families.

Above all, you have resisted by refusing to disappear. Zionism wills you to be gone, and through your resistance, you have denied them this dream.

As South Africans, speaking up about the life or death of the Palestinian people is also about salvaging our own dream of a moral society that will not be complicit in other people's suffering. There are, of course, other instances of oppression, dispossession, and marginalization in the world. Yet, none of these is as immediately recognizable to us who lived under, survived, and overcame Apartheid. Indeed, for those of us who lived under South African Apartheid and fought for liberation from it and everything it represented, Palestine reflects the unfinished business of our own struggle in many ways.

Thus, I and numerous others who were involved in the struggle against Apartheid have come here, and we have witnessed a place that reminds us of what we have suffered through. Archbishop Desmond Tutu is, of course, correct when he speaks about how seeing the conditions of the Palestinians "reminded me so much of what happened to us black people in South Africa. . . . I say why our memories are so short? Have our Jewish sisters and brothers forgotten their humiliation?" But yet, in more ways than one, here in your land, we are seeing something far more brutal, relentless and inhuman than what we have ever seen under Apartheid.

As South Africans who resisted Apartheid, we understood the invaluable role of international solidarity in ending centuries of oppression. Today we have no choice but to contribute to the struggle of the Palestinians for freedom. We do so with the full awareness that your freedom will also contribute to the freedom of many Jews to be fully human in the same way that the end of Apartheid also signalled the liberation of White people in South Africa.

At public rallies during the South African liberation struggle, the public speaker of the occasion would often call out: "An injury to one?!" and the crowd would respond: "Is an injury to all!" We understood that in a rather limited way at that time. Perhaps we are destined to always understand this in a limited way. What we do know is that an injury to the Palestinian people is an injury to all. An injury inflicted on others invariably comes back to haunt the aggressors; it is not possible to tear at another's skin and not to have one's own humanity simultaneously diminished in the process. In the face of this monstrosity, the Apartheid Wall, we offer an alternative: Solidarity with the people of Palestine. We pledge our determination to walk with you in your struggle to overcome separation, conquer injustice, and to put an end to greed, division, and exploitation.

We continue to draw strength from the words of Nelson Mandela, the father of our nation and hero of the Palestinian people. In 1964 he was found guilty on charges of treason and faced the death penalty. He turned to the judges and said: "I have cherished the ideal of a democratic and free society in which all persons live together in harmony and with equal opportunities. It is an ideal which I hope to live for and to achieve. But if needs be, it is an ideal for which I am prepared to die."

Naeem Jeenah

Executive Director of the Afro-Middle East Centre, South Africa

"Becoming pro-Justice; becoming Anti-Apartheid"

The 1980s was a decade of intense political activity by a range of anti-apartheid forces in South Africa (and from outside South Africa), and one of severe repression by the apartheid state. It began in 1980 with nationwide school and university boycotts that continued for the better part of the year, and was followed by a decade of "rolling mass action" that included ongoing student uprisings, protests, trade union strikes, large-scale community mobilisation, and rejection of puppet structures installed by the government.

The period included a number of armed operations by members of the underground structures of the liberation movement: the African National Congress's uMkhonto we Sizwe (MK); the Pan-Africanist Congress's Azanian People's Liberation Army (APLA); the Black Consciousness Movement's Azanian National Liberation Army (AZANLA); as well as smaller groups such as the Muslim organisation Qibla. That decade also saw the formation of two large national coalitions against apartheid: the National Forum and the United Democratic Front (UDF). The former brought together a coalition of Black Consciousness- and Africanist-aligned groups within the country, together with a number of leftist groups and trade unions; the larger UDF was composed of a range of civic, student, trade union, and other groups that were mostly aligned to the banned and exiled African National Congress (ANC). A number of national and provincial states of emergency were also declared by the government at different times in the 1980s, and repression across the country increased, with assassinations, detentions, and torture becoming commonplace.

It was in this decade that I became politically involved. My entry into political activism and the South African liberation struggle was not through any of the groups mentioned above, however; I joined the Muslim Youth Movement (MYM) in 1980, when I was fourteen years old and a high school student. The MYM, at the time, was one of two national Muslim organizations or social movements in the country – the other being the Muslim Students Association (MSA) – that had become, by the early 1980s, the unofficial student wing of the MYM.

Both MSA and MYM were engaged in South African liberation politics, but they also both had a strong focus on international solidarity. Unfortunately, much of this international solidarity was directed at "Muslim" causes, but it served as my introduction to the struggle of the Palestinian people for their liberation. These two organizations, together with another two Muslim organizations that were politically active, were the most vocal on the Palestinian issue through the 1980s and into the 1990s. The Palestinian cause (Israeli oppression) was mentioned by other resistance organizations in South Africa – especially leftist groups – on rare occasions when they issued a statement about it, or in statements on imperialism or American support for South Africa's apartheid regime, or a mention of Israel when talking about states busting sanctions against apartheid South Africa. Perhaps understandably, the greater concern for these groups was the struggle in South Africa, which intensified in the 1980s. This despite the fact that the Palestinian Liberation Organization (PLO) was lionized among South African activists; and the liberation movement in exile – particularly the ANC – had close relations with the PLO. The space for Palestinian solidarity was thus left to the Muslim political groups, and was, therefore, often cloaked in religious symbolism.

However, for a young high-schooler, perhaps what had a more serious impact on my consciousness regarding Palestine was not the focus on Palestine itself, but these organizations' emphasis on the Islamic imperative to struggle for justice, to fight against oppression and to work for the liberation of all people. The notion that one should be willing to give one's life to support any struggle by oppressed people to liberate themselves had a profound impact on my mind and on the rest of my life. It influenced my thinking not only regarding Palestine, but on a range of issues – from international solidarity to women's rights. The apartheid state realized the potential of international solidarity, and how it could be mobilized against the South African state itself, and thus suppressed attempts at expression of support for the Palestinian and other freedom struggles.

Later, in 1998, four years after South Africa's first democratic election, I was part of a group that founded the first Palestine solidarity organization in South Africa; the Palestine Solidarity Committee (PSC) that was not religion-based but brought together anti-apartheid activists from different political traditions and different faith orientations (and those of no faith orientation). After the formation of the PSC, the MYM encouraged its members to join the PSC and similar groups and to engage in solidarity activities through these (secular) organizations rather than through the MYM.

The second crucial factor that helped me "become pro-Palestinian" was a consequence of the first. My involvement in the MYM and MSA meant that I was also involved in South African liberation politics in different ways. Understanding the form and character of South African apartheid also helped many anti-apartheid activists recognize the apartheid that existed in the Palestinian context, as implemented by Israel. We were using the terminology of Israel as an "apartheid state" long before the recent reports by human rights' organizations; long before, even, the 2001 World Conference Against Racism (WCAR) where South African activists, sometimes using the analysis of Israeli scholar Uri Davis, forced "apartheid" onto the agenda as a way of describing Israeli policies. The civil society march of tens of thousands of people during the WCAR ended with a (largely symbolic) launch of an "International Anti-Apartheid Movement Against Israel".

What we South Africans saw Israel doing in both the Occupied Palestinian Territories and within Israel itself very easily resonated with us victims of apartheid; for us, it *was* apartheid – even before we looked at the legal definition in the Convention for the Suppression and Punishment of the Crime of Apartheid, or engaged in the kind of careful analysis of Israeli laws that Davis had undertaken or, later, that done by a Human Sciences Research Council (South Africa) project with the help of international law experts, or, more recently, the reports produced by a number of human rights organizations. To us, Israel looked like apartheid and Israel felt like apartheid, and its victims sounded and felt like Black South Africans. We who lived as Black people under apartheid know it when we see it, we know what it feels like on our bodies, what it tastes like in our bloodied mouths. We therefore had no option but to fight it. Just as in a previous period South Africa had been regarded as the moral issue of the day, Palestine became *the* issue that for us symbolized all struggles for justice, equality, against exploitation and colonization. It is unsurprising, then, that well-known South Africans such as Archbishop Desmond Tutu and numerous political, trade union, religious, and other leaders spoke so easily about how the plight of Palestinians reminded them of South Africa; and why Nelson Mandela, in his now-famous statement, said, "We know too well that our freedom is incomplete without the freedom of the Palestinians".

For us, fighting the Palestinian struggle was, perhaps, less a case of "solidarity" and more a case of continuing the struggle we had been engaged in for decades. And so my South Africanness is the second factor that ensures that I have been, for decades, pro-Palestinian.

When I was twenty, and still an angry young student activist, I met someone who profoundly altered my understanding of struggle and of solidarity, Shamima Shaikh (who later to my surprise did me the great honour of agreeing to marry me). Shamima, in the words of one of our greatest poets, Don Mattera, "epitomized compassion". He made this comment after one of my lectures during which he had counted the number of times I had used the word "compassion". For me, Shamima also epitomized Che Guevara's comment that "the true revolutionary is guided by a great feeling of love". Struggle, I learnt from her, was all about love, gentleness, and compassion – not about anger, frustration, and despondency. And solidarity too is about love.

Pakito Arriaran, a Basque ETA volunteer, expressed this clearly in his last letter before being martyred in the mountains of Salvador fighting for the FMLN: "Solidarity is the tenderness among peoples". I find it difficult, therefore, to call myself pro-Palestinian, because tenderness and love makes one part of those to whom one expresses these feelings, not just "pro-" them. Solidarity, as the late revolutionary president of Mozambique, Samora Machel, insisted, "is not an act of charity: it is an act of unity between allies fighting on different terrains toward the same objectives... an assertion that no people is alone, no people is isolated in the struggle." And Mandela's quote that "our freedom is incomplete..." encapsulates the essence of solidarity: it is not about doing for others; it is very much about doing for ourselves. Our lives and destinies are inextricably linked with the lives and destinies of all oppressed people. That understanding makes solidarity an act of love – for those with whom we express solidarity, as well as for ourselves. Solidarity is not about things like humanitarian assistance, pity, or giving; it is a political act. Even more than that, it is a political process that creates political and loving relationships.

Before I heard any of these wonderful revolutionary quotes, I learnt these lessons from my partner, through her love and compassion for all people – with a special kind of love for the Palestinian people. She, then, was the third factor that ensured that I became, and remain, "pro-Palestinian".

The effect of the South African struggle for liberation on the understanding and perspectives of South African activists did not stop at a comparison of the systems of oppression in the two apartheid contexts; it extended as well to an understanding and appreciation of the nature of struggle, of visions of liberation, and of strategies for liberation. The Palestinian liberation struggle is one against colonialism and apartheid. We believe that the strategic options available to Palestinians are many and that, as in the case of South Africa, outsiders should not impose strategies on or dictate to oppressed people who are struggling to free themselves from colonialism. During our struggle, we had insisted that South Africans would decide how we would resist apartheid, what strategies and tactics we would use, and how we would determine our progress in that struggle.

Similarly, we insist that Palestinians must themselves decide how they will conduct their struggle and, as people in solidarity with them, we will respect and support their choices. This is why I, and other South African comrades who have been anti-apartheid strugglers, argue that the minimum forms of support that solidarity activists should give to the Palestinian people are: 1) campaigning for boycotts, divestments, and sanctions as part of the global BDS movement, and the global isolation of Israel – militarily, politically, diplomatically, economically, culturally, and academically; and 2) support for any forms of resistance chosen by Palestinians against the occupation, colonialism and apartheid of the Israeli state, including armed resistance if or when that is their choice. During the era of apartheid in South Africa, we asked for solidarity from people around the world, but, at the same time, we jealously protected our right to decide our own forms of struggle and our own strategies for liberation.

When international law gives occupied and colonized peoples the right to resist occupation and colonization even through armed means, when that was a choice that our liberation movement made in our context – a choice that we continue to celebrate, how can a South African condition their support for the Palestinian people by stipulating what forms of struggle they find acceptable and by demonizing violent forms of resistance?

Often, when speaking about Palestine, I used to be asked by young Zionists, in South Africa and elsewhere, why Palestinians did not choose peaceful/non-violent means of resistance. "If only they followed the example of Nelson Mandela," was a common refrain. First, such a statement reflects a profound disrespect for Mandela, who was sentenced to life imprisonment not because he called for non-violence but because he was one of the founders of the ANC's armed wing, uMkhonto we Sizwe; the charges that he and his fellow treason trialists faced had to do with their promotion of armed resistance to the apartheid state. It is a profound insult to my brother who was killed by apartheid police (and to all our martyrs who sacrificed their lives in order that we might be able to overcome apartheid). The last pictures of him show him lying on the ground with an AK47 rifle alongside his body.

For many South Africans, the manner in which our democratic government since 1994, led by the ANC, has repeatedly let down the Palestinian people and their struggle has become a source of disappointment. Despite the past relationship between the ANC and the PLO, the ANC government, more than a quarter century after taking power, has yet to implement economic sanctions against Israel. Indeed, there are state-owned companies that source products and services from Israeli companies, including security equipment. South Africa still hosts an apartheid ambassador and an apartheid embassy. There has been some change in this regard over the past few years; South Africa has now downgraded its representation in Tel Aviv, campaigned strongly against the holding of the Africa-Israel Summit (subsequently cancelled), led the battle against Israel's accreditation to the African Union, and is poised to call for a recognition in multilateral fora of Israel's practices of apartheid, considered crimes under the Convention for the Suppression and Punishment of the Crime of Apartheid. For a state and a ruling party that claim to support the Palestinian people and struggle, it has taken far too long to get to this point, and there is much more that needs to be done.

While the focus of the apartheid designation of Israel is on international law, as it correctly should be, South Africans feel a personal connection to the issue because of our own experience. We therefore also hope that Palestinians will achieve their liberation as we did. However, we are conscious of the manner in which South Africa, post-apartheid, has been unable to provide the kind of restorative justice that we had expected, has not adequately dealt with the land question, has ignored the national question, has seen inequality in our country worsen as successive governments have adopted neoliberal economic frameworks, and exists in a context where, while we have achieved political liberation, economic justice for the vast majority of South Africans remains a dream repeatedly postponed or cancelled. In a sense, South Africa's ending of apartheid can be regarded by Palestinians as a dry run for their own continuing struggle, a live scenario-planning exercise that can be used to assess what we did right and what we did wrong, and how these lessons might benefit the Palestinian struggle, so that Palestinians may emerge into a post-colonial and post-apartheid era that does not mirror South Africa's mistakes and failures but ensures that they do not happen again.

Apart from the concrete solidarity that we can offer the Palestinian people, this is possibly our other great contribution to the Palestinian struggle: the appeal not to make the mistakes we made.

Zahid Rajan

Publisher and human rights activist, Kenya

"Wearing a Badge of Honour: The Kenyan Palestinian Story"

Recently I was speaking to a member of the newly formed Malawi Palestine Solidarity Movement, and asked how their organization was getting along. He lamented that their billboards in their capital city of Blantyre had been vandalized. The billboards showed Nelson Mandela as saying, "Our Freedom is incomplete without the liberation of the Palestinians". He sounded depressed and downhearted, to which I replied, "Welcome to the Palestinian struggle – wear this setback as a badge of honour!"

It is said that in every crisis lies an opportunity, and therein lies the genesis of my becoming "Pro-Palestinian". Israel's extensive use of white phosphorus munitions during its twenty-two-day military operations in Gaza, from December 27, 2008 to January 18, 2009, named "Operation Cast Lead", had horrified the world once again. How could I not act? I asked myself

By 2011, I had had a partnership with the Alliance Francaise (AF) in Nairobi for a number of years on co-hosting different cultural events, and now I thought of approaching them to host a Palestinian Film Festival. The AF had been hosting annual Israeli film festivals. My first meeting with the coordinator was tricky. AF is a locally registered NGO and was established to host cultural shows regardless of political affiliations. After listening to my idea, they explained that they already were hosting the Israeli Embassy and would find it difficult to host us. But I argued our case, saying they were taking sides and that we also had the right to tell our side of the Palestinian story. And so they agreed, asking me to send them a formal proposal with a possible list of films. Simultaneously I constituted a small committee of about ten people under the banner of the Kenya Palestine Solidarity Committee (KPSC). As a committee we were clear that because of the low level of awareness of the Palestinian struggle in Kenya our main task would be "Education, Education, Education", and our tools would be films and discussions. The film screenings would attract more people to the organization and enable us to grow slowly but surely.

A week before the start of the film festival I requested AF for wall space to display posters of the Palestinian struggle. The answer was an emphatic NO! Yet when the film screenings began, the audience response was truly amazing. My partner had privately predicted that I would be looking at an empty hall and yet during the entire week we did not have standing space at the screenings! We had clearly filled a void in the Kenyan people's interest in, and support for, the Palestinian struggle! During the panel discussions I was repeatedly approached by the organizers to avoid "politics" and refused permission to distribute leaflets explaining the broader context of the Zionist occupation.

Despite approval of the list of films I had submitted, on the second or third night I was called in by the AF management and told I could not continue screening some of the films as I had not sought "screening rights". Some of the film makers had allegedly called them and said they were not happy at their films being screened at our festival. Note – they did not say that I had not sought screening rights. While in principle their argument made sense, it was clear that other forces were at play. Attendees from the Israeli side refused to sign the registration sheet, or filled in fictitious information, and were there simply to report on our activities. Clearly we had touched a raw nerve. But internally the tensions had taken their toll on some of our committee members who had been intimidated by the negative happenings. Over the next three years they quietly withdrew from the KPSC. Lessons learnt: i) We had filled an important gap in creating awareness of the Palestinian struggle in Kenya.; ii) Israel has a strong diplomatic, political, and cultural presence in Kenya and would always be a thorn in our side; iii) The absence of a Palestinian diplomatic presence in Kenya clearly made us vulnerable.

Over the next few years I read more about the Palestinian struggle and spent time establishing contacts with other solidarity movements around the world, particularly in South Africa where the BDS movement is very strong. Come 2014 and forces began to coalesce again, and with the support of a few comrades we founded the Kenya Palestine Solidarity Movement (KPSM), with its acronym in Kiswahili "Kenya na Palestine" (Kenya and Palestine). On 24 October 2014, we partnered with a new youth NGO, "PAWA 254", for our first film screening of "Roadmap to Apartheid". The event was attended by about thirty persons followed by a short discussion session.

The next three years were spent mainly on creating awareness both at home and abroad of the existence of KPSM through our social media platforms. In 2017, we became aware of the Israeli Apartheid Week (IAW) https://bdsmovement.net/iaw. This is a tool for mobilizing grassroots support for the Palestinian struggle for justice at the global level. It is a mechanism to raise awareness about Israel's apartheid system, and to mobilize support for strategic BDS campaigns to help bring an end to Israel's occupation of Palestine.

In 2017 we held our first Israeli Apartheid Week. Here too we had our fair share of challenges and successes, and learnt more about the capture of local NGOs by the US government. In late 2016, I approached PAWA254 again. I explained to them how #Apartheid/Israel worked and the kind of challenges they might face if our experience with Alliance Francaise was anything to go by. I was assured that there would be no such backtracking, and that the planning process could begin. Time flew by, and after resending emails for a month, I called them. No reply. Then a message appeared on Skype saying "We can't host the IAW". What?! No explanation, no apologies and no further communication?! The penny dropped – the Empire had struck again. My main contact remained non-communicative.

After recovering from the shock, it was time to stop agonizing and start organizing again. By that time I had become aware that Amnesty International, which had recently opened an office in Kenya, had highlighted "Land Day 2017". This was a campaign that had begun in 1976 when Israel had expropriated 2000 hectares of land surrounding Palestinian villages in the Galilee. Israel's response to the Palestinians' protest march was six killed, one hundred wounded, and hundreds arrested. I approached the Amnesty office here in Nairobi, and to my pleasant surprise, got a positive response. They agreed to host the IAW 2017! Other members of the committee now also got galvanized and the IAW expanded into events at three different venues: one in the Central Business District where we screened a film; another in the newly formed Mathare Social Justice Centre; and one at Amnesty International Kenya. We screened five films at Mathare and Amnesty: "Occupation 101", "Jerusalem – the East Side story", "Frontiers of Dreams and Fears", "Omar", "Tears of Gaza", and "Leila Khaled – Hijacker". A spin-off was the relationship we developed with the IAW international team. They sent us a template for a poster they had developed. The IAW were so delighted with our adaptation of the poster that some of our inputs got adopted in the international campaign for 2017. Amnesty however did not allow us to use their logo on our publicity material, citing fear of jeopardizing their newly established presence in Israel.

The 2018 IAW week expanded to a 14-day awareness campaign at four different venues, themed "Afro-Palestine Solidarity" week. We decided to engage as many diverse audiences as possible in different parts of Nairobi. We held screenings at two venues in the largely working-class area of Eastlands, and at two venues in the more middle-class area of Westlands. The films we screened were: "Junction", "5 Broken Cameras", "The Wanted 18", "The Idol", and "Speed Sisters".

In 2018, through internal fundraising we produced merchandising: branded T-shirts, stickers, posters and educational material. One particular highlight was an exhibition in the Amnesty premises by the Brazilian cartoonist Carlos Latuff. The staff and visitors at Amnesty were captivated by the cartoons, and many spent lunch breaks and evenings viewing the exhibition.

That year the screening at the 'Eastleigh Mall' in a largely Somali-inhabited area attracted the largest audience. The area's member of parliament, the Honorable Yusuf Hassan, graced the occasion. The screening was an emotional event as anger against #Apartheid Israel became palpable. Though this was a very successful screening we were aware of the fact that in Kenya the Palestinian struggle was still being identified as a "Muslim" struggle.

There were two spin-offs from the IAW 2018: one was a film screening at the Law Campus of the University of Nairobi. The event was well attended with a mix of films and robust discussion forums. The students' campus group has now metamorphosed into a country-wide 'National Student Caucus'. The second was a monthly film screening at the British Institute in Nairobi. We held eight monthly film screenings from April to November, as well as keeping the Palestinian cause active in the mind of the public with regular postings on social media. Among the films we screened were "Divine Intervention" and "The Time that Remains" by Elia Suleiman, and "Anti-black Racism and Israel's White Supremacy" by Abby Martin of the Empire File documentary series.

The year ended with the establishment of a Palestinian Embassy in Kenya. This diplomatic presence would make our solidarity work so much easier. The new incoming ambassador, His Excellency Hazem Mohamed Shabat, graciously hosted the steering committee for dinner soon after his arrival and put the embassy at our service for our activities in Kenya.

Lessons learnt in 2018: We had created an awareness of the Palestinian struggle in the minds of diverse audiences, and had achieved part of our campaign to "Educate, Educate and Educate". However, we had not been successful in attracting enough people to join the committee and expand our capacity to organize on an even larger and more effective scale. A lot more work was needed.

The year 2019 turned out to be a year of surprises. We were approached by Suraya Dadoo, based in South Africa, about the possibility of hosting a Palestinian author/intellectual to tour Kenya. Naturally we were very excited and settled on Ramzy Baroud, who is based in Seattle, USA. The visit took place from June 25 to 29 2019, and consisted of five public engagements across different sites in Nairobi, also a book signing of his latest book, *The Last Earth*. Ramzy Baroud's visit was well received in Kenya especially by the Human Rights sector. The week's activities generated a great deal of awareness of the Palestinians' struggle, history, and contemporary issues. We expanded our media reach and Horizon TV and Switch TV were particularly supportive.

In 2019 we hosted a very successful "Quds Day" at the CID Training School. The event was attended by between fifty and seventy people, mainly from the Islamic faith consisting of men, women, and young children. We produced T-shirts, posters, and banners bearing the slogan "Silence is not an Option". Those who attended included representatives of social movements, international solidarity movements based in Nairobi, and political parties.

In the early part of 2020, before the pandemic lockdown, we had a live television discussion on Horizon TV, an online Muslim TV station in Nairobi. Ambassador Hazem M. Shabat and the secretary of KPSM, Kenne Mwikya, were the guest speakers.

In 2021, together with some KPSM members, I formed a youth-based, grassroots pro-Palestinian organization and named it "Kenyans for Palestine" (K4P). We have held to date two film shows, "5 broken Cameras" and "Stones Cry Out". "Stones Cry Out" depicts the story of the brutal eviction of Christian Palestinians and became a topic of much discussion. It helped dispel the propaganda labeling the Palestinian struggle as a Muslim religious struggle.

K4P is engaging robustly with the BDS movement and has been successful in convincing a local restaurant, "Falafel", to avoid stocking food ingredients sold by an Israeli company in Kenya called "Baraka Israel". We have also produced informative leaflets on creating awareness of the BDS campaign in Kenya.

In October, Maren Mantovani from the BDS National Committee and "Stop the Wall" movement visited Kenya, further enhancing the message of being "Pro-Palestinian" and creating greater awareness of the Palestine/Israel situation. Maren visited Kenya as part of her 4-month outreach to various countries on the African continent. Her visit has been very productive for K4P, and has given us added impetus and ideas for activities for the Palestinian cause in 2022.

In September 2021, I was among a group of people that established the "Pan-African Palestine Solidarity Network" (PAPSN). PAPSN's first campaign was to lobby the African Union (AU) to reject the proposed "Observer Status" granted unilaterally to Israel by the Chair of the AU. This resulted in a robust campaign by African States calling for the rejection of this abhorrent proposal, and led to the deferment of the final decision to an AU Heads of States meeting in February 2022. PAPSN plans to hold its first "Anti-Apartheid African Conference" in Dakar, Senegal in early February 2022.

On November 29 2021, the embassy of Palestine in Nairobi hosted K4P and friends of Palestine in commemoration of the "International Solidarity Day for Palestine". The day was commemorated by a film screening of "The Great Book Robbery", the awarding of appreciation gifts to the Steering Committee of K4P, and a sumptuous dinner afterwards.

In conclusion, we in the solidarity movement in Kenya are committed to the liberation of Palestine. We face many hurdles and challenges, but the Palestinian people face a ruthless and brutal occupation in Palestine. As is said, "Under Apartheid South Africans lost their land; but the Palestinians are losing their country". If the Palestinians have not given up after seventy-three years of oppression, the least we can do in Kenya is to show our solidarity with the Palestinian cause, and urge the world to put an end to the illegal, racist, violent Apartheid Israeli government. Long live the Palestinian struggle! Amandla. Palestina Huru, Afrika Huru!

NORTH AMERICA

Penny Johnson

Writer/activist, US, lives in Ramallah

"Three Questions on the Path to Palestine"

My solidarity with Palestine began with a question. I was standing in a movie queue in San Francisco in 1967 waiting to see Alan Bates and Julie Christie in *Far from the Madding Crowd*. I had abandoned a dreary linguistic summer school class at Stanford University for San Francisco's "Summer of Love", along with about 100,000 other young people. Some of these were also waiting in line: hippies, women in maxis and minis, long-haired and beaded males, peace signs and ponchos galore, and smiling youth with a whiff of marijuana on tie-dyed clothes. In front of me, three such movie-goers were celebrating Israel's victory in the June War – "We smashed them", one said. Hearing their elation, I began to wonder weren't we all anti-war? And who was this "we"? And more profoundly, who were they?

These questions lay dormant for a year or so as the "Summer of Love" was forgotten amid the tumultuous events of 1968, beginning with the January Tet Offensive by North Vietnam and the National Liberation Front, and including the assassination of Dr Martin Luther King and the subsequent uprising by African-Americans in 100 cities across the United States. And at my university in Houston – Rice University – we were also grappling with racism on campus as the first black student ever to be admitted to the University was dismissed. We founded a chapter of the Students for a Democratic Society (SDS), in which the entwined struggles of African-Americans for equality and justice and the anti-war movement occupied our minds and hearts – and which, as I argue in this essay, led many of us to solidarity with liberation movements across our troubled globe.

Reflecting now on this time of protest, I can see solidarity with Palestine developing most quickly within the Black Consciousness movement. The turn of young Black activists in the Student Non-Violent Coordinating Committee to pan-Africanism was clearly a path of Palestine. Like others of my anti-war generation, these activists were our teachers.

However, I must emphasize my own youthful ignorance and uncertain path to knowledge in that time we call "the sixties". The adage, "If you remember the sixties, you weren't really there" has more than a grain of truth. Did I know, for example, that Malcolm X visited Gaza in 1964? Or that ten years later, Muhammed Ali visited

Palestinian refugee camps in Lebanon and gave a stirring press conference in Beirut? No.[1] Closer to home, was I aware of the heated conflict between the young Black leaders emerging from the SNCC and an older generation working in liberal civil rights organizations over (the former's) support for Palestinians? Only in the broadest of outlines. I learned (some years later) that it was the Drum and Spear Press, founded by activists from the Black Consciousness movement, that published *Enemy of the Sun*: *Poems of Palestinian Resistance* (in 1970), after many publishers had turned it down. Reading backward I can see that the rush of events in those days and my own youthful ignorance inevitably precluded deep knowledge but fostered an almost intuitive solidarity, born from horror at the American atrocities in Vietnam, for all those movements opposing US imperialism (a word we in the '60sgeneration learned on the hoof).

My understanding of the Palestinian liberation movement increased as I attended graduate school (although not necessarily classes) at the State University of New York in Buffalo. That May (1970), the killing of students at Kent State and Jackson State led to widespread student strikes and massive demonstrations. Students from the Arab world active in these protests – I particularly recall Ali from Yemen – helped me understand the links between Vietnam and Palestine, ties cemented by the growing spirit of internationalism among young activists. It is hard now to conjure up this spirit but I can recall that when we occupied the President's office at the University to protest ROTC and war research on campus, someone quickly picked up the phone to call students in Bangkok sitting in another university president's office. Strange that now, in our supposedly interconnected world, we are in many ways more divided.

It was not of course that every anti-war activist gravitated towards solidarity with Palestine. I found this out when I left graduate school, again with another question. It was the 1973 October War and students gathered in the conference hall for a discussion that rapidly turned into impassioned support for Israel, seen as besieged by multiple more powerful enemies. When I got up to speak on Israel's occupation of Arab lands and Palestinian lives, my voice trembled as I encountered a wave of hostility from fellow students. Again, a war and again a question: how to make Palestine and Palestinians visible to those who had a commitment to justice but were blinded by the dominant Israeli story?

I left once more for San Francisco soon after, eager to join friends who had also fled academia and the East Coast, and worked in a small but vigorous publishing collective called *People's Press*. We all made our livings outside our shabby office (I found work in a press clipping service), but gave as much of our time as we could to the Press. The Press's commitment to all of us learning every skill – Harold Kahn, a distinguished scholar of Chinese history at Stanford, specialized in book packing – led me to learning layout by hand through working on *Women of Vietnam*, alongside the book's exacting author Arlene Eisen Bergman.

But a third question comes to me now: How did we at the *People's Press* decide to write a primer on the Palestinian people? We must have begun to talk seriously about

---

[1]   I learned the details of these visits and much else in Michael Fischbach's recent incisive *study Black Power and Palestine: Transnational Countries of Color*, Stanford, CA, Stanford University Press, 2019.

it in 1975, perhaps after the evacuation of US troops from Vietnam – the victory for Vietnam that had been at the forefront of our activism, dreams and downright obsessions for so many years. The Press's first publication in 1969 had been an influential primer, *Vietnam: A Thousand Years of Struggle*. Perhaps, someone must have said, it is time to address the Palestinians.

But again why did we turn to Palestine? The Press had an ongoing book project on the liberation struggle in Angola (*With Freedom in Their Eyes*, published in 1976), but this was not simply a case of looking for the next liberation struggle in line. Palestine was a troubled subject within the many concentric circles that we sometimes called the "New Left" and sometimes simply "The Movement", and we felt it needed to be addressed.

So not only at the Press but in the nascent Palestine Solidarity Committee in the Bay Area, we begin to think Palestine. One day a thump at the door of the Press revealed a clandestine book – *Prairie Fire* by the Weather Underground – that included a chapter on Palestine. Encouraging, even for those of us who questioned Weather Underground's colleagues (well, we called them comrades) in the Middle East Research and Information Project (MERIP), which I was later to join, both on account of its own publications and what the editors recommended. Ibrahim Abu Lughod's seminal work *The Transformation of Palestine* informed our work as did other contributions by Palestinian and Arab scholars in the United States, the beginning of a wave of publications on Palestine and the Arab world.

Our Roots Are Still Alive: The Story of the Palestinian People was published in late 1977, collectively written with a postscript that I penned after a solidarity trip to Lebanon that spring. Re-reading and reflecting on the book for this essay, I wince at some of its naïve flaws, favouring, for example, simple heroism over the multiple tragedies in the story of the Lebanese civil war and the Palestinian role therein. But there is much that still strikes a chord in my older self.

My understanding deepened with my work in the Association of Arab American Graduates (AAUG) in Massachusetts from 1979 to 1982, where, as communications director, I edited and wrote a newsletter and fired off various protests to the mainstream media, occupations that would follow me to Palestine. The AAUG was exciting, both intellectually and politically, its annual conferences a meeting place for scholars and activists not only from the US but from the Arab world and beyond. Edward Said was active in inviting academic colleagues to join a delegation that Naseer Aruri and I led to Palestine in 1980, a time when Birzeit University and other educational institutions were shuttered by military order. Naseer was a deeply informed and humane professor of political science, raised in the village of Burham in the West Bank, and I was extraordinarily fortunate to be his colleague. Our group of literary scholars and one lone scientist was met at the airport by Israeli physicist and leading peace activist Danny Amit – a reminder now of a vibrant earlier time of solidarity.

Upon return, these academics and other colleagues founded an association to defend Palestinian universities. Back at my desk at AAUG, requests – one could call them orders – from colleagues at Birzeit University informed my work ("We need buttons," commanded Beshara Doumani from across the sea). And the 1982 war in

Lebanon brought us back to the spirit of the movement against the Vietnam War, with teach-ins and mass protests.

It was this summer that brought me to Palestine for good, although I thought I was coming for only a year to develop a campaign for academic freedom for Palestinian universities "from the other side." I worked first in public relations and with the inestimable and much-missed Albert Aghazarian, as well as the University's semi-clandestine prisoners' committee (later the Human Rights Action Committee), for which I visited lawyers, wrote endless press releases, and learned what I have termed "the art of waiting" as we sat in the tin shack outside the military government and court for endless hours, waiting to glimpse our students (I could never match the attentive patience of committee member and philosopher Hugh Harcourt).

That lone year morphed into four decades of life in Palestine, most of my adult life. Am I still "pro-Palestinian"? I would not shed this label but I would complicate it as my affiliations with place and people have grown over time, whether with colleagues, friends, communities, and family, including my marriage and cherished partnership with Raja Shehadeh.

And who am I as I engage in "pro-Palestinian" activities? Like a number of Birzeit University faculty and staff, I was swept up in the Palestinian delegation to the Madrid Peace Conference – now thirty years ago – and to the subsequent negotiations in Washington, aborted by the Oslo agreements, negotiated so hastily and with such disastrous effects to this day.[2] I am both a citizen of the most powerful nation on earth (unless China takes this mantle in the near future), and a "citizen" of an enclave that announces itself as a state where I have voted in several elections (always for a losing candidate). My affiliations rest in my closeness to people, and in deep ties to a ravaged but still lovely land. Perhaps someday we will place our local commitments to our bio-region and our wider one to our planet. For now, Palestine does not belong to me but I belong to Palestine.

---

[2] My memoir of Madrid, "Not to Surrender or Forget: The Madrid Peace Conference Thirty Years On," was published in *Jadaliyya*, https://www.jadaliyya.com/Details/43284

Dimitri Lascaris

Lawyer, Canada

"Why I Fight for Palestinian Human Rights"

In 1981, the US television network ABC aired a four-part mini-series entitled *Masada*. *Masada* was a fictionalized account of the historical siege of the Masada citadel by legions of the Roman Empire in AD 73. The siege ended when the Roman armies entered the fortress, only to discover the mass suicide of the Jewish defenders when defeat became imminent. The final scene of the mini-series shifted to the modern era, and showed members of the Israeli Defence Forces declaring their oath of allegiance to the State of Israel on top of the Masada citadel.

At the time that the mini-series aired, I was a seventeen-year-old high school student living in London, Canada. My parents, who had emigrated to Canada from Greece several years before my birth, knew nothing of Israel/Palestine, other than that Jesus was born and died there. They had grown up during the Second World War on an impoverished farm near Sparta, and had come to Canada with little money, no high school education and a limited understanding of the world beyond Greece.

In effect, *Masada* was my introduction to the Holy Land. Watching the mini-series caused me to become enraptured by Israel, so much so that I authored a poem about the battle of Masada for my Grade 12 literature class.

Four years later, in the summer of 1985, I embarked on a grand adventure. I was bored with my university studies, and although I had not yet completed my degree program, I dropped out of university with the intention of becoming a writer. At that time, I was acutely aware of the limits of my own experience, having spent my entire life living with my parents in London, so I decided to travel to Europe on my own, with the savings I had accumulated working as a waiter, a janitor, and a security guard while pursuing my studies. I had no particular plan for what I would do upon my arrival in Europe. I simply wanted to immerse myself in cultures and places I had never before experienced, and write.

After arriving in England on a flight from Toronto, I meandered by train down to the Mediterranean region. I spent several weeks in Greece, where I visited the ancient ruins that dotted the rugged countryside.

I then took a ferry from the island of Rhodes to the island of Cyprus. I lingered in Cyprus for several days. While in its capital, Nicosia, I visited the Green Line that separated the Turkish-occupied North from the rest of the island nation.

While contemplating my next destination in Cyprus, I remembered Masada. With a profound sense of anticipation, I purchased an airline ticket from Larnaca to Tel Aviv.

When my flight landed at Ben Gurion Airport, the airplane came to a stop on the open tarmac. I and the other passengers were instructed by the flight crew to vacate the airplane and wait on the tarmac for further instructions. As we lingered near the fuselage of the parked aircraft, airport staff emptied our luggage from the aircraft's cargo bay and placed our luggage on the tarmac. Israeli security officials who were standing nearby then instructed the passengers to collect their luggage and wait for further instructions.

As soon as I retrieved my large knapsack from a pile of suitcases, a security official asked me to accompany him to a van parked near the aircraft. I complied. He then directed me to enter the back of the van with my knapsack. He followed me into the vehicle.

Once inside the vehicle, the security official began to interrogate me. He wanted to know if I was Jewish and whether I was travelling alone. When I disclosed to him that I wasn't Jewish and that I indeed was travelling alone, he demanded to know why I had come to Israel.

I was bewildered by his questions. I explained that I simply wanted to explore the region because I was fascinated by its history. He was not satisfied. He told me that he could not understand why a young man who is not Jewish would travel alone to Israel. All I could do to assuage his concerns was to repeat to him that I was attracted to the rich history of Israel and wanted to learn more by seeing it with my own eyes.

Exasperated by my answers, the security official directed the driver of the van to take us to an inspection facility beside the airport terminal. There, I was strip-searched. My belongings were scrupulously examined. Having found nothing on my person or in my knapsack which aroused his suspicion, the security official eventually allowed me to proceed to the customs and immigration counter inside the terminal. There, I was granted a visitor visa and authorized to enter the country.

My first stop on my inaugural trip to the Holy Land was the city of Tel Aviv. I visited its beaches and was struck by the fact that many of the Israelis who were lounging on the sand were listening to Greek music.

Tel Aviv seemed to me to be a modern city, but I was in search of ancient sites and holy ruins. The place that I was most excited to see was Jerusalem, so after two days in Tel Aviv, I grabbed a bus to the ancient city.

Upon my arrival there, I checked into a youth hostel in the Arab Quarter of the Old City of Jerusalem. The Arab Quarter lies within the boundaries of East Jerusalem.

The year was 1984. At that time, East Jerusalem, which is Palestinian territory under international law, was occupied by the Israeli military. The occupation had begun seventeen years earlier, in 1967. In 1980, Israel's Parliament, the Knesset, passed the Jerusalem Law, which declared that "Jerusalem, complete and united, is the capital of Israel". This declaration was determined to be "null and void" by UN Security Council Resolution 478, adopted months later.

Strolling around the old city of Jerusalem, the first thing I noticed was the disparity in the living conditions between the Arab Quarter and the Jewish Quarter. Relative to the Jewish Quarter, the Arab Quarter seemed impoverished. The buildings in the Jewish Quarter were in a much better state of repair and preservation. The streets were much cleaner as well.

One of the first historical sites I visited in Jerusalem was the Church of the Holy Sepulchre. It lies in the Christian Quarter of the Old City. According to tradition, the Church contains the two holiest sites in Christianity: the site where Jesus was crucified and Jesus's empty tomb.

While I was visiting the Church, I was approached by a Greek Orthodox priest who worked and lived in the Christian Quarter. His name was Father Dimitri. We struck up a friendly conversation. He kindly gave me a tour of the Church.

The next day, while sitting on a bench outside Zion Gate (one of the Gates to the Old City), I heard a commotion. When I looked in the direction of the ruckus, I was shocked to see Father Dimitri grasping the hair of an Orthodox Jewish man. Father Dimitri was kicking him in the stomach. I rushed to the scene of the fracas and separated Father Dimitri from the Jewish man. In amazement, I asked Father Dimitri what had happened. He replied "That Jewish man spat on me. I know that Christ said to turn the other cheek, but I'm a Spartan!"

The following day, after eating a falafel, I came down with a severe case of food poisoning. I began to vomit. I then became feverish and sweated profusely. The owners of the hostel, two Palestinian brothers, became concerned for my well-being. While I was lying awake, sweating and trembling in my bed that night, they approached me and asked me in broken English whether I wanted them to drive me to a hospital. I accepted their offer.

En route to the hospital, the two brothers, who were speaking Arabic to each other, became embroiled in a heated argument. I spoke no Arabic and, sitting in the back seat wrapped in a blanket, I had no idea what they were saying. The brother who was driving the vehicle pulled the vehicle over to the side of a dark road. I became terrified.

At that stage of my life, my image of Palestinians, based entirely on depictions of them in the mainstream Canadian and American media, was that many of them were terrorists who harboured an implacable and irrational hatred of Westerners. I feared that the brothers might be debating whether to kidnap or kill me. Minutes later, however, they calmed down and continued driving me to a hospital.

Once at the hospital, the brothers delivered me to the emergency ward. While waiting to see a doctor there, orderlies rushed by me pushing a stretcher. An Orthodox Jewish man, screaming in pain, was lying on his stomach on the stretcher. I saw a knife sticking out of his back.

Hours later, after receiving treatment from a doctor, I began to feel better and was released from the emergency ward. I returned to the Old City, where I vowed never to eat another falafel – a vow I have kept to this very day.

The next morning, after catching a few hours of sleep, I decided to visit Hebron in the occupied West Bank. I wanted to see the Tombs of the Patriarchs, which are located there. The Tombs are in a cave which, according to the Abrahamic religions, was purchased by Abraham as a burial plot.

I decided to travel to Hebron on a Palestinian bus departing from East Jerusalem. The bus was full of Palestinian workers who resided in Hebron but worked in Jerusalem.

Unbeknownst to me at the time, the Israeli military had recently placed the city of Hebron under a curfew due to unrest there.

Upon the bus's arrival in central Hebron, the Palestinian workers rushed directly to their homes. Within minutes, they had disappeared. I found myself alone in streets strewn with rocks. All the shops were closed and boarded up in the middle of the day. There was no one from whom I could seek directions, so I began to wander the empty streets in search of the Tombs.

I soon came upon a memorial in a square. The memorial, which was surrounded by barbed wire and had red paint splattered all over it, had been erected in honour of six Jewish students who had been slain a few years earlier in a terrorist attack. One of the slain students was, like me, from Canada.

I continued walking the streets until I spied an Israeli military checkpoint in the distance. Upon seeing me, an Israeli soldier standing at the checkpoint raised and pointed his assault rifle at me and ordered me to stop. He approached me and asked me what I was doing in the streets. With my arms raised in the air, I explained to him that I was a tourist from Canada who had come to Hebron on a Palestinian bus to visit the Tombs of the Patriarchs. I said I was lost. The soldier then lowered his weapon. He told me that I was "crazy" to be walking the streets of Hebron during curfew. He directed me to the Tombs of the Patriarchs and urged me to return to Jerusalem on an Israeli bus at the conclusion of my visit.

My first trip to the Holy Land is filled with memories such as these. Until that voyage, I had known nothing of this ancient place and the peoples who inhabited it, other than what I had seen on American and Canadian television. When I departed Israel and Palestine after ten days there, I knew that what I had seen and heard had changed my impressions of these peoples considerably, but it would take me years, and several more visits, to achieve clarity as to those changes.

For several more months, I meandered across Europe on overnight trains, travelling alone. Throughout that time, I wrote a lousy, coming-of-age novel which no one wanted to publish. As my limited funds were running out, I decided to return to Canada and complete my university studies.

Shortly after the resumption of my studies at the University of Western Ontario, I met Leslie, a young Jewish woman from Toronto who, like me, was in her final year of studies. We began to date. Soon, our relationship became serious. Leslie decided to introduce me to her family. She invited me to stay at the family home in Toronto during Passover. I accepted.

Leslie's parents and younger brother warmly welcomed me into their home. They explained to me the traditions of Passover. During my stay with them, I accompanied them to a synagogue, where, at their request, I donned a prayer shawl and a skull-cap. In my conversations with them, I learned of their love for Israel.

The summer following that year of studies, Leslie and I decided to travel to Israel together. I have two enduring memories of that visit. One of those memories is of me lying on my back in the salty waters of the Dead Sea while reading a newspaper. The other was a stroll with Leslie through the Arab Quarter of Jerusalem's Old City. At one point, as we were walking hand in hand, we heard a ruckus in the distance. We looked up and saw several heavily armed Israeli soldiers shouting at two elderly

Palestinian shopkeepers. While staring coldly at the shopkeepers, Leslie said to me, "I hate those people".

My relationship with Leslie ended a few weeks later.

I returned to Israel and Palestine twice more. One of those trips occurred in 1989, during the summer after my first year of law school. On that trip, I travelled once more to Greece, Cyprus, and Israel, where I spent most of my time in Jerusalem's Old City. Upon my arrival in Jerusalem, I discovered that the Palestinians of East Jerusalem were still living under military occupation, and that the living conditions in the Old City's Jewish Quarter continued to be markedly superior to those of the Arab Quarter.

As a result of my first three trips to Israel and Palestine, I no longer had a positive view of Israel, but I felt no particular sympathy for the Palestinian side either. Rather, I had become one of those many Westerners who ignorantly view the animosity between Israelis and Palestinians as a complex, intractable, centuries-old conflict that no amount of foreign mediation could resolve.

After my trip to Israel/Palestine in 1989, I did not revisit the region for another twenty-six years. During that time, I graduated from the University of Toronto law school, started my legal career on Wall Street, returned to Canada, and became a plaintiffs-side class actions lawyer who specialized in prosecuting cases of securities fraud.

The financial crisis of 2007–2009 was a seminal moment for my political evolution. As a securities class actions lawyer, I had a front-row view on the vast mortgage-related fraud that nearly brought the global economy to its knees. I came to understand that our economic system was rigged for the benefit of the privileged few, and to the detriment of the great majority of my fellow citizens.

When Barack Obama emerged as a presidential aspirant in the midst of that crisis, I was so moved by his soaring rhetoric of hope and compassion that I temporarily left my legal practice in Canada and returned to the United States to canvass for his campaign in poor, predominantly African-American neighbourhoods in Indianapolis and Pittsburgh. When Obama emerged victorious in the Presidential election of November 2008, I was moved to tears.

Then came Operation Cast Lead. Within weeks of Obama's election, the Israeli government of Benjamin Netanyahu launched a devastating attack on Gaza. For three weeks commencing in late December 2008, Israel's military relentlessly bombarded the besieged, impoverished and densely populated Palestinian enclave, massacring nearly 1,000 unarmed civilians – including 288 children. By contrast, retaliatory rocket attacks by Hamas killed three Israeli civilians.

As the world watched the unfolding horror, Obama did nothing. For that and other reasons, I became deeply disappointed in the candidate to whom I had just lent my support. Moreover, as a result of Operation Cast Lead, I began for the first time to feel real sympathy for the Palestinian cause.

My sympathy for the Palestinian people was greatly strengthened by Israel's even more horrific attacks on Gaza in the summer of 2014. This time, Israeli forces massacred nearly 1,400 Palestinian civilians – including 526 children. By contrast, six Israeli civilians were killed in retaliatory rocket attacks by Hamas. During Israel's ferocious bombardment of Gaza, it repeatedly attacked United Nations schools whose coordinates had been provided to Israel's military by UN officials. This prompted UN Secretary General Ban Ki-moon to "strongly condemn" Israel and to declare that he was "appalled" by its attacks.

Yet again, Obama did nothing.

In early 2016, I returned to Israel, this time as a lawyer and for professional reasons. I was then prosecuting a class action against a Canadian mining company, Nevsun Resources.

Nevsun had used forced labour at its flagship gold mine in the deeply impoverished country of Eritrea. I and my colleagues had launched the class action on behalf of Eritrean labourers who had been forced to work at Nevsun's Eritrean mine. Through our investigation, we learned that several of those labourers had escaped Eritrea and travelled to Israel by land. They were now living in the country as refugees. In April of that year, I travelled to Tel Aviv to interview them for evidentiary purposes and to explain to them the basis of the lawsuit.

In Tel Aviv, I personally interviewed several of these labourers over a period of one week. Quite apart from the horrors they had experienced at Nevsun's mine – including a torture technique known as "the helicopter" – they spoke to me as well of the racism they had encountered in Israel and experienced on a daily basis. They confessed to me that they were anxious to leave the country, and that what they really wanted was to emigrate to Europe.

When my work was done in Tel Aviv, I travelled to the occupied West Bank at the invitation of a Palestinian-Canadian artist, Rehab Nazzal.

I had met Rehab while she was pursuing doctoral studies in Canada. In December 2015, Rehab was shot in the leg by an Israeli sniper. At the time that she was shot, Rehab posed no threat whatsoever to anyone and was simply photographing an Israeli "skunk truck" while it was pouring an extremely noxious fluid onto the homes of Palestinians in Bethlehem.

Over the period of a week, Rehab gave me a tour of life in the West Bank.

She introduced me to an aging, Palestinian farmer whose land had been encircled and taken from him by Israel's illegal "separation wall". With Rehab's assistance, I spoke with Palestinians living in Hebron's old city. They described to me how Israeli settlers living illegally in their community routinely dumped garbage and foul liquids on their heads from the upper floors of residential buildings. Rehab and I visited Canada Park, built on the remains of Palestinian villages destroyed in the Nakba. I saw an ancient cemetery in East Jerusalem where Israeli settlers had desecrated many graves. I spoke with a well-respected Palestinian lawyer whose home had been bulldozed by Israeli forces, leaving him and his family to live in a tent erected next to the ruins of their home.

All of this so deeply disturbed me that I resolved to act.

At the time, I was the Justice Critic in the Green Party of Canada's shadow cabinet. Upon my return to Canada, I drafted a resolution calling for the Green Party to endorse the use of boycotts, divestments, and sanctions (BDS) to bring an end to Israel's brutal, decades-long occupation of Palestinian territory.

After drafting the resolution, I asked party leader Elizabeth May, who was then the only Green Party MP in Canada's Parliament, to co-sponsor my resolution. To my disappointment, however, she declined to do so. She was fearful, she explained, that the pro-Israel lobby would attack the party relentlessly if we adopted such a resolution.

Because of Elizabeth's popularity and influence within the Green Party, I became convinced that my BDS resolution would fail to pass. I nonetheless resolved to put the resolution to a vote of the party's members. For me, this had become a matter of principle and I could not, in good conscience, abandon the resolution.

By the time the Green Party's policy convention was convened in Ottawa in August 2016, the pro-Israel lobby had learned of my resolution and had begun indeed to smear the Green Party, as well as me personally. For the first time in my life, and despite having had a distinguished legal career, I found myself accused of antisemitism and support for terrorism.

Fortunately, these scurrilous accusations motivated Palestinian solidarity activists and groups to mobilize in support of my BDS resolution. Foremost among them were Independent Jewish Voices Canada and Canadians for Justice and Peace in the Middle East. They eloquently campaigned for passage of the resolution and sent representatives to the Green Party convention as observers.

On the convention floor, when the resolution came up for debate, no less than the party leader herself, Elizabeth May, led the opposition to the BDS resolution. I, in turn, spoke as sponsor of the resolution and appealed to the conscience of the members to support an oppressed people whose only hope for freedom and justice was the vigorous intervention of civil society: Western governments are uniformly supportive of Israel, despite its innumerable crimes against Palestinians. Without the support of civil society, I argued, Palestinians would be doomed to suffer.

To my astonishment, the party members who participated in the final vote endorsed the resolution by a wide margin. This made national headlines in the corporate press. By and large, the coverage was negative.

The next day, Elizabeth May threatened to resign. In a panic, the party's Federal Council hastily convened a special meeting of the members, to be held in Calgary four months later. This was unprecedented. The obvious purpose of the meeting was to persuade party members to rescind the BDS resolution so that the party leader would withdraw her threat of resignation.

I was deeply disturbed by the decision of the Federal Council to convene another meeting. The members had spoken after an open and vigorous debate in Ottawa. Participatory democracy – one of the Green Party's six core values – had prevailed. The leader's threat of resignation seemed to me to be a transparent attempt to coerce the members into acting contrary to their conscience.

I decided to commit the next three months of my life to defending the resolution. With the wonderful assistance of Palestinian solidarity activists from around the country, I conducted a speaking tour in fifteen Canadian cities and participated in two moderated debates on the BDS resolution. With the assistance of activists, we raised thousands of dollars to defray the transportation costs of party members who wanted to travel to Calgary to attend the special meeting for the purpose of defending the resolution.

As news of these collective efforts spread, party leader May invited me to enter into negotiations over a possible compromise resolution. The negotiations led to an agreement that the BDS resolution would be replaced with a resolution that omitted the acronym "BDS", but which called unambiguously for sanctions against Israel, including an arms embargo and a ban on the importation of products made in Israel's illegal West Bank settlements. The new resolution contained many other provisions that were absent from the original BDS resolution. In my opinion, the "compromise" we struck resulted in an even more vigorous statement of support for Palestinian rights.

In advance of the Calgary special meeting, the Green Party announced to the membership that the negotiations had succeeded and that the new resolution had the support of the entire shadow cabinet, including the leader. May withdrew her threat of resignation, and the new resolution passed in Calgary with overwhelming member support. It was subsequently ratified in an online vote by over 90% of the Green Party members who voted.

As a result of this widely publicized victory, I suddenly became well-known to the Palestinian solidarity movement in Canada. This was not something that I had planned or foreseen. In fact, if I hadn't travelled to Occupied Palestine months earlier, I doubt that I would have challenged the party leader on the issue of supporting sanctions on Israel.

Nonetheless, I now found myself in the unexpected position of having considerable political capital and credibility within the Palestinian solidarity movement. It seemed to me that I had a moral choice to make: either I could go back to the activities that had preoccupied me prior to this victory for human rights, or I could use my newfound stature within the Palestinian solidarity movement to advance the cause of Palestinian human rights much further. I chose the latter.

Since then, I have represented numerous Palestinian solidarity activists in legal proceedings. I have performed that work on a pro bono basis because the vast majority of activists who need legal representation cannot afford to pay a lawyer. In one of the cases I have taken on, Dr David Kattenburg, a member of Canada's Jewish community, is challenging the legality of "Product of Israel" labels on wines produced in Israel's West Bank settlements and sold in Canada. Since that litigation was commenced in 2017, we have received favourable judgements from Canada's Federal Court and its Federal Court of Appeal, but the government of Canada refuses to give up. As Dr Kattenburg has made clear, we will take his complaint to the Supreme Court of Canada, if we have to.

Rafi Silver

Ex–IDF, Canada

I was born in the United States and migrated to Israel in 1971. I joined the Israeli army a few years later, and what the army experience gave me was a real education in the Israeli/Palestinian conflict: an education in lies, brutality, and inhumanity that I had never imagined possible. I had bought into all the myths and fabrications that the Zionist ideology of the environment I grew up in had fed me. Sometimes a person's or a nation's narrative will purposefully distort history, and sometimes it will just leave out critical parts that are too inconvenient or uncomfortable to acknowledge. No one likes to see his/her true side when there are elements in it that are ugly. We all try to sugarcoat or ignore the bad things we have done. Confronting that side of us is the only path to reconciliation and peace within ourselves. This is true not only on the individual level but certainly on the national or societal level as well. It was certainly the case in Israel/Palestine, and being in the Israeli army – inadvertently I might add – exposed the lies and distortions I had bought into. Suddenly I began to see the "Other" as a person just like me, instead of the "enemy" I had been taught about.

This dissonance between what I had been taught and what I was seeing first hand with my own eyes became starker with each new encounter with Palestinians. It is no wonder that armies historically, in every society, do not allow their soldiers to fraternize with the other side. Once you see yourself in another person and can begin to feel their pain you cannot kill them. At that moment you cease to be the robot that army discipline tries to make you into, and you are no longer an effective tool of the state to pursue some abstract or racist policy.

I had some of those experiences in my regular service in the army from 1974–6, but the much stronger and more impactful ones were when I did my reserve duty in the 1990s. There I really saw the consequences of the occupation and the price that was being exacted on the Palestinian population on a daily basis, in countless ways. It didn't even have to be the brutal beatings or killings which happened frequently. It could be nothing more than the humiliation at checkpoints, the invasion of homes, the denial of free movement, or access to medical care. It was the capriciousness that was most striking. The inability of the overwhelming number of soldiers around me to see a Palestinian as a human being just like anyone else was the hardest to take. The blatant racism, hypocrisy, and self-justification were enough to make me sick. The Jewish narrative, the Jewish victimhood no longer carried any weight. It was as if I was witnessing a nation spitting in the face of the lessons of the Holocaust. There were all sorts of false justifications: "security", "nowhere else to go", "the whole world hates us", and the like were always in the air. These false justifications were pervasive throughout Israeli society and they set in motion a process that culminated in total disregard for the life of a person who didn't belong to our "tribe", a process that could be witnessed on a daily basis by anyone who cared to look. The most discouraging part was that so few of my fellow soldiers cared to look at all. I was never quite sure if they couldn't look or wouldn't look. I suppose it didn't matter since the end result was the same.

I began to realize that I was a part of the problem, and that I was a part of an inhumane system that had placed its knee on the neck of another people. All of the myths I had swallowed without question were exploding one after another. It really began when I served for a month in Gaza in 1992, and reached its peak a few years later when I served in Hebron. It was then in the mid-90s that I came to the conclusion that I had to leave that country. It was then that I realized that I had been tricked and manipulated, sometimes by others and sometimes by myself, and that I could no longer reconcile myself to it.

I can remember to this day the look in the eyes of a small Palestinian child staring at me in absolute terror as I walked by. This child was the same age as some of my own. I wanted to pick her up and comfort her, but realized that that would have just terrorized her more. I can remember running through a refugee camp in the middle of the night, imposing a collective punishment on 10,000 people for the actions of one person, thinking to myself how I was on the wrong side. I can remember clearly that dark, rainy November night in the middle of a refugee camp where I came within a hair's breadth of shooting a Palestinian child because of my own fears. I can remember listening to a fellow soldier callously telling a young Palestinian mother with two small children to stand in the rain while he denied her entry to her home for no other reason than that he could. I can still see the face of an Israeli policeman who approached me at a checkpoint, and told me to stop the next Palestinian car. I did. He got in the back of it, put a gun to the driver's head, and told him to take him to the settlement where he lived. He thought nothing of terrorizing someone, who in his eyes was barely a human being, in order to get a free ride home. I can remember a time when I was a witness to the brutal treatment of an elderly Palestinian man in the Gaza strip by an Israeli Border policeman. All of those incidents, and many more, cumulatively burst the bubble I had bought into, or had created myself over the past number of decades. Suddenly, everything I had believed in seemed wrong, and I wanted no part in it whatsoever.

I searched for answers as to why there was not, and still to this day is not more widespread resistance to this kind of treatment of Palestinians by the Israeli state. Not only has there not been any significant opposition within the country, but neither is there very much from Jews in the diaspora. That lack of opposition was the final bubble to burst for me. We were certainly not the Chosen People. We were certainly not any better than anyone else. We were certainly not less brutal, hypocritical, or manipulative than any other nation.

It is ironic that most likely I would not have come to this understanding without the army experience. For sure, other people have, but I was not one of them. I needed that personal, up close, eyewitness experience to wake me up. I wish I could say that I had the insight and the understanding to be able to read the map that had been laid out in front of me right from the beginning, but I didn't. I fell victim to the manipulations and fabrications of the state just as so many other people do. I don't blame myself because I know I am no different from millions of others who have fallen into these traps. At least now I can see the traps much better and can avoid them much more easily.

I was raised a secular Jew, and was taught to be proud of my heritage, culture, and history. The message that I was part of something bigger than myself was central, also that I had a responsibility to continue the Jewish tradition. All of that was key to becoming the person I am today. However, the most important value that supersedes all of the rest, that I was taught from an early age, was "**Justice, Justice, You Shall Pursue**" [Deuteronomy 16:18]. That value did not mean pursuing justice only for Jews, nor did it mean giving Jews more rights or benefits than anyone else. But sadly that value has been forgotten in the Israel of today. Instead we see an apartheid regime; sophisticated yet brutal, intelligent yet unforgiving, oblivious to, or ignorant of, the ancient teachings of the Jewish people.

For me the pursuit of social justice is the essence of Judaism, and my role in this struggle is what defines me today as a Jew. The ideology that propelled me to Israel and the army fifty years ago has revealed its true nature, and I choose justice over fear, racism, a sense of entitlement and superiority, and over an unwillingness to see the Other as the same as oneself. That is the true spirit of being a Jew.

Naomi Wallace

Playwright, US/UK

"My Dutch Mother, and Palestine."

I didn't learn anything in my Kentucky high school about Palestine, nor the decades long resistance to its occupation. I do remember that in the USA in the 1970s and '80s, to even say the word "Palestine" meant that you were some left-wing nut sympathetic to terrorists. So early on, in my small circles, I was labelled a "terrorist sympathizer". This continued well into my adult life and career as a playwright and screenwriter.

Palestine, the country, the idea of it, and its history I learned largely from my Dutch mother, Sonia De Vries. Sonia fiercely believed that the anti-colonial resistance there was one of the most important of ongoing struggles for justice. Simply put, Palestine was, to my mother, the centre of the world. Not in the geographical sense but as a unifying concept and ideal fundamental to a moral universe and to one's own moral compass. Herein the brutal forces of racism, colonialism, and class oppression intersected and could not be untangled without dismantling the whole occupation.

While still in the graduate playwriting program at the University of Iowa, I wrote "In The Heart of America", about two soldiers, one Palestinian-American and the other white and poor, from Kentucky, who fall in love in the midst of the US war against Iraq. In the play I made connections between US racism at home and abroad, and attempted to connect various US wars through language and metaphor. I was discouraged by the head of the theatre department from going forward with the play but I did. The play was later premiered in the UK at The Bush Theatre, directed by Dominic Dromgoole.

I continued my own studies of Palestine and its history through the works of Ilan Pappe, Rashid Khalidi, Edward Said, Michel Warschawki, Saree Makdisi, Ghassan Kanafani, Sara Roy, and others. And through the Palestinian struggle I learned more about racism and war in my own country, about the intimate connections between Black liberation and Palestinian liberation. In 2002 I co-organized a trip to Palestine with half a dozen other US playwrights in order to connect with our colleagues in the Occupied Territories. The playwrights on that trip included Tony Kushner and Kia Corthron.

I have written numerous plays for the theatre about the Middle East and Palestine, and about US wars of aggression. One play that has been performed in the US, UK, and Egypt is "The Fever Chart: Three Visions of the Middle East". It is a trilogy, and two of

Becoming Pro-Palestinian

these short plays are about Palestine and contain Palestinian characters as leads. This trilogy is both surreal and poetic, but very much about the absurdity and violence of colonialism and war, and how intimately these effect our lives.

Abdel Fattah Abu-Srour, Lisa Schlesinger, and I were commissioned to write a play for the Guthrie Theater in Minneapolis a few years ago titled "Twenty One Positions: A Cartographic Dream of the Middle East". The play is about two Palestinian brothers, one living in the US, and one in Palestine. It is a very dark comedy with songs. The Guthrie's dramaturg in residence at the time accused us of "supporting terrorism" when he first read the play – and they declined to publish it.

I recently co-adapted Ghassan Kanafani's novel "Returning to Haifa" with Ismail Khalidi. The adaptation was commissioned by the renowned Public Theater of New York and was set to be directed by the then head of the theater, Oskar Eustis. Due to the intervention of the Public's board the project was cancelled. This adaptation finally received its world premiere at the small, award-winning Finborough Theater in London three years ago. While Faber and Faber agreed to publish the adaptation, my own US publisher – who had published my plays for over twenty years – refused, writing to me that he considered Kanafani to have engaged in "terrorist activities".

Censorship around the question of Palestine is still very much alive in American theatre today, though writers such as Betty Shamieh and Ismail Khalidi are working to change that, as well as US cultural critics and historians such as Robin D. G. Kelley.

My mother Sonia died last August at the age of ninety-one. In one of the last photos I have of her she is standing at an anti-war monument in Amsterdam, her fist raised. Palestine, for her, was the motion of blood through her heart. She was a passionate activist who believed that we are more than the idea of our individual selves and therefore a harm to one is a harm to all. And occupations anywhere were a brutality against our collective freedom to be, and to love.

EUROPE

Lori Allen

Anthropologist, university teacher, and editor, US, lives in UK

I first learned about Palestine and was gripped by the Palestinian liberation struggle – eventually absorbing it as my own – from my starting point as an ignorant undergraduate at the University of Chicago. From a working/middle-class family with no experience of study abroad – meaning, outside of Kansas City, Missouri – I was already rather out of place in this university. I was being jarred like a pinball, flung from new idea to new experience, lights flashing and bells clanging, exhilarated and bruised by the challenges. In this chaos of young adulthood, I found my way into the gobble hole[1] of Palestine. It didn't end the game so much as launch me outside the machine.

As with so many things in life, when I look back, it seems both random and logical, if not fated. Luck, both good and bad, plays a part in every defining moment, which is never just one moment but a synthesis. The culmination of my choices and external influences – authorities rebelled against, fears tripped over, encouragements and inspirations gratefully received and cleverly seized upon – brought me to Palestine, something that is both far from my origins and resonant in many ways.

Being out of place at the University of Chicago is relevant to the story. I was perhaps more of a blank slate than many of my peers who, at the age of eighteen or twenty, knew more about world politics than I, and were often more politically formed than I was at that age. So many of them grew up in academic families, discussing Marx around the dinner table with their professor fathers and filmmaker mothers; forming considered opinions of communism while living in Russia; discussing the news on family camping trips through Mexico with political activist parents. Me, I grew up irritated and bored by non-stop discussion of cars and their parts or the prices of daily items – far from the dramas of global politics. Having no familial, ethnic, or religious ties to the Middle East, to Islam, to Greek Orthodoxy, or to Judaism deepened my openness to the complexities and obviousness of Palestinians' demands for freedom. It may be just that blankness, less smudged by propaganda or heritage, that allowed me to begin to understand and care about Palestine and its history of injustice.

As a Junior (third year) undergrad, I stepped into an interdisciplinary class – part International Relations theory, part global history – that was taught by a range of

---

[1] A technical term for a hole that can end a pinball game or award huge points.

professors, including people with deep knowledge and personal experience of Palestine and Israel. Other professors were introducing me to the histories of feminism, Gandhi, and anti-colonial resistance, which jibed with my expansive, inchoate, and inarticulate rage at patriarchy, oppression, and discrimination. In this challenging and motivating learning environment – the University of Chicago is famously a place "where Hell does freeze over" and "fun comes to die" but ideas and knowledge matter a lot – the IR/ history class opened for me the box of questions and clues that spurred me into learning more about Palestine.

At its start, I was uninformed enough to not object when a kippa-wearing classmate instructed me to refer to the West Bank as Judea and Samaria. And although I was raised a Catholic, forced to attend church weekly and sometimes more frequently, I had no idea of the ideological weight of different terms. I considered the comments of my classmate with as much willingness to hear as I had willingness to ponder what I was reading from other perspectives. Eventually, I acquired enough information to think more critically about what Zionist terminology does to obscure history and sympathy. But that took time, experience, and the patience of strangers who were willing to walk me through it all.

So this is a story of chance encounters and human connection.

As part of this IR/history class, we were invited to develop a research project, learn how to write a grant proposal, and compete for money to do fieldwork. I think a professor suggested a topic in words like, "You're interested in women and revolution, why not go to Palestine?" And with the shrugging shoulders of someone who doesn't know enough to be wary, I said "OK". I got a grant to cover my travel and lodging for a couple months and off I went, settling in Abu Dis, a village near East Jerusalem.

It was towards the end of the first intifada and pre-Oslo Accords that I travelled to Palestine. My first and last El Al flight. I really had no idea what I was doing or what to expect. A soldier's gun dug into my ribs on a bus ride to Haifa. All the reading I had done could not prepare me for the strange acceptance that Israelis had of life surrounded by soldiers carrying guns – in buses, hitchhiking, in the malls, on postcards. All the reading I had done could not prepare me for the anger I felt upon learning that the ex-husband of my Palestinian host could not travel from one neighbourhood to the next freely and without fear because he had been a political prisoner and Israel decided he could not travel freely and without fear. I had read so much about the role of women in the first intifada, about women wresting boys from the hands of Israeli soldiers, proclaiming "they are all our sons" – I read every story of female heroism I could find (revelling in their romanticism with the simple certainty of a newly-minted feminist). All this reading could not prepare me for the insistent tones and straightforward words of the Palestinian women I talked to across the West Bank – describing their suffering and their *sumud* [steadfastness]. I had never encountered power like that. The power that comes from individuals working in concert, working to bring more people into their collective efforts.

There is much that a white working/middle-class Midwesterner from a large Catholic family could resonate with in Palestine. Many of the people I met came from large families like mine, and many of their mothers also started their mornings wondering what meal to prepare that day. Babies were doted on, always a focused source of entertainment, as they'd always been in my family. How much the sister-in-law paid for that purse or that kilo of veggies was always a matter of female discussion. Siblings in large families were shaped by their place in line. I learned the phrase "*akher al-anqud*" – the last grape on the vine – to describe the last child in a family (last and sweetest, or most spoiled, depending on one's place in their line-up). On a future trip, I became good friends with another youngest daughter of many with an authoritarian father, with whom I shared a rebellious spirit modestly expressed.

There were many differences, too – in the intensity of people's generosity, openness, and modes of appreciation. It took me a while to learn to hold my tongue before offering a compliment or admiring something, lest the object be given to me. (I got a tape of Arabic pop and a pair of earrings out of my cultural blunders.) My naturally suspicious nature dissolved in the enthusiasm of families' invitations to their homes. The fact of my position as a US citizen paying taxes to a country that has encouraged Israel's settler-colonial project gave me a sense of obligation. I knew intellectually that I had a responsibility to mitigate these horrors. What nurtured my sense of connection emotionally was the time that people took to share their experiences, to show me the pain and the pride that resistance engenders, and their belief in the importance of helping me understand.

It was the summer of 1992. I bumbled my way around the West Bank, asking inappropriate and probably boring questions of very busy women. These were people who were working for national and women's liberation, while managing their families and dealing with the daily grinds of life under military occupation. How to get children to school through military checkpoints manned by hostile Israeli youth; what to do with kids whose universities the occupation had shut; how to prove they had a right to live in their house in their city through a bureaucracy set up to thwart them; how to make a living while finishing a master's degree. And so on.

I was shocked, impressed, and most overwhelmingly, outraged – an energizing emotion. Outraged at the bald injustice of it all. "How could 'the world' let this occupation go on?!" I kept asking myself. The red-faced expression of someone who doesn't know enough to be cynical.

I spent much of the next few decades learning and trying to explain just that: how the world lets this injustice continue. Through a BA thesis on women and nationalism in Palestine, a Master's thesis on Israel's torture of Palestinian political prisoners, a Ph.D. thesis on violence and society during the second intifada, and two books on the ideologies of human rights and international law that constrain the political imagination about Palestine globally.

That IR/history class and first research trip set me on a path that has defined most aspects of my life. Where I have travelled, studied, and taught; what languages I learned and what I read and write about; who my friends are and who I married; what I want to offer to the world; what makes me saddest, angriest, and most frustrated (my books have the words "cynicism" and "false hope" in their titles); what continues to motivate me (the novel I am writing is about the better futures that could have been and might still be).

Palestine is still an exception when it comes to accepted standards of academic freedom. Palestinians are denied jobs, their cases for tenure jeopardized, their classes cancelled because they are Palestinian. As an academic whose work focuses on Palestine and Palestinians' perspectives, I have been subject to forms of critique, criticism, and attempts at censorship that are obtuse and plainly political, having nothing to do with the quality or subject of my research. Once, a senior scholar at an ivy league institution asked me a pointedly political question having nothing to do with the subject of my lecture at a job talk – probably illegal. Most who write about Palestine have experienced similar and worse. My scholarship is an attempt to understand the institutional, social, and ideological mechanisms underpinning the long history of this kind of discrimination and liberal exceptionalism. My latest book, *A History of False Hope: Investigative Commissions in Palestine* demonstrates how western actors have rejected Palestinian demands for freedom while claiming to uphold democratic principles. It's the galling hypocrisy of liberals that always confounds me.

There are so many people in the world who also recognize the outrageous injustice. Except for people who are ideologically committed to Zionism, American imperialism, and/or Islamophobia, it really doesn't take too much exposure to the facts to see that the military occupation is brutally inhumane and unjust, that Israel is a racist state. These are facts repeatedly confirmed by so many human rights reports, but a week touring the occupied Palestinian territory and talking with Palestinian citizens of Israel make it all so obvious. I am gratified by the stream of random folks I meet who have cared enough to do something for Palestine and for Palestinians, to speak out and vote and boycott, to teach and preach and donate. This despite the propaganda machines of racism, Zionism, and liberalism that churn misinformation into widespread beliefs that it's too complicated, that there are two equal sides with Israel being the more equal, that you have no right to say anything if you are not Israeli, that "the conflict" is unsolvable.

The stream of people visiting the youth centre in the refugee camp where I spent a lot of time while doing research for my Ph.D. are diverse and international. Students, teachers, ministers, writers. These people understand or come to understand that none of this conflict, this settler-colonial project, is inevitable, necessary, or right. One of these volunteers, a high-school Latin teacher dedicated to her students and archaeological remains in Rome, has devoted years of her life to Palestine and Palestinians. Teaching English to stay-at-home moms and young men stuck feeling they have no future in the West Bank, raising funds for youth projects, giving her own money to struggling young families, lecturing with passion and painstakingly produced power-points to share her knowledge and perspective with others. She is exceptional in her energy, but also representative of so many people who do what they can for the cause of Palestinian liberation and whose "only" connection to Palestine is a concern for social justice.

I sometimes get sad when Palestinian friends express their frustration and impatience at the ignorant people around them, at having to explain their lives and histories. And I am gloomy when I hear anyone from an oppressed community make it a point of pride to reject that burden of political pedagogy. I understand where it comes from: "Why should I have to explain this? Why is it my responsibility to address their privileged obliviousness? Why do I have to exhaust myself battling their lack of information and attention?" But I also know what I would have lost, and (in all humility) what the struggle for Palestinian liberation would have lost in the way of at least one more active supporter, had strangers not patiently shared their stories, feelings, and knowledge with me. For solidarity to grow, we must be willing to accept the contingency of people's starting points, and to recognize that their structurally conditioned ignorance can be changed through a mix of curiosity and connection.

Helga Baumgarten

University teacher, Germany, lives in Jerusalem

"Becoming Pro-Palestinian"

My first direct encounter with Palestinians and the "Palestinian Problem" occurred in Lebanon in summer 1972. The context was rather extraordinary. An American friend of mine had refused to be drafted to fight in Vietnam. He did his alternative service in Lebanon, and invited me to visit him in this beautiful country. As a good German, I checked immediately for books on Lebanon in the bookstores in Tuebingen, where I studied at the time.

All I found, however, was a book on the Palestinian Resistance by Gerard Chaliand, published in 1972. So from the start Lebanon for me turned into a country where the Palestinian Resistance was active.

Also, during my studies at an American university between 1969 and 1971, one of my friends was a young Lebanese student (the one and only Lebanese at this university) who had been active with the Arab Nationalist Movement (*Harakat al-qawmiyeen al-Arab*). When I arrived in Beirut, I visited my Lebanese friend and his family in Bourj al-Barajneh, and he introduced me immediately to Palestinian activists in the Resistance.

Back home in Germany, I decided to go for a Ph.D. thesis on the presence of the Palestinian Resistance in Lebanon. In order to prepare myself for this new project – fascinating for me not least because there had been no work done on this topic, and hardly any literature in English, French, or German was available – I came back to Lebanon in spring 1973, with the intention to spend a few months in the country to find out if the idea was realistic.

Shortly after my arrival in Beirut, on April 9/10, the Israeli army, supported by Mossad, carried out an attack against Palestinian militants in Beirut, killing Yusuf an-Najjar, Kamal Adwan, and Kamal Nasser. This led to an important insight for someone like me, coming from Germany. There, the background of Germany's responsibility for World War 2 (fifty million dead!), coupled with the attempt to exterminate all Jews in Europe, dominated everything. The result, not surprisingly, was unconditional German support for the state of Israel.

What I experienced in Beirut in 1973 ran, however, counter to the official German discourse: It wasn't Israel that was being attacked, rather Israel was the aggressor, and the Palestinians were their victims, together with the Lebanese, above all Lebanese in the poorer quarters of Beirut and in the South, i.e. first and foremost Shi'a Muslims.

As a young academic, dedicated to the attempt to establish historical truth through critical research, I decided to spread the information I had gained during my stays in Beirut, through writing and publishing. My impression at the time was that people in Europe, above all in Germany, simply did not know what was going on in Israel and the surrounding states, especially in Lebanon, or had been misinformed by the press.

I started fieldwork for my Ph.D. thesis in early 1975, when I went again to Beirut. The period I spent there was dominated by the Lebanese Civil War, by the Israeli invasion of South Lebanon in 1978, by continuous Israeli attacks, mostly air-raids, and, last but not least, Syria's intervention in the Lebanese Civil War and the destruction of the Palestinian refugee camp Tell al-Zaatar, north of Beirut.

Without doubt, these events deepened my support for the Palestinians, above all those living in the refugee camps. Apart from my research, I started teaching special classes in Bourj al-Barajneh refugee camp. After the destruction of Tell al-Zaatar camp, I also volunteered in the Palestinian hospital in Fakhany.

I stayed in Lebanon until summer 1979, when I went back to Germany with a car-load of photocopies of important papers of the resistance, covering the years from 1948 until 1979, and with many cassettes, on which I had recorded countless interviews with Palestinian leaders and activists from all the organizations *(tanzimat)* of the PLO.

While my solidarity included all Palestinians, I soon started to differentiate between the leadership – often very authoritarian, the Palestinian bourgeoisie – often interested above all in profits -- and the simple people who lived mainly in the refugee camps. Also, I supported the goal of national liberation, while at the same time having clear reservations about extreme nationalism. After all, I was a leftist and based my readings of history and politics on historical materialism as developed by Karl Marx.

Back in Germany, I started to teach, in parallel to writing my thesis, first at the University of Gottingen, then at the Free University of Berlin.

In 1983, I got my first chance to visit the occupied West Bank and East Jerusalem. By this time, I was married to Mustafa al-Kurd, the Palestinian musician, *oud* soloist, and composer from East Jerusalem, who after 1967 had single-handedly developed Palestinian political songs in protest against the occupation.

We lived with Mustafa's mother and met the whole family. Mustafa's mother was a living example of a simple Palestinian woman who never had the chance to go to school, poor, a widow who had raised her five children on her own after her husband died. She was wholeheartedly engaged in resisting the occupation, following the activities of her son Mustafa. She continuously participated in protest demonstrations in the Old City, and particularly in al-Haram al-Sharif. But while being a pious Muslim, she was never extremist. On the contrary she demonstrated an amazing openness on all matters. Also, she was extremely intelligent, understanding events and developments more deeply than many of her compatriots who had university degrees. Undoubtedly Umm Mustafa strengthened my support of simple Palestinian people, and deepened my critical attitude towards often self-proclaimed leaders, the newly rich, and old bourgeoisie.

This first visit to Occupied Palestine also gave me the chance to establish direct relations with the Israeli left, above all members of Matzpen and of the Communist

Party, all of them old friends of my husband. This obviously raised the hope for a future in which Palestinians and Israeli Jews would be able to live together in equality and freedom.

In 1985, after I had submitted my thesis and received my Ph.D. degree, we moved to East Jerusalem for good. Since then, I have lived a somewhat hybrid life between Jerusalem and Germany, mainly in Stuttgart where my family lived, and Berlin, where I had taught and lived with Mustafa, and where our son Darwish was born.

Our life in Occupied Palestine was soon disrupted by the First Intifada which started in December 1987. The Intifada again increased my commitment to the Palestinians, who united and rose against the intolerable occupation regime, which by then had already lasted twenty years too long. It was amazing to experience the committed resistance of people, again simple people from all over, coupled with the attempt to build an independent Palestinian existence in East Jerusalem, the West Bank, and the Gaza Strip, an existence without settlers, without the Israeli army everywhere, without oppression – simply a life in freedom. Obviously, I supported all this wholeheartedly.

My husband recorded a cassette *Awlad Filastin* (Children of Palestine), with songs of the Intifada. The lead song was "A Stone and an Onion and a Bucket of Water". He was briefly arrested, and his cassettes confiscated. But his lawyer and friend Lea Tsemel managed to get him out of prison, the Moscobiyeh in Jerusalem, after only two days.

The hopes of Palestinians, which had run so high in 1987/1988, were mercilessly crushed by Israel, starting with Rabin's order to break the bones of the demonstrators, and culminating in a second crucial order, which made all activities of the Popular Committees illegal. By that time, the PLO leadership under Arafat had taken over.

In November 1988, the Palestinian National Council voted for a two-state solution, i.e. for the establishment of a Palestinian State in the areas occupied by Israel in 1967, East Jerusalem, West Bank, and the Gaza Strip. For a leftist, this clearly signaled the end of the hope for a shared future for both peoples in all of historic Palestine.

The Two-State-Solution met widespread support among Palestinians and among all the organizations of the Resistance, with the exception of the newly established Hamas, which was not ready to give up the goal of the liberation of all of historic Palestine. Things changed, however, when the PLO/Fatah-leadership under Yasser Arafat signed the Oslo accords in 1993. Intellectuals like Edward Said, but also the leadership of Hamas, criticized the Palestinian leadership for surrendering historic Palestinian demands for liberation, freedom, and independence. Above all, they criticized the acceptance of Israeli settlements in the Occupied Territories in return for the mere promise of a state to be established after five years. Developments since 1993 have proved these critics right.

As the perennial optimist into which life in occupied East Jerusalem had transformed me, I had initially shared the hopes that Oslo might after all prove a historical turning point. However, Rabin's lack of reaction to the massacre committed by a settler in Hebron inside the Ibrahimi mosque, as well as his missing a historic chance to act against the settlers and remove the settlements, doomed Oslo and crushed the hopes of many of us.

After the killing of Hamas leader Sheikh Ahmed Yassin in 2004 by an Israeli missile, and the death of Yasser Arafat by poisoning, a new era started, an era which also affected the solidarity movements. While until then, international solidarity gave generous support to the Palestinians, in the Oslo years many of the solidarity movements came to Palestine as leaders of international NGOs. Solidarity thus gained a financial value that often prevented the necessary critical attitude. This included the local NGO community, which was driven into accepting the programs of international NGOs, while abandoning their own goals which should have supported Palestinian society.

Obviously, this also affected the way my solidarity, up to that time unshaken, developed.

Criticism of the new leadership, their politics, their strategies – or better, lack of strategies – moved centrerstage. At the same time, support for Palestinian society, for the people, above all for those continuing resistance, continued and even increased.

Through my teaching at Birzeit University, I had the chance to work with young Palestinians from all over. I tried to introduce them to critical scholarship, to continuous questioning of what political leaders were doing, above all to relentless criticism of the Palestinian security services. The song that students in all my classes had to learn was Ziad al-Rahbani's "Change the system, it isn't working". At the same time, I attempted to introduce this young generation to international examples of liberation and resistance: Vietnam, Cuba, South Africa, but also Algeria.

Quite a number of my students moved on to do a Master's degree and/or a Ph.D. in Germany, or elsewhere in Europe, or in the United States. Many of them came back to teach at Palestinian universities.

All through those years, I continued to write and publish many articles and a number of books. Also I had the chance to give lectures all over Europe, with a focus on Germany, Austria, and Switzerland. More and more people learned what was really going on in Israel/Palestine, and many were moved to participate in solidarity actions (for example helping with the olive harvest, working as volunteers in hospitals, or studying at a Palestinian university), and then to further spread the message.

Still, German policy towards Israel, like Austrian and Swiss policy, has not really changed. While criticism is raised here and there, it remains verbal criticism, not followed up by any real action. And in the end, it is the Palestinians who are blamed, who remain the eternal "terrorists". In this respect, it is the Hamas movement that has replaced Fatah as the main terrorist culprit preventing a "solution" of the "conflict".

While I cannot help but continue writing and publishing and hoping for change, the picture has become much clearer than it was in the '70s. Today there is no lack of knowledge about what is going on in Israel/Palestine; but political leaders and the majority of the media simply refuse to see reality as it unfolds on the ground. They prefer to align with the strong, i.e. the State of Israel, and neglect the weak, i.e. the Palestinians.

Also, an old problem has continued until today. The renewed discussion of the massacre of Tantura with the publication of new oral history material at the end of 2021 made this blatantly clear. Reports by Palestinians of their experiences, whether about massacres or about the Nakba in general, are only accepted internationally once Israeli academics, journalists, or film-makers have dealt with them. It is the subalterns, the Palestinians, who until today are widely considered to be untrustworthy.

This has been my experience throughout my academic career. For example, Walid Khalidi's work was not accepted until it was confirmed by Benny Morris and Ilan Pappe. There has been an implicit, and often explicit, pressure, to rely on Israeli sources, even when Palestinian sources and references have been available. Even recently, I went through a shocking experience with the editor of a left-liberal German newspaper. After I gave a Palestinian source for the events I was analyzing in the article, I got a call asking if I was serious in relying on such a source. I insisted, the article was published, but that was the end of our cooperation. While such an attitude has been an ongoing problem, at least it is now openly addressed, not least by young Palestinian journalists and academics.

Last but not least, there is the experience of young Germans born to Palestinian parents in Germany (or for that matter Switzerland or Austria), and who grew up there. By now, we have a number of documents describing their shocking experience of feeling forced to deny their roots and their attachment to Palestine, as described in Sarah El-Bulbeisi's outstanding book [2020, in German]. Even more shocking are the repeated incidents where young Germans with a Palestinian background are denied employment or get their contracts cancelled because of pro-Palestinian statements which are regularly labelled as "antisemitic", as the experience of medical doctor and TV journalist Nemi El-Hassan in 2021 shows.[1]

So a lot of work remains to be done. Many more people have become pro-Palestinian since the early '70s, and support for the Palestinian struggle for freedom, justice, equality, and dignity has increased. And people like me, who have known Palestine, Palestinians, and their fate for so many years, must continue their work, despite everything, until Palestinians have gained their freedom.

[1] Michael Sappir, "The Inquisition of Nemi El-Hassan", *+972*, October 6, 2021.

Sophia Deeg

Teacher, translator, Germany

"How I Became and Why I Continue to be Part of the Universal Movement for Palestinian Rights"

It must have been in the early '90s, when everyone was euphoric about the Oslo peace accords. I admit, I was not specifically interested or well-informed about Israel/Palestine.

At the time, I volunteered in a Munich activists' venue, housing initiatives by people from different countries, mainly from the Global South, and Germans like myself. Having witnessed fierce racist attacks against migrant workers and their families in East and West Germany, we felt we had to take a stand with those who, after the wall came down, were under unprecedented threat. What we saw in the early '90s in East and West German towns was the re-emergence of the horrors we naively imagined "unthinkable nowadays". In the East, migrant workers from Vietnam, Romania, Ghana, Iran, Bangladesh were being chased, threatened, and their shelters set on fire by neo-Nazis, while German neighbours watched and applauded, and police did nothing. In the West, the homes of Turkish migrant workers and their families were set on fire, some of the inhabitants killed, others severely wounded, again with half-hearted reactions from officials. We felt we needed to insist on the basic principle of equal rights. So I joined an association for the defence of foreigners' rights. Our main task was to provide foreigners in Munich with legal advice by specialized lawyers.

One evening, after volunteering, I came across a small event organized by Fuad, a Palestinian activist in our venue. Ronni, an Israeli guest, sat behind a table adorned with a Palestinian flag. She was beginning her talk about the Oslo peace accords. Her crystal clear analysis shed a totally new light on what I had read in the media about the recent agreement between Israel and the Palestinians.

Even though I'm a critical reader of mainstream media, I never imagined that there could be such a wild discrepancy between them and what I had just learnt from an Israeli activist. In the weeks that followed I spoke about this with my Palestinian students (I was a teacher at a college for foreign students). What they told me about the reality on the ground confirmed what Ronni had said. I also did my own research. Understanding what the Oslo Accords were really about greatly upset me. Though celebrated as peace talks that did justice to both sides, the Accords had in fact been brokered with a weak Palestinian leadership that had replaced the principled negotiators who had emerged from the 1st Intifada. The Palestinian leaders brought in by the US and Europe seemed ready to give away everything just for the sake of being "in power" inside insignificant bantustans under Israeli control.

When I visited Israel/Palestine in 1996 and 1998, these were indeed the sad facts on the ground, though most Palestinians I met in the West Bank, Israel, and Gaza were still full of hope that a free, democratic, independent Palestine was imminent, and that they would live in peace, as equals with their Jewish neighbours. I remember a moment somewhere in the West Bank when we, some Europeans, were being greeted by children who took us for Israelis. They came running towards us, waving and smiling and welcoming us in Hebrew.

In March 2002, when I visited again, this time as a journalist and with activists of the worldwide farmers' movement, La Via Campesina, who were responding to the call of a desperate Palestinian civil society, we witnessed the IDF's re-occupation of the West Bank. If only for a few days, I lived under military siege with about twenty other internationals, locked up in a hotel in Ramallah. For the first time in my life I heard bombs exploding close by. For the first time, I saw snipers. An Israeli sniper aimed right at me, our eyes met, he lowered his gun and shook his head. We, civilians from different countries, had finally dared to break the siege, waving white pillowcases and towels. Our mission, proposed by Palestinian doctors, was protecting a hospital in Ramallah against an imminent attack by the IDF. Tanks approached threateningly. Palestinian ambulance drivers gestured helplessly towards us as they were prevented by the IDF from saving those who lay wounded.

Later when we internationals, together with the Palestinian hospital staff, tried to block the entrance of the hospital, there suddenly was a commotion and a young Palestinian lying on a stretcher was laid down at our feet, right between us and the Israeli soldiers, and the paramedics began to wail, to pray. I didn't understand the words but the meaning was obvious. There was a small hole in the young civilian's chest, his sweatshirt stained with dried blood. For the first time in my life, I saw someone who had been killed: a young man shot at by another young man. The sniper who had decided not to shoot at me?

The ambulance had been blocked too long.

We, international witnesses, were at least able – this one time – to prevent the army from entering the hospital and dragging out wounded "suspects".

Only a few days earlier, two of us had been in Gaza. We had met refugees in miserable camps and spoken with academics, professionals, experts, who had happily given up their jobs and careers all over the world to return home and build the free Palestine of their dreams. And we met Haidar Abdel Shafi (1919–2007), the Gazan medical doctor, founder of the Palestinian Red Crescent, and chief negotiator at the Madrid and Washington peace talks. Any kid you asked in the streets of Gaza "Where is Dr Haidar's house?" would show you the way. In 1996, he had been elected to the Palestinian Legislative Council (PLC) as the member with the highest number of votes. He was known to be rather left-wing, but virtually everyone in Gaza understood that he was absolutely independent from partisan interests. Everyone – whether followers of Fatah, Hamas, or any other political party or ideology – knew that he stood uncompromisingly for Palestinian rights as expressed in UN resolutions and International Law. He had resigned as a deputy in the Palestinian Legislative Council to protest the failure to deal with corruption in the Palestinian Authority. Following the outbreak of the Second Intifada, he urged the Palestinian Authority to organize the Intifada rather than distance itself from it. When we met him in 2002, all his efforts – and those of other Palestinians – had failed. But the gentleman who welcomed us in his house in Gaza was neither bitter nor resigned. I guess this was because he was true to himself and to the Palestinian people, which he remained to his death. He would never – as so many other leaders of liberation struggles have done – yield to pressure and accept the role of sub-contractor of external powers striving to control popular liberation movements and prevent real empowerment for those oppressed and dispossessed.

Only days after meeting Haidar in Gaza we discovered a powerful joint civil society effort: activists from different countries and continents came together in East Jerusalem, heeding the decision of the 1st World Social Forum in Porto Alegre to support the Palestinian struggle. For the first time I participated in the planning of direct actions organized by people who hadn't known each other before. During that meeting in Jerusalem, some fifty internationals decided to enter the West Bank as the population there was being overwhelmed by military force, without any international protection or witnesses.

We used our privilege: our "powerful" passports. I understood then that it is a sad, an unjust privilege, as is any privilege. But I also understood that you can use it to *live* equality, even if just for a fleeting moment, assuring each other without words, that we will not forget the promise inherent in this joint experience of those with rights and those deprived of rights. Equality is what we keep striving for together, while we continue on this path in different contexts and different parts of the world.

As it turned out in the months and years to come, some internationals who used their passports in this way were not protected by the "shield" of a European, a US, or an Israeli citizenship. Though practising non-violent resistance, some of them were shot at, maimed, or even killed, as was Rachel Corrie while she tried to prevent an Israeli soldier in his enormous armoured vehicle from flattening a Palestinian home in Gaza. She died under the weight of the horrific machine. Rachel became a Palestinian, a refugee at the European or the US/Mexican borders – one of all those who refuse to accept for themselves or for others inequality, injustice, oppression, exclusion, poverty – while there is enough for all of us.

Today, the Palestinian cause seems more universal than ever. Wherever I go, wherever I support struggles like those of the "sans-papiers" or those against racist police violence in France, I meet activists who are in solidarity with the Palestinian cause. Whether it is for refugees' rights or against racism and colonialism, the Palestinian struggle is part of these struggles.

The omnipresence of Palestine struck me for the first time in 2002 when I met activists of the International Solidarity Movement (ISM), farmers from Europe and Latin America, Italian anarchists and many others in the West Bank, joining Palestinians in their struggle against the occupation. What motivated us, internationals, and motivates us to this day? An important point is that *together* – Palestinians and internationals – we develop ideas and strategies.

The Palestinian struggle is intrinsically part of worldwide movements challenging inequality, injustice, and oppression. Over the years, I discovered the logic of why Indian peasants robbed of their land identify with the Palestinian cause as *their* cause; why the inhabitants of neglected French suburbs, once colonized and still treated as second class citizens, targeted by racist state violence, often chant: "All of us – we are Palestinians!"

I understood the power behind some small, fragile boats that were the first to reach Gaza since decades in 2008.

I remember the night in August that year. I knew that the first of these boats had set sail and was approaching Gaza. Hoping against hope, I dialled Huweida, one of those who had defended the hospital in Ramallah in 2002, and now was with the boats. She answered.

"We are approaching Gaza ...! I see the coastline".

And then, miraculously, more boats followed, with a heavy load of activists. Heavy with determination, they made it through to Gaza. They were greeted by incredulous, overjoyed Gazans, people, young and old, who had never seen a boat approach their coast except Israeli war ships come to shell them or prevent Gaza fishermen from fishing.

When in 2005, the Boycott, Divestment and Sanctions strategy was proposed by a broad coalition of Palestinian civil society, I felt this was another creative step on the way towards equality. In many countries around the globe, trade unions, students' associations, religious congregations, as well as artists, academics, and athletes support BDS: the right of return, equal rights for all Israeli citizens, and the end of the occupation. Among BDS supporters, as with ISM and the Boats to Gaza, there are many Jews who feel strongly about their Jewish tradition to stand in solidarity with the oppressed.

What fascinates me about BDS: We, campaigners, are free to discuss and apply this coherent strategy of solidarity to the realities of our respective societies. It is not a desperate appeal, as in so many other cases, to more or less blindly support a cause *as framed by the supporters* or by a political party or a leading figure. BDS challenges the cooperation of national or international companies and institutions with the occupation of Palestinian land, the ever expanding illegal settlements in the occupied territories, the cruel consequences for every Palestinian there and in exile. While doing research about precisely how all this is interconnected, we understand: We are not "far away" from where these human rights and international law violations happen. And the people we talk to in the streets can see this as well.

On days when something horrific happens somewhere in the world, this makes it into the headlines for a few days. There will be an outcry, maybe tens of thousands join protests in the streets, and then the catastrophe vanishes from the headlines as if it was no longer a disaster for those exposed to it. But BDS makes it clear on a daily basis, that, indeed, what happens in Palestine is an *ongoing* Nakbeh. The urgency to act doesn't diminish when, for a while, Israeli bombs aren't raining on Palestinian civilians.

This ongoing conversation, strategizing and acting together continuously, as in the BDS campaign and other movements for equality, is the basis for real hope, not just for Palestinians, but for all of us.

Elisabetta Donini

Physicist, retired university professor, Italy

"Letter to a Palestinian Friend"

In remembrance of Salwa Salem,
to whom I hold deep gratitude
for the generous friendship with which she allowed
me to know the fascinating story of her life as
a Palestinian woman

Salwa Salem, *Con il vento nei capelli. Vita di una donna palestinese*
a cura di Laura Maritano, Firenze, Giunti 1993.

Dear Ruba,

I do hope you accept the proposal I am about to make to you. Some weeks ago, I received an e-mail from Rosemary Sayigh, who invited me to contribute to a collection of testimonials from several persons she had invited to describe "how and why they became 'pro Palestinian'".

I was immediately attracted to accept the invitation: it would be an excellent opportunity for me to rethink – after more than thirty years – how important sharing initiatives with both Palestinian women and the few Israelis who opposed the Occupation became in my life. At first I was afraid that I wouldn't be able to express myself adequately in a language I don't master. But suddenly I realized that Rosemary herself was suggesting an "easy" approach, i.e. "much like a letter to a friend". Such a possibility would help me feel at ease, if I could find the "right" person to write to. It is to you, Ruba, that I turn. First I knew you as Salwa's dear daughter, but over the years, our friendship has become independent of Salwa, and strong.

A Feminist Approach to Involvement with Palestine

To describe when and how the fate of the Palestinian people became a major concern of mine, I have to go back to the late 1980s, precisely to 1987. The starting point of my engagement was shaped by the indignation I felt at the news of the siege of Palestinian camps in Lebanon by Amal militias.[1]

This indignation gave an ethical and political impulse to my searching for a way to give concrete solidarity to those who were at risk of dying of hunger in the camps. Because of the context in which I was immersed at that time, this new urge was immediately shaped by the priority that self-identification as a feminist was taking in my life.

That's why from the very beginning I tried to share my new engagement within the women's movement. I hope, Ruba, that you understand what I mean when I recall the interlacement of ties with Palestine and the feminist approach that guided my experiences from the beginning, even if you chose to intersect your Palestinian roots with an academic interest in women's and gender studies.

A precise date and place mark a "before" and "after" with respect to how I became involved in Palestinian issues: Verona, February 13, 1987. I had been invited to participate with other feminists in a debate about "Woman, Science and the Future". The discussion revolved around two main issues: the Chernobyl disaster and the growing social and scientific engagement in the race for artificial human reproduction. In both cases we all agreed that to trace a feminist path to "change the world" – as we used to say then – we had to affirm our complete autonomy from male values and priorities, above all from the patriarchal way of knowing, based on the claim to dominate nature. However, this consensus turned into bitter dissent among some of us when we dealt with concrete aspects such as the Palestinian camps.

Dramatic news continued to arrive from Lebanon about the siege through which the Amal militias were trying to force Palestinian refugees to surrender or die of starvation. It was reported that it was women who took charge of looking for food, sneaking out of the camps, risking their lives, often being killed. I remember feeling so grieved and angry that I argued that these events concerned us, and that we had to move from outrage to action. There were some who argued that we could not as women take charge of all the crimes in the world; and that, as women, we mustn't fall into a position of responsibility for remedying all evils. Our first task was to develop gender self-awareness. Otherwise we'd spend all our energy in a fruitless attempt to remedy injustices resulting from men's behaviour.

I came out of that debate very sad and disappointed. I kept wondering why it was not possible to act in solidarity with others while continuing to develop a feminist consciousness. Eventually I decided to share my reflections with the women's movement in the form of an open letter published in the communist newspaper *Il Manifesto*. The letter, titled "Women in Beirut", was featured on the front page of the newspaper on February 22, 1987. I summarized our Verona meeting's discussion in terms of two divergent visions around feminist action: there were those for whom mobilizing to stop the siege of Palestinians in Lebanon would mean women's enactment of their long term patriarchal role as self-sacrificial subjects; while others felt that taking action against violence and colonialism around the world would give the women's movement

---

[1]   See Rosemary Sayigh, *Too Many Enemies: The Palestinian Experience in Lebanon,* London and New Jersey, Zed Books 1994.

momentum for a new type of feminist autonomy and a fuller awareness of women's power. Faced with this contradiction, I tried to stress that emotions such as indignation are an integral part of our being in the world.

During those days, in the wave of the demonstrations against the missiles that had linked women in Greenham Common and Comiso, the appeal "War out of history" was circulating, promoted by several organizations. It was in this context that I made a proposal: "Why don't we enact a concrete initiative, setting up an international women's camp in Beirut, to bring the war out of the present, where death is an everyday experience?" My article was published on a Sunday. I had spent that weekend attending women's meetings where I had the opportunity to gauge reactions, both critical and supportive. Comrades in the women's movement called me to express their agreement with the idea of a "Peace Camp", and we decided to meet soonest at the Turin Women's House. I was really surprised how many women came, and how committed they were to the project.

After that, things advanced very fast: in May we organized an international meeting in Turin with the provocative title "*It is not enough to say enough*". This also enabled us to better understand the specificities of the Palestinian events in Lebanon. Thanks to the discussions we had there, it became very clear to us that we had to go to the roots, we had to travel to Palestine.[2] Three of the group decided to spend their holidays in Palestine/Israel, so as to broaden our contacts, while in September seven of us went to Lebanon and another group followed in November. At the end of 1987 we were ready for our summer camp in Palestine; and in August 1988 68 women went to Jerusalem to attend meetings with Palestinian and Israeli women, separately and together.

How Our Collective Identity Took Shape

At this point I can no longer evade the discomfort I feel with respect to the theme of this book "Becoming Pro-Palestinian". Did I in fact become pro-Palestinian? I and my comrades did not identify with national affiliations; on the contrary the core of our common perspective was to strengthen an anti-patriarchal and anti-militaristic sense of self. We tried to relate to both Palestinian women and to the Israeli ones who did not accept the cruel injustices of their state towards Palestinians and the claims of domination professed by their country as sacred. In this context, what happened was rather that Palestine became a turning point for the feminist movement in Italy, divided between those with a prevailing internationalist and anti-colonial agenda and those who were more invested in gender issues, both with regard to Palestine and at home.

In December 1987 the first "Intifada" began in Gaza; it was immediately clear that this would become a wide popular uprising with women and youth leading protests and taking centre stage in the struggle. A month later, in early 1988, a small group of Jewish women from Israel came out into the streets in Jerusalem, giving birth to the "Women in Black" movement, which quickly spread throughout Israel and around the world. The preparatory trips we made in 1988 enabled us to arrive at the Peace Camp

---

[2] Some guests were most important to lead us to this different approach: Leila Chahid from Palestine, Felicia Langer from Israel, Nawal El Saadawi from Egypt...

in August having already met the "Women in Black", and having recognized ourselves in their feminist, anti-militarist and anti-nationalist initiative.

Building Bridges, Not Walls

Many peace activists adopted these words to express the meaning of their choice. In this perspective I think it is up to us to support any effort to keep channels of communication open, particularly when the harshness of division is growing. I do not mean by this that both sides are equal: on the contrary, rights must be recognized on one side and injustice on the other.

To clarify what I mean, I refer to a particular case: mid-January 1991, the First Gulf War began. We wanted to keep in touch with the groups in Palestine/Israel who were part of our network, so we decided to ask them to write on how they were living these days of war. We had found a magazine, *Inchiesta*,[3] that was eager to publish these essays, and quickly came out with a special issue.

Our proposal quickly received positive responses. We were surprised, having thought it wouldn't be easy to accept our invitation while missiles fell, moreover in a context of double injustice, since Palestinians didn't have the same war equipment. The quick consensus from both sides surely expressed the desire to have a voice.

To discuss details about the texts they were preparing, we often tried to speak on the phone. Our Israeli friends would tell us about the emergency of missile attacks or the need to take refuge in shelters, which made them understand – perhaps for the first time – what the life of Palestinians was like. Indeed a Palestinian friend said, "At last they feel what we feel". However each side continued to believe that building a dialogue was worthwhile.

"An Arab Woman in Black"

Thirty-one years have passed. The everyday conditions on the ground for Palestinians have worsened, and the dialogue we initiated couldn't continue. Many events have unfolded since then: the First and Second Intifada, the Boycott, Divestment and Sanctions movement, the intersectional struggles that unite Palestinians with other indigenous and black liberation movements across the globe. However, in recalling those days, memory goes back to the special issue of *Inchiesta*. That work still holds a special place in my heart, as it epitomizes the shared efforts of women across various divides aimed at building a future of coexistence beyond national affiliations. There was an article that struck us deeply as Italian feminists, entitled "I Laid a Rose on My Husband's Grave" by Ibtihaj Khoury, a Palestinian woman in Acre who had longed to join the Women in Black movement, but didn't ask because she thought it was only for Jewish Israeli women. Invited to join, she said, "I believe a vigil of Jewish and Arab women constitutes power .... we create a powerful image of Jewish and Arab women who oppose war and have joined forces to fight against racism. Coexistence is part of

---

[3] "Pace e guerra in Medio Oriente. Percorsi di donne", *Inchiesta*, n. 91–92, gennaio-giugno 1991, pp. 1–112.

our message. . . . One day a man stopped at our vigil and gave each of us a red rose. I was moved to tears. I went to the cemetery and laid the rose on my husband's fresh grave, with the thought, "This rose is a gift from women who believe in some of the ideals to which you dedicated your life when you were elected as a Communist Party member to the Acre Municipal Council, to serve Jews and Arabs alike".[4]

In Search of Liberation and Freedom

Just when we were preparing our trip to Jerusalem for the 1988 "Peace Camp", the journal *Il Manifesto* published an interview with Zahira Kamal, a well-known activist of both the women's and Palestinian independence movements. "In search of liberation and freedom" were the words she used to characterize the double aim of the Palestinian women's struggle. This was the best encouragement we could receive to stay true to our beliefs as feminists, while respecting the priorities and sensibilities of other women who became central in our feminist politics.

After such a long time the experience of peace ties with Palestinian and Israeli women remains for many of us an important approach. It is up to younger generations to continue according to their point of view, while retaining what they recognize as appealing in the world we have tried to build.

Acknowledgement

While writing this text, I became increasingly conscious of the fundamental role that Ruba was playing in it. In fact, she not only helped me in better shaping my thoughts, but she acted as my interlocutor in a real exchange. I am very grateful to her for accepting this dialogical relationship.

[4] For the original publication in English see *Challenge,* July 1990; for the Italian translation see *Inchiesta* quoted in footnote 4, p. 77.

Jane Frere

Artist, Scotland

"Discovering Injustice Beyond the Myths"

As a research-based artist I am drawn to significant topics addressing aspects of the human condition, its confrontation, its vulnerability. Increasingly I have come to understand the importance of human rights, human dignity – the essence of humanity.

With this in mind I have been deliberating whether or not I should describe myself as being "Pro-Palestinian" and concluded that to be "pro" or in favour of one ethnicity over another exacerbates the schism at the core of nearly all conflicts. Believing myself to be an artist on the side of all humanity, instead of "pro-Palestinian" I prefer to describe myself as "pro-Humanitarian".

However, that begs the question, and many do ask me, why then single out one particular aspect of history – the conflict between two distinct groups of people, Palestinians and Zionists – for an art project that reflects the grotesque injustice of one side.

By choosing to focus on one aspect of the conflict have I highlighted only those injustices meted out towards a single ethnic group? Paradoxically, this is a question that is made more apposite when considering that my initiation to the Palestinian/Israeli issue happened through a chance encounter with Israeli pilgrims in a notorious Nazi concentration camp in Poland.

Early in the new millennium I had been working as a creative producer with two Polish theatre companies in Lublin. During that period, I made several visits to Majdanek, a Nazi concentration camp on the outskirts of the city.

Unlike the infamous destination Auschwitz, which has over two million visitors a year, Majdanek receives relatively few visitors, especially in the dark winter months, which made my visit particularly chilling. Using my video camera almost as a shield to give me fortitude, I ventured alone into the labyrinth of barely lit spaces, contemplating the evidence of extreme cruelty and excruciating human suffering. Intending to make a video artwork, I pored over hundreds of pairs of shoes, mounds of spectacles and human hair, clothes, children's toys, anonymous belongings that have become synonymous with the Holocaust.

On my last visit, while leaving the crematorium, I encountered a group of Israeli pilgrims. Before their departure, they had planted a sea of miniature blue and white

Israeli flags on a sloping bank of one of the trenches that had been used for mass execution. I had been so absorbed by the tragic events that had taken place here in another era, that then to be hurled back in an instant to the present by a random vision of fluttering blue and white flags left me in a state of incomprehensible confusion.

I knew this flag, it too was synonymous with crimes against humanity, contemporary crimes against an indigenous population trapped by a cruel occupation of their land and by the occupier's ensuing litany of broken human rights conventions. I found myself in a quandary, as just a short time before I had been sharing profound sorrow with these same Israeli pilgrims in empathy for their lost relatives.

As I watched their coach depart I was unable to reconcile myself with the idea that they would be returning to their appropriated land, a blood-soaked and arguably stolen land since, contrary to the myth, it had never been *"A land without a people for a people without a land"*.

The words of the renowned Palestinian intellectual Edward Said came to mind, "Victims of Victims", but I knew there was a great deal more to this simplistic aphorism and if I were to settle the brooding storm of confusion and perplexity in my mind, I would have to engage in a period of in-depth research trying to come to terms with a complex history, on the one hand overlooked or else so distorted and suppressed, which yet remains at the root of the perpetual conflict in the Middle East.

When contemplating a significant art project, before my pencil even touches the paper, I spend much time at the outset in a research mode seeking clues – almost like a detective – in order to arrive at a concept which frames the subject. Without an understanding of the source of a conflict, we cannot hope to make sense of current events.

My starting point was history. I began by focusing on the Israeli revisionist "new" historians, namely Ilan Pappe and Benny Morris. I soon came to realize how important it is to understand something of the source of conflicts. How little I knew about the role my own country played in the injustice imposed upon an entire people – the infamous Balfour Letter in 1917 declaring the British government's support for the establishment of a "national home for the Jewish people" in Palestine. Rarely mentioned is that this support was given on condition that "nothing shall be done which may prejudice the civil and religious rights of existing non-Jewish communities in Palestine, or the rights and political status enjoyed by Jews in any other country."

There are so many aspects to this conflict which are misunderstood. Could art through its language of symbolism and metaphor help to bring understanding, so often obscured by political agendas? I was struck particularly by the way the Nakba, as important to the Palestinians as the Holocaust is to the Jews, has been and continues to be denied, if not entirely erased like the hundreds of villages destroyed, evidence of their existence concealed, while their original inhabitants still languish in refugee exile.

For an artwork to do justice to such cataclysmic events would require an artistic concept of epic proportions. I decided that taking a solely intellectual approach to the research based on third party accounts of history and other people's experiences would not give the work sufficient weight or depth. I needed to be amongst Palestinians living, observing, feeling daily challenges under occupation – or worse, the suffocating and debilitating lives of those in refugee camps.

Wax – visceral, fragile, and yet resistant, its translucent and warm tones associated with anatomical studies – was the medium I chose for the sculptural installation. I visualized wax coated figurines, suspended by thousands of transparent threads in animated positions, diminishing in size to give the illusion of a vast throng receding into the distance, becoming the symbolic representation of Palestinians driven into exile in the murderous campaign of 1948.

To create the impression of a tsunami of humans fleeing towards an unknown destination required thousands of individually made wax figures. To give them an identity, imbue them with their own history and soul, I felt it would be more poignant if they could be made by the hands of Palestinians.

I devised a series of related workshops, an educational programme around the making of the figures which also included the gathering of oral histories from family members, which gave a personalized opportunity to observe aspects of their history and identity. The workshops were spread out across the region inside and out of refugee camps where I specifically chose to stay with families so that I could get some sense of life as a refugee languishing in shocking often impoverished conditions.

The collated histories via handwritten testimonies, audio and video recordings, accounts of loss, fear, and hope of return, were often in response to mundane questions: Why did they leave? By what means of transport? What could they carry with them? What were they wearing? The answers not only helped to give identity to the figures but equally they reminded many youngsters of just what their parents and grandparents went through.

In the words of Professor Duncan Macmillan, Scotland's foremost art historian and critic in his review of the Edinburgh Art Festival of 2008, my role as the artist was that of an inspired enabler, but what mattered was "only the truth of the stories enshrined in this remarkable work."

The Process

As a means of introduction for the participants making the figures, the workshops were started with a PowerPoint presentation describing how the idea was formed and most importantly establishing my reasons as a foreigner for taking such an interest in their history. Winning trust while firing enthusiasm for the work from the outset was vital.

To begin with the images from Majdenek and a brief description of the Holocaust was controversial and a risk. Few people had any knowledge or understanding of what had taken place and the response was often that of outrage and incomprehension. How could Europeans, supposed champions of civilization and democracy, have committed such barbaric atrocities, and in such recent times as the 20th century? Some of the questions, made all the more poignant as I stood in front of people whose lives have been so desecrated and disempowered by external forces, remained unanswered.

Why was it that Palestinians had to suffer for what might be construed as atonement for a crime committed by foreigners in distant lands? Why were they still paying the price without any resolution or compensation? Why, by comparison to so many other disenfranchised and oppressed human beings, had they been forgotten by the international as if sacrificed and left in permanent limbo?

These sessions provoked lively discussions which pushed my resolve further to ensure that the work should be of such power enough to give a voice not only to the older generation – the witnesses of 1948 – but equally for the millions of Palestinian refugees to this day who remain forgotten and invisible.

As I stayed in more homes, the more tears I collected through heart rending accounts from the various stages of the exodus in 1948, listening to first-hand accounts of the systematic expulsion of Palestinians from areas of the country through large-scale intimidation tactics: the setting fire to homes, the terrorization ensuring that communities would flee through tactics of coercion, rape, torture, murder, the planting of mines in the rubble to deter return. I decided there had to be additional elements to supplement the visual.

Hundreds of handwritten testimonies were included, forming hanging scrolls bearing the imprint of the personal testimonies, and creating a forest of words of witness, exhibited in rooms adjacent to the wax figures themselves.

Equally, hearing of hundreds of villages that were erased – literally wiped off the map and in some instances superimposed with settlements and new Jewish names – led me to create a sound installation of fragmented, layered voices reciting the lost names.

I believe that art in its many forms can act as a catalyst by drawing attention to the challenges facing society's most vulnerable in ways that will connect with the audience on an emotional level – the place where beliefs and attitudes are formed and changed. Art can stimulate empathy and when an empathic connection with the experience of the most marginalized is established, there is at least the potential to generate positive change.

The principal aim of "**Return of the Soul**" was at the very least to encourage such questioning and to create an awareness that a majority of Palestinians had been systematically expelled from their land, a truth that has been concealed through obfuscation and repeated myths to the present day.

In his book *Why Only Art Can Save Us*, the European philosopher Santiago Zabala remarked on the "Return of the Soul": "The participation of Palestinian refugees in the creation of the figures accounts for the Nakba and also belongs to it and in doing so it discloses its ongoing emergency. Again Frere's work rescues us *into* an essential emergency, one that determines both the most significant event in the history of Palestinians and their current conditions."[1]

The whole experience of becoming deeply involved with the Palestinian people I worked with for "Return of the Soul" made such an impression on me that I did not want to leave. You cannot be a witness, a tear collector and then walk away, forget and move on. The emotional memory remains too strong. It becomes less about sadness and despair but turns into outrage at the unfairness of it all.

I kept thinking about my slide presentations posing uncompromising questions. Although the history of the European Jews is deeply complex, The Holocaust, which

---

[1]   Santiago Zabala, *Why Only Art Can Save Us – Aesthetics and the Absence of Emergency*, New York, Columbia University Press, 2017.

was my starting point in Poland, was a uniquely European atrocity; yet it is the Palestinians who are being punished and sacrificed as if they were nothing but an inconvenience in the prevailing world order. That's where my despair lingers and for a time it became imbued in the essence of everything that I did as an artist.

After the "Return of the Soul" was shown in my own country, Scotland, and in East Jerusalem, Beirut, and Amman, I returned to the West Bank and experienced once more the oppressive impact and a sense of incarceration staying close to that obscenity – the Israeli apartheid wall. It imprisons, it crushes morale, it extinguishes hope. But although ugly and oppressive, I found the wall's surface from an artist's perspective intriguing. It is full of words, peeling paper, colours, and texture, and this informed a new approach to my painting and drawing.

Conceptually, the layering of marks reminded me of a palimpsest, where text is worn away but can never be completely erased. Actually the map of Israel reminds me of a palimpsest, the imposition of a new map over an existing one, but history cannot be entirely eradicated and most importantly for those whose inalienable human right is to hold on to their identity, everything must be done to preserve it.

There is nothing to compare with the experience of having been there, of discovering how different the realities are beyond the distorted truths and myths. I discovered very different stories. Not only the obvious unfairness of one's place on this world being crossed out, the shrinking map redrawn by the decade, but the practical injustices inflicted on Palestinians in their daily lives.

My work in Palestine rewarded me with lasting friendships with people whose dignity and that special quality – *sumud* – are remarkable, and whose energy and determination to succeed against the odds one cannot but admire. If being Pro-humanitarian makes me Pro-Palestinian, so be it.

Chris Giannou

Surgeon, Greece

I grew up in Toronto, Canada, the son of Greek immigrants who had fled the Greek civil war. At an early age, through the influence of my family, I became attuned to world events. I read widely and discovered the Shoah and the Sharpeville massacre long before these became mainstream topics. I followed closely happenings in the Third World: the anti-colonial and anti-imperialist struggle, the Cuban revolution, the independence of Algeria, the American war in Vietnam, and the civil rights movement in the US. I became committed, personally, to a sense of political and social justice.

My Toronto high school participated in a "mock" United Nations General Assembly, each school representing a different country; students met every fortnight to discuss UN resolutions dealing with everything from disarmament to Palestinian refugees. Palestinian refugees! This was around the time of the 1967 Arab-Israeli war. Western media talked of "the Arabs, Abdel Nasser, Egypt", but the Palestinians had disappeared from public discourse.

My studies took me to Mali, Algeria, France, and Egypt. Shortly after the Second World War, when decolonization was the order of the day, there occurred a wave of "re-colonisation", notably the institution of apartheid in South Africa, and the dispossession of the Palestinians through the establishment of Israel. Hannah Arendt, a refugee from Nazi Germany, claimed that the post-war "solution of the Jewish question . . . namely, by means of a colonised and then conquered territory", succeeded only in producing "a new category of refugees, the Arabs". For me, this was the arch example of the victims of centuries of Christian persecution perpetrating an injustice on another people, the Palestinians. Hypocrisy rampant!

In July 1980, having completed my Master of Surgery in Cairo, I arrived in Beirut and joined the Palestine Red Crescent Society. The PRCS ran hospitals, clinics, and an ambulance service. It functioned much like the ministry of public health that the Palestine Liberation Organisation had established in Lebanon during the civil war.

Most of PRCS personnel were Palestinians living in Lebanon as well as Lebanese, but also Palestinians from other regions, as well as Arab nationals who had come to Lebanon to join the "Palestinian Revolution". Eventually, progressive doctors and nurses from South Asia joined the PRCS, as well as European volunteers on a short-term basis. I was a full-time employee of the PRCS and received a monthly salary, like my Arab colleagues, and was the only "Westerner" so employed besides an Australian nurse, Jean Calder, specialized in the care of disabled children.

I became the chief resident of general surgery at the main PRCS surgical centre in Beirut, the Gaza Hospital. The consultants were Palestinian and Lebanese surgeons already experienced in treating the war wounded during the civil conflict in Lebanon and the various Arab-Israeli wars. One Lebanese colleague had worked with the Algerian FLN during the war for independence. I learned my war surgery at the hands of these senior consultants. I spent weeks living in the hospital during the shelling between East and West Beirut, and was responsible for organizing the triage of mass casualties.

On 17 July 1981, Israeli warplanes bombed West Beirut for the first time, and we expected an invasion of Lebanon. Having completed our day of surgery, a meeting was called by Dr Fathi Arafat, President of the PRCS. He had received an order to send a surgical team to the southern town of Nabatiyeh in preparation for a possible Israeli assault.

The PRCS already had hospitals in Sidon and Tyr. Only Nabatiyeh was not covered. Nabatiyeh was the only section of Southern Lebanon where Palestinian and Israeli forces came face to face, the rest of the buffer zone in the south being occupied by United Nations peacekeeping troops, deployed after the Israeli invasion of 1978. The name "Nabatiyeh" instilled fear into anyone's heart in Lebanon then. Dr Arafat asked for volunteers to go. I raised my hand.

An Egyptian anaesthetist, four Palestinian male nurses and I left for Sidon that evening. We worked in the hospital there that night and departed for Nabatiyeh early next morning. There was one small private hospital in Nabatiyeh that functioned more like a clinic.

Israeli bombardment continued throughout the southern regions, with Palestinian and Lebanese nationalist forces responding with rockets. After a week, a ceasefire was announced. I remained in Nabatiyeh, with the PRCS renting the private hospital. During the next year, I worked as the director of the hospital as well as the only surgeon in the region. I came to know the military and political leaders of the Combined Palestinian and Lebanese Forces (*qawat al-moushtaraka*), as well as the inhabitants of nearby villages, almost entirely Shi'ite, and largely depopulated because of frequent Israeli bombardments. I saw the remnants of the Palestinian refugee camp, with the destroyed school where tens of students lay buried under the rubble.

As an Arabic speaking foreigner and doctor whose services were free of charge, I gained the confidence of many of my neighbours. The Jermuk Brigade, known popularly as the "students' brigade", was the chief Fatah and PLO contingent in the region. The officers were all university graduates and their interaction with the civilian population was exemplary, clean of the errors committed by other Palestinian groups in Lebanon. "If this brigade had been here before, we would never have had any problems with the Palestinians" one of my Lebanese neighbours told me.

In June 1982, a botched assassination attempt on the Israeli ambassador in London by a renegade Palestinian faction became the pretext for the Israeli invasion of Lebanon. We had to evacuate Nabatiyeh after about a week of fighting, and I soon found myself in the government hospital in Sidon just across from the Ain al-Helweh refugee camp, the largest in Lebanon, along with several PRCS nurses, and several thousand civilians who had taken refuge in the hospital. The city fell to Israeli forces and only the refugee camp remained unoccupied. The hospital was hit by a tank shell, which ruptured the water lines; we were obliged to drink intravenous fluids. I operated on the floor of the ground floor since the operating theatres were located on the fourth storey and were exposed to shelling. Leaflets were dropped by Israeli airplanes, announcing a ceasefire and calling on the people to go down to the seaside. But shelling resumed during what was supposed to be a ceasefire, and people did not know what to do. A group of Palestinian combatants came to me in the hospital and said that they would leave Ain al-Helweh and go over the mountains to continue the fight there. The next morning, thinking that the resistance of the camp was over, I took advantage of another announced ceasefire to evacuate as many patients and civilians from the hospital as possible. We marched down towards the city and, at the main central road, were stopped by the first line of Israeli soldiers. I managed to return to the PRCS hospital located on the main street.

My PRCS colleagues were taken prisoner the next day and I soon joined them in the St Joseph Convent School turned prison. Two Norwegian medical workers, Steinar Berger and Oyvind Muller, who worked in a rehabilitation centre for mentally and physically handicapped children, accompanied me down to the beach for my "security check", and were taken prisoner as well. The convent school playground held about 800 men, including all the male members of the PRCS. We were kept there for several days in very difficult conditions: summer heat, little water or food, no facilities to relieve ourselves, random beatings, and interrogations. I was interrogated on five occasions there, but suffered no physical abuse. This was not the case for many of my colleagues and other fellow prisoners. At least eight prisoners died during our stay in the convent school. We were then taken by bus to a fruit conserve factory south of Sidon, where I underwent another interrogation, and was struck by a passing soldier who "did not like the way that I looked at him". The two Norwegians and I were then placed on another bus, along with a number of other prisoners, and taken to the Megiddo prison in Israel.

After a week, and the intervention of the Norwegian and Canadian governments, we were taken to Tel Aviv and released to our respective embassies. I returned to Canada and was interviewed by the media, as were the Norwegians in Oslo. In addition, I gave testimony to a Canadian parliamentary Foreign Affairs Committee, telling what I had witnessed: the destruction of residential areas, the thousands of civilian dead, the use of cluster bombs in civilian areas, and the mistreatment of prisoners of war. This went counter to Israeli propaganda on the conduct of the war and was highly controversial. I also insisted on the necessity of a political solution, on the mutual recognition of Israel and the Palestinians, and on a two-state confederation.

The largest Arab population in the United States lives in Detroit, just across the river from Canada, and people there watch Canadian television. I was soon contacted by the American-Arab Anti-Discrimination Committee, a lobby group, which organised an appearance for me before the House Foreign Affairs Subcommittee and then a speaking tour in the US. A second speaking tour of American universities followed. For many American students, this was the first time that they heard of the Palestinian point of view.

In the meantime, combat in Lebanon and the siege of Beirut continued. Finally, a ceasefire intervened and Yasser Arafat and the rest of the PLO leadership agreed to leave the city. Some combatants left by land to Syria, others by ship. Only Palestinians with Lebanese residency were allowed to stay in Beirut. Wounded Palestinian combatants who had to leave Lebanon were evacuated on a ship contracted by the International Committee of the Red Cross. I happened to be in Cyprus then and, as a Greek- and Arabic-speaking PRCS surgeon, was told to organize the reception of the wounded in Cyprus and, later, in Greece. Only two weeks later, the President-elect of Lebanon, Bashir Gemayel, was assassinated by a Lebanese leftist, Israeli troops entered West Beirut, and a Lebanese right-wing militia perpetrated the Sabra and Shatila massacre.

In early 1983, I went to Tripoli, north Lebanon to set up a PRCS hospital in one of the refugee camps there. A split had occurred in Fatah, the dissidents supported by the Syrian regime. Interfactional fighting had broken out in the Beqaa Valley and we feared that it would spread to the Tripoli area, especially after two PLO leaders, Yasser Arafat and Abu Jihad, had arrived in Tripoli. Fighting eventually broke out, we evacuated the hospital and set up a field hospital in the basement shelter of a school in the city. After three and a half months of combat, a ceasefire was reached, Arafat and loyalist troops left the city, and I evacuated 100 wounded on an ICRC ship to continue their treatment abroad.

During the battle, one of six Israeli prisoners of war taken during the 1982 invasion and held by the PLO fell ill. I was called upon to treat him. Dodging Syrian bombs, I was taken to an old house in the port area where the POWs were being held. The next day, two ICRC surgeons and two PRCS surgeons examined the POW patient. We four surgeons wrote out a psychiatric report and, along with two ICRC delegates, I presented the report to Yasser Arafat, pleading with him to hand the prisoner over to the ICRC. He replied that negotiations were underway for a prisoner exchange. In effect, five days later an exchange of the six Israelis for 5,000 Lebanese and Palestinian prisoners in still-occupied South Lebanon took place, including my PRCS colleagues taken prisoner with me in 1982.

After the Tripoli evacuation, I was named medical director of the Palestine Hospital in Cairo, and after a year, was sent to Sanaa, North Yemen to set up another PRCS hospital. About 3,000 Palestinian combatants and their families who had evacuated Beirut in 1982 were now housed in Sanaa, where there was a desperate shortage of good hospital care. The hospital opened in 1985; about 90% of patients were Yemeni citizens, who were treated free of charge as an example of solidarity with Yemen for the hospitality shown the Palestinian combatants.

It was during my time in Sanaa that three Palestinian refugee camps in Lebanon came under siege by the Lebanese Amal militia as part of the ongoing struggle between Arafat loyalists and the Syrian regime. Rashidieh in the South and Borj el-Barajneh in Beirut already had functioning hospitals. Sabra fell during the first round of combat in May 1985; the Gaza Hospital no longer functioned, but Shatila camp resisted and remained under siege, but without a hospital. I managed to obtain a transfer to Shatila to set up a hospital. I finagled my way to Beirut and Shatila in October 1985 and remained there until January 1988. The "war of the camps" was a dreadful and painful experience for both the Lebanese Shi'ite and Palestinian communities, who lived side-by-side and included numerous mixed marriages.

Several battles took place, much of Shatila was destroyed by bombardment, the inhabitants starved during the siege, but the camp resisted. The hospital played a major role in the "steadfastness" (*samud*) of Shatila and maintaining people's morale. As one young fighter told me: "If a bomb falls on my head, that is the will of God. But if I am only wounded, I know that there is a surgeon and a hospital to save me." During the six-month battle, we organised three vaccination campaigns of the children in the bomb shelters. The outbreak of the first intifada in the occupied Palestinian territories put an end to the siege: it was politically impossible for the Amal and Syria to continue. With the raising of the siege, I left the camp to write my memoir of the experience, *Besieged: A Doctor's Story of Life and Death in Beirut.*

Matts Grorud

Animator/director, Norway

"*Ka'ek wa simsim* with Norwegian Brown Cheese"

I have many people to thank for becoming pro-Palestinian. First, my mother who jokingly told me when I was ten years old, that in this life I could choose freely whatever I wanted to do or believe in, except on the issue of Palestine... There was no choice.

But I don't think I needed my mum's smiling remark. The story of the Palestinians and their situation has been closely related to my own life since my mother started working for NORWAC[1] as a nurse in Lebanon during the wars in the 1980s. Since then there has never been any question where my heart lies.

I remember seeing pictures from the Palestinian camps in Lebanon when she came back every three to four months. Names of camps I would learn properly later: Bourj al-Barajneh, Ain al-Helweh, Rashidieh, Nahr al-Bared. In the photos I saw kids my own age smiling among rubble. My mother told me that when there was finally peace in Lebanon we would go together.

I often think about the many generations of Palestinians that have been living in the camps since 1948; and about the generations of people who are not Palestinians who are part of a solidarity movement for the Palestinians. My grandparents were pro-Palestinian, my parents worked in the solidarity movement for Palestine, and I hope that my own children will one day feel the same warm connection.

In 1989 my mum got a job working at the Palestinian hospital in Heliopolis, Cairo. This time the whole family came along. I remember the many receptions with small pizzas, scarves with the Palestinian flag, pictures of Al-Aqsa; and being star struck as a twelve-year old making drawings for Fathi Arafat, who we knew was the brother of Yassir Arafat, the man whose pictures were everywhere.

That year we also went to Raffah in Gaza and I remember being put in a dentist's chair, and suddenly the doctor was inside my mouth fixing a cavity. Palestinian medical efficiency! It was during Christmas and I remember that it snowed that year in Jerusalem. On all the street corners there were kids our age showing the Victory-sign with their fingers, smiling to me and my brother and sister while passing Israeli

---

[1] NORWAC (Norwegian Aid Committee) was formed in 1994 to carry out health-related work in Palestine, Syria, and Lebanon.

soldiers. We bought *ka'ek wa simsim*[2] at the Damascus gate and ate it with our Norwegian brown cheese. I still remember the taste and the smell, and sitting on the stairs by the gate.

My best friend Abu Hassan Bairakji from Bourj al-Barajneh in Beirut once told me that as a child he drank Palestine from his mother's tits. . . I think my own mum had the same impact on me. My whole upbringing seems in so many ways to have rotated around Palestine, and for this I am forever grateful.

In 1995 I was nineteen years old, and it was finally possible to go to Lebanon. We went for two weeks with the Palestine Committee in Norway. The trip was led by my mother and the priest Øyvind Sagedal. I could finally see with my own eyes the Lebanon I had only seen in photos. We went to Sidon, Beirut, Tyre and Baalbek. We visited different camps, kindergartens, NGOs, the Women's Union, and Beit Atfal al-Sumoud.[3] We went to a river near Sidon to eat, and to Jeita Grotto, stayed at the Mayflower Hotel, and saw the beautiful gardens of the American University of Beirut. For many years we had been writing to a Palestinian girl my own age, Nihaya, whom we were finally able to meet.

Everywhere we went, which was mostly the camps, people greeted us with a warmth and hospitality I had never known before.

In 2001 I finished my education in animation/film in Norway. I was twenty-five years old, and there was a program organized by the Palestine Committee to stay in Bourj al-Barajneh or Rashidieh camp, and work with a local NGO for six months. I was curious to understand more, and experience what it was like living in a camp, and make friends there. I have always been interested in history, and in Lebanon there's plenty of this everywhere.

In Bourj al-Barajneh I was quickly invited to visit Salim's family. Several of his uncles and aunts had studied in Russia or Eastern Europe, so I was served good drink, and got a different start to my stay than I expected. It was the first opening to a world of different experiences and lives.

I started to work in a small kindergarten run by a local NGO, and made friends among the women working there. I was introduced to their families, and was quickly adopted by all their relatives and neighbours.

I would work in the morning and spend the rest of the day drinking coffee and smoking cigarettes, watching Oum Kulthum and Abdel Halim on TV with Salim's uncle and his mother Naqie. I would wait for Salim to wake up later in the day, drink more coffee in Abu Husam's grocery shop, whose son played football in Malmø, Sweden. I'd sit with Abu Hassan's sisters Hanan and Rana waiting for Abu Hassan to return from work at "Elegant Cleaning" in Hamra. I was on rooftops with Fahed as he showed me how he trained his pigeons. I sat with Bassam and his sister Ghada, with their mother and brothers stopping by. I visited Yasar and her husband Naser, and their beautiful daughters Yara and Nour.

---

[2]   Palestinian crusted bread rings with sesame seeds.
[3]   An NGO established to bring up Palestinian orphans.

I played football for the "Haifa" team, and we travelled to the other Palestinian camps to play against their teams. I became good friends with the captain Hisham and his family -- his wife Hind and children Sara and Adham, and his strict, yet smiling uncle Haj Salah, whose communist brother, Hisham, would laugh at his strong religious views. In the evenings I visited Yehia and we drank coffee on the stairs to the roof. We laughed at the rat that passed each evening on her way to the roof. I got my hair cut in the saloon of Salim's cousin Saleh, who had the funny nickname "Sarsur" [cockroach], and was the gentlest man I ever met. I had more coffee at Hisham's sister Suad's place. It made a deep impression on me that she was missing a finger on one of her hands and figured it had to do with her participation in the Communist Party and years in Russia.

I learnt about Salim's father, who was martyred in the 1979 Israeli incursion in South Lebanon, and how Salim as a young boy moved to Moscow and got educated there. I learnt about Abu Husam, who lost most of his family during the 1980s wars. I learnt about Ghada, who wanted to become a graphic designer, until war put a halt to her dreams. I heard how Bassam learnt his good English listening to Michael Jackson on his Walkman, and was taught how to dance"Michael" by the young guys in camp. I learnt the jokes about the Syrian army and President Hafez al-Assad. Perhaps the funniest were about Abu Ammar. I learnt about the older brother of Abu Hassan, shot by the Amal militia during the siege of the camps (1985–1988). I learnt about Bilal's father, who was a driver for UNRWA and able to move out of the camp. From Hanan, I learnt about her close relationship with her grandfather, the stories he told about pre-1948 Palestine, also the seeds he carried in his jeans pockets, and how he was the strongest man from their village Kweikat.

In the camps I learnt how to sit on rooftops for hours and talk, and learnt that you could laugh, maybe it wasn't important why, but that you laughed together. On the few trips out of the camp – either with the football team or the once yearly trip to the mountains – I learnt the true meaning of a "Dance Party". The youths started dancing the minute they entered the bus in the morning, continued dancing while it moved and in the parking lots as we stopped for breaks, more in Faraya, our destination, and then the whole way back! It was the same with the weddings in the camps. When there was joy, there was no holding back, you danced until you dropped!

It may seem as if everything was all fun and games in the camp. I was in my early twenties and to me this was very much the part of life I was shown. But as I stayed longer I learnt what lay underneath the smiles, the proud greetings and the hospitality: there was an ever present seriousness and sorrow. People's past lives and inner feelings and the hardships facing them every day were revealed to me as a friend.

I would feel this pain at the morning coffee on Amlieh Street, drinking with guys who didn't have work that day – or not at all. I could feel this when my friends on the rooftops looked into the horizon after their pigeons, when the evening prayer was called. I would feel this when my friends told me that the forever smiling Abu Husam had lost his family in the wars; and when I heard how Bassam's love married someone else because he didn't have money to provide for her. I would feel it when Abu Hassan told me about the racism he faced at work; and when Yehia asked me for a small loan to pay for medicine for his cancer.

But for most of the time I felt the overwhelming warmth of my friends and their families in the camp and always the smile and eagerness to share a cigarette or a coffee, and always *them* asking *me* if I needed something. I was not used to this custom, and I blushed to feel I was at the receiving end in the camp.

After living a year in the camp I finally had to leave. I have never cried as much as that last night talking with Hanan and Abu Hassan before their father Lutfi drove me to the airport early in the morning in their beat-up old car. I have never been more proud than when Hanan told me, "*Enta ibn al-mukhayem*" ("You are a son of the camp"). Until today I carry that remark with me.

In 2010 I used my experiences of living in Bourj al-Barajneh camp to write a script for an animated feature film called "The Tower". During the eight years making the film, I was lucky enough to return to the camp and meet up with my friends again. I asked them whether the script resonated with their experiences growing up in the camp. I went to Sidon to see friends of mine and my mother's there. It was important for me to hear what they thought of the script, and whether my depiction of life in the camps felt true to people who had experienced everything themselves.

I also used other sources to dig into the past, such as the beautiful book, *What it Means to be Palestinian* by Dina Matar, *Cyclamens from Galilee* by Elias Srouji, Fawaz Turki's *Soul in Exile*, and the *Nakba Archives* compiled by Mahmoud Zeidan and Diana Allan.

The film *The Tower/Al Bourj* was released in 2018. Though the production was entirely European I included as many Palestinian voices as possible. We did the Arabic version in Haifa, and to me this was a remarkable and beautiful part of the project: having Palestinian actors from inside Palestine play the voices of their brothers and sisters in the Lebanese camps. With the help of Salim Jabal and Ahlam Canaan we were able to have a superstar cast for the film: first Laila Najjar who played Wardi, the main character in the film, but also others such as Mohammad and Saleh Bakri, Makram J. Khoury, Mouna Hawwa, Morad Hassan, Hanan Hilow, and Shaden Kanboura.

For the musical recording in France we had a mixed ensemble of Palestinan and French musicians; I was so proud to have Palestinian musicians -- Mahmoud Karzon, Marina Eichberg, Youssef Hbeisch, and soprano Dima Bawab -- on board. There are many more I should mention that the making of the film put me in touch with, and there are so many memories we share. One of the fondest was when Marina and Mahmoud played for the recording while watching the film. I understood that what we had made together touched them deeply.

Later we toured the film for about two years, screening it all over the world in cinemas and at festivals. It touched me deeply to hear from diaspora Palestinians how their grand or great-grandparents also had their keys with them, and how they would recognize the different alleys of the camp, despite the fact that in the film it's all done with puppets and cardboard. We screened the film in several of the camps in Lebanon and the West Bank, from noisy football pitches to indoor rooms with fans, scout assembly halls, and kindergartens. These screenings were always very different from the showings in European cinemas, with more noise, laughter, and singing.

So the journey of becoming pro-Palestinian has been until now a very big part of my life. It's the personal meetings I've had with young and old that strike a chord in my heart. Working as a volunteer with kids in the camp who now must be grown up, with kids of their own; my friends -- some still in Lebanon, and many who have managed to travel abroad. Thinking about Abu Hassan, my best friend from the camp who now lives in Helsingborg, Sweden. How despite everything he made the best out of his life, and now has four kids and a job. But I also keep thinking of the injustice of how his mother Rozette would have had better treatment for the cancer that killed her had she not been a "refugee". I keep thinking about how his father Lutfi has been unable to travel to Sweden to see his son and grandchildren, or return to Kweikat in Galilee. And my good friend Abu Hassan, the most brilliant and funny guy I know, what troubles he has had to endure because he grew up in exile and carried a travel document from the UN instead of a passport.

This injustice that so many Palestinians suffer due to the ongoing occupation fuels rage. But more importantly, I feel love for everyone I was lucky enough to meet on this road starting in my childhood until today – love and respect – and the feeling that I am in debt for everything that I have been given in the Palestinian camps, and when meeting Palestinians in the diaspora.

Roger Heacock

Historian/university lecturer, France, resident in Ramallah

"Choosing Palestine"

Laura, my life's companion, and I were long-time American internationalists, politicized and radicalized by the Vietnam War and second-wave feminism. I had been a supporter of the Palestinian cause ever since I discovered the Nakba through the account, in the mid-1960s, of a fellow student, who in 1948 had experienced the massacre of part of his family in Lydd, and the expulsion of the rest. In the early 1970s, I came to know the PLO in Beirut, where, with Greek activists, I went to seek possible support for the struggle against the fascistic Greek military junta, prior to their overthrow in 1974. We went to Nicaragua in solidarity with the Sandinistas after the 1979 *triumfo*, then to Paris, to engage with France's transition to socialism following the election of François Mitterrand as president in 1981. Vain dreams! As we lived, studied, taught, and worked in Paris, and raised two small children, we dreamt of lending our skills and energies to the cause of peoples faced with the oppressions of capitalism, colonialism, imperialism – in other words, the Third World. We saw Palestine, in other words, as one of a network, social, national, and ideological, of popular struggles for justice.

In 1982, Israel waged war on Lebanon, intent on expelling the PLO from the country and in the process gaining and maintaining control over Lebanese water resources. (In the event, they largely achieved those dual goals; the latter, however, only for a couple of decades until their withdrawal under fire in 2000.) Like so many friends of the Palestinians, we were riveted to the news of the invasion and Lebanese and Palestinian resistance in that summer of 1982. By September, many cadre and fighters of the PLO had been dispersed throughout the Arab world, the leadership relocated to Tunis. Tens of thousands of Palestinian refugees were now defenseless in the face of their Israeli and their many Lebanese enemies. Hundreds of Falangist militiamen made their way to Shatila refugee camp in the Sabra neighbourhood of Beirut, their way opened to them by the Israeli armed forces, who coordinated and facilitated their task with 24-hour floodlighting, and perpetrated one (but only one) of the worst massacres since 1948. The Sabra-Shatila massacre reminded us of America's recent Vietnam debacle: an overweening, over-armed, technological giant killing massive numbers of Lebanese and Palestinians, mainly civilians, largely from the air, violating end-of-conflict agreements and authorizing the slaughter of many more civilians, this time mainly children, women, and old people; a racialized killing spree. And the United States fully supported Israel in its violence against the peoples of the area generally, and Palestinians in their own land in particular.

This massacre tipped the balance, and we decided we would devote our energies to supporting the Palestinian people, rather than simply a distant and abstract Palestinian cause among causes. It seemed natural to head for the "inside", under Israeli occupation, where millions of unarmed, exposed people lived and struggled. Having first scouted the West Bank and found that Ramallah was replete with schools in which our children would be happy, we left our work in Paris (at the university and in women's health), then drove and sailed down in August 1983 from Venice to Haifa, with a few addresses in our pockets. Alerted to the allegedly ubiquitous presence of Israeli agents on these Greek vessels ("they are everywhere!" in the words of one Gazan lawyer, a fellow passenger), and, to be frank, succumbing to a short-term form of paranoia, we threw overboard such "compromising" texts as Raja Shehadeh's very moderate critique, *The Third Way*, and the telephone numbers of contacts in occupied Palestine. Our intention was to stay, if possible, two years rather than one, the first one being certainly needed for us to settle in. In the event, the two years became thirty-five.

Ramallah was already a centre of cultural, social, and especially political activism, and we both soon found work, modestly paid, but given the moderate cost of living at the time, enough to support us. The first to offer us work was the Friends School in Ramallah, where we taught history, or French, or health sciences. By the time of the first anniversary of the Sabra-Shatila massacre, I was also working with *al-Haq*, the human rights organization (then known also as *Law in the Service of Man*), and we heeded the call by the PLO for commemorative and protest marches everywhere. Our little group of *al-Haq* employees, and hangers-on, including our six-year old daughter and (on shoulders) two-year old son marched down from the centre of Ramallah, via Qalandia refugee camp, through Beit Hanina to East Jerusalem – a total of 12 km, which took us several hours of course, but at a leisurely pace, a clear illustration of how close, how symbiotic was Jerusalem with the West Bank hinterland. We waited for a bus to take us back, and when we asked the driver if he was going to Ramallah, he answered, "No, no, you'll have to take the Arab bus." This was our precocious and decisive discovery of the unique feature of Israeli rule: everything, animal, vegetable, and mineral, has an ethnic identity.

The children quickly became *'atfal al hara* (children of the neighbourhood) and roamed freely among neighbours, venturing on their own to the nearby Manara (the central square), and when of age (beginning kindergarten), walking to school: as foreigners, they had a choice between a variety of perfectly adequate schools, with teaching in Arabic. The Friends School in Ramallah was then, as now, a prized local educational institution; it also served to give the children of (whether voluntarily or forcibly) exilic Palestinians an opportunity to revive their roots, often living with their grandparents; and like its sister institutions, the school was a centre of largely symbolic but deeply committed nationalist activities. Of course, Palestinians are people just like others, something one's activism on their behalf can lead one to forget. They have their share of mistrust of ideas, persons, and things unknown, and in particular, xenophobia. But by and large, our acceptance was rapid and comprehensive, and we were included in activities of all sorts by way of outings, collective childcare, and, of course, planning for political change in the face of this unusual and pervasive form of colonization.

The endearing personal environment also made it possible for us to find useful professional activities. Laura, a midwife, was first employed by the Arab College of Nursing in al-Bireh (now a part of Al-Quds University), while I, in addition to Al-Haq, worked part time for al-Najah National University in Nablus. Both the Arab College and al-Najah were known to be conservative, pro-Jordanian institutions (administration, not student bodies), but this did not prevent them from giving foreigners jobs in which they might prove to be useful to the Palestinian cause. Indeed, those early contacts with students at al-Najah, years before the uprising, convinced me that the occupation was not and would never be taken lying down, which was the implicit message of Israel, with its claim to being a "liberal" occupier, practising an open bridge policy, yet unable and unwilling to do anything for the population, with the exception of their very effective, vigorous, often violent measures in the twin areas of security (for Israelis) and tax collection (which financed the Occupation and filled the coffers of the state). As a result, Gaza and the West Bank became a veritable and rather anarchic – or, more accurately, self-managed – "wild west", a testing ground for experiments in the field of primary health, legal proceedings, and education in such disparate fields as music and literacy. We were, in other words, drawn into a very traditional, still somewhat pastoral lifestyle, yet replete with ideas, initiatives, and people. We sensed that the change in question was holistic – the quest to change human beings in tandem with political emancipation – and that the issue which had drawn us to Palestine was augmented by a multidimensional striving for improvement in the interrelationships among people along with the self-evident need for a decisive break from the Occupation.

Ramallah and the mountainous West Bank, Gaza with its single locally-owned hotel on the beach, the Cliff Hotel, turned out on the personal level to be a wonderful place to raise children. Indeed, we soon had a third one, and would drive all over greater Palestine (no permanent checkpoints at the time, around the Strip, Jerusalem, or '48 Israel, one and all navigated freely "from the [Lebanese] border to the [Egyptian] border, and from the [Jordan] River to the [Mediterranean] Sea." Leaving Ramallah, one could shop in the Old City of Akka in the morning, spend the night in Gaza, and return to Ramallah via Jerusalem, West and East, all in a matter of 48 hours, even including a quick float in the Dead Sea at 'Ain Feshka if one really wanted to stretch it. Indeed, Palestine was, compared to so many other places, a truly idyllic place in which to raise children and invest our revolutionary energies. Although nobody imagined the turmoil to come, popular committees were flourishing, certainly attached to the various political factions, but deeply committed to the full panoply of rights, for youth, women, workers, farmers: in short, every section of a society.

Once we found jobs in other universities, Birzeit University's departments (health and history) became interested, even anxious to hire us; within a couple of years, I was part of the history department; Laura held out some years longer, finding direct action and advocacy; the women's health coalition, the school for community health workers of the Union of Palestinian Medical Relief Committees, were more to her liking during the initial years of struggle. Palestinians in the mid-'80s were true "pessoptimists". They didn't see how or when they would get rid of the occupation, or even stop the never-ending expansion of the Israeli settlements. And yet, their determination, their belief in liberation found hope in the experiences of so many third world peoples, all of whom by now had won their independence. It seemed illogical that these fruits of struggle would be denied the Palestinians, and in their daily lives they acted out their rejection of the status quo in a thousand ways. As the years went by, we found our decision to move to Palestine fully justified. Without ever taking ourselves for Palestinians, we developed in those early years deep bonds with people from all walks of life: from colleagues at work, to politically like-minded folks, to the shepherdess who nourished her goats in our large backyard, to the neighbourhood baker, the Hebronite family who sold Jericho bananas in Ramallah, the parents of our children's schoolmates and their teachers, the collective taxi (*service*) drivers taking us to Nablus, Jerusalem, or the Jordan valley. And many others peopled and enriched our existence as we got our full-bodied taste of the real Palestine, so different from the abstraction of the cause, so much more contradictory and yet so much more dynamic, and beckoning to our family with young children, encouraging us to have another, to dig our roots deeply in the newly discovered land, and to give up on our cozy Parisian home, and the thought of careers in health and education back in the west. Long before the intifada broke out in December 1987, our attachment to the people and the land had, whether or not we were fully conscious of it, determined that we were there for the long haul.

This increasing determination to stay was most certainly also fuelled, and decisively so, by the newly inaugurated geopolitics of the region and the struggle. By expelling the PLO leadership and fighters from Lebanon, Israel was completing the job begun a decade earlier by king Hussein of Jordan: forcing an oppressed people to turn inward rather than outward in their quest for freedom and self-determination. Palestinians were kept far from the borders; the Arab states had long demonstrated their utter incapacity to give them their promised freedom. And yet the quest for liberation burned just as brightly. Logically and inevitably, the inside (and specifically, Jerusalem, the West Bank, and Gaza) inexorably moved towards becoming central in the struggle. Indications were that the leadership in Tunis was as yet unconscious and rather contemptuous of this development: they certainly acted that way. And so the movement of ideas and practices in the occupied Palestinian territories accelerated, driven by individuals, groups, and professions whose potential was hitherto untapped, and eventually reaching its explosive, critical mass in December 1987. Thereafter the PLO, as well as the other great socio-religious movement, the Muslim Brotherhood, moved to catch up and recuperate their lost footing. Although the Palestinians in their revolution of stones had never renounced their allegiance to the leadership, the role of the inside, in which we resided, was asserted progressively before its outbreak and has never been renounced. This was then the environment in which we spent our first years in Palestine, consolidating our own relationship to the country and its people, and conscious of the potent energy of the context in which we lived out our daily lives as individuals and as a family.

Our long, exhilarating, and yet exhausting time in Palestine was thus initiated by a shock – Sabra-Shatila – a settling in to our large old house and garden (the 70 Jordanian dinars monthly rent, then worth about $200, was considered too high!) – and, most significantly, acceptance into the society, its schools, and its professions, all in the shadow of and aimed at ending the occupation. Thus prepared, we and our three children went through the collective feat of the uprising against occupation, the first Gulf War with the threat of chemical attacks, the hopes and illusions of Oslo, the second intifada, the successive elections in the Palestinian Autonomy, the death of Yasser Arafat and advent of the stewardship of Abu Mazen: in short, the many hopes, fears, traumas, and joys we shared with Palestinians and their friends the world over, for thirty-five years. Having been arrested and expelled on various occasions, but never for cause, and unable to blunt our determination to return (with the help of Palestinian and Israeli lawyers), in 2018 we were denied any hope of visa renewal and thus forced to leave, it would seem for good since the alternatives are too constricting, and require the constant input of lawyers, waiting for a response from the occupier, and waiting at the bridge with baited breath to see if this time we can get in. With this panorama of years passed, friends gained (and lost to death), and horizons broadened immeasurably for us and our deeply Palestinized children, and despite the terrible disappointments in the political, social, and economic evolution of our Palestine, Laura and I can say without hesitation that we have no regrets. We were not serving an illusion, but a vision that requires years, decades, generations to bear fruit. Change, like hope, springs eternal, and to this rule Palestine is no exception.

Anni Kanafani

Kindergarten teacher/director, Denmark, lives in Lebanon

There was nothing about Palestine or the Middle East in our history textbooks either at school or in college. When Israel was established in May 1948, the Danes, like most other people in the "civilized" world, were completely ignorant about what had happened to the Palestinians, how they were forced to leave their homeland, Palestine. People in Denmark only got to know that in 1948 a country called Israel was established for the Jews.

In 1960 I participated in an international teachers' and students' conference in Yugoslavia. There, for the first time, I was confronted with the Palestinian tragedy through meetings with Palestinian students. Back in Denmark, I continued to correspond with them, and to discuss their problem with fellow students. I started to talk about the expulsion of the Palestinian people from their homeland at the International Peoples' High School, but in Elsinore (close to the castle, where "Hamlet" is being staged each year.)

I first went to Syria in September 1961, to see with my own eyes and hear with my own ears. When I decided to continue to Lebanon, a Palestinian student leader in Damascus gave me a letter to Ghassan Kanafani. When I was introduced to him, he was the cultural editor of the Arab weekly *Al-Hurriya*. When I asked him if I could visit some refugee camps, Ghassan fell silent. Then he *shouted*, "Do you think our Palestinian people are animals in a zoo?"

From there he started to tell me about his people and his country: How on November 29 1947, the UN, in violation of its own charter, partitioned Palestine against the will of its Arab population, which at the time made up two thirds of the total population of the country. Then Ghassan began to tell me about his beloved Palestine, and how he was forced to leave it in May 1948, together with his parents and five brothers and sisters. That is how my relationship with the Palestinian cause really began.

I stayed in Beirut and started to work in a Lebanese kindergarten, and the relationship between Ghassan and me began to develop through the Palestinian cause. I compared the struggle for the liberation of Palestine to the resistance movement's struggle in Denmark and other European countries against the German Nazi occupation during the Second World War.

Israeli massacres against the population of Gaza have continued ever since 1948. Ghassan wrote a short story *"Letter from Gaza"* in 1955, about one of the Israeli atrocities. Gaza is surely the world's biggest prison. What has been happening to Gaza and its people since 1948 is intolerable. The US and the EU countries could put pressure on Israel to stop the continuous attacks on Gaza, but instead they defend Israel, and are blind to the suffering of the Palestinian people. I don't understand how US presidents and their allied world leaders can sleep knowing that every day young children and civilians are being massacred by the Israeli army's terror weapons.

The steadfastness of the people in Gaza should be admired by everybody, and their will to continue the struggle is fantastic.

The way I was raised as a child by my parents has influenced my way of thinking and behaving in support of oppressed peoples everywhere, and against war and exploitation. I have always dreamt of a beautiful and just world for all children to live in. Ghassan and I dreamt about establishing kindergartens and cultural centres for children and youth in the Palestinian camps. In the past forty-seven years our dream has gradually come true, though unfortunately only after Ghassan's martyrdom, when we founded the Ghassan Kanafani Cultural Foundation [GKCF] in his memory.

Ghassan always said "The children are our future" and therefore it became evident that a big part of GKCF's work should focus on the Palestinian children for whom Ghassan held such admiration and respect and in whom he had such great faith.

Information on the GKCF supplied by Leila Kanafani, daughter of Anni and Ghassan:

In 1969 Anni approached UNRWA trying to convince them to establish kindergartens in the Palestinian refugee camps, but UNRWA replied that they did not have the mandate to do so. Anni and Ghassan considered, together with friends, establishing something independently.

On July 8 1974, on the date of the second commemoration of Ghassan's martyrdom, GKCF was founded as an official Lebanese NGO, and Anni became the vice-chairperson. The main aim was to commemorate Ghassan by publishing his works and carrying on in his spirit the struggle for a free and democratic Palestine.

Among the Foundation's goals are: Establishing and running kindergartens for children aged 3–6 years and habilitation centres for children with special needs in Palestinian camps (and other deprived areas); establishing and running libraries/art centres and clubs for children aged 6–16 years; integrating activities between children with special needs and other children; training teachers and other staff members; promoting cultural and social activities (among these have been yearly exhibitions of children's artwork).

Since 1974, GKCF has established six kindergartens for children aged 3–6 years, two habilitation centres for children with special needs, four libraries for children aged 6–18 years, and three clubs all situated within or on the outskirts of Palestinian refugee camps in Lebanon. The Foundation's work involves the inclusion of children with special needs, as well as the integration of the different facets within the projects, parents and community participation, health and social awareness, cooperation across borders, and advocacy. The pedagogy in the different projects is based on the *holistic approach* and creative learning and art education. It is through constant development and ongoing training of staff that GKCF is able to maintain a high professional standard.

In August 1982, during the Israeli invasion of Lebanon, Anni took part in an international hearing in Oslo (Norway), under the patronage of the former Irish minister of foreign affairs and with the participation of officials from different countries, lawyers in international law, journalists, doctors, and others. The hearing resulted in a *White Book*, made public, condemning Israel for war crimes in Lebanon.

Since her first chance meeting with Palestinians almost five decades ago, Anni has dedicated her life to a just cause, a cause she strongly believes in: the Palestinian cause.

Monica Maurer

Film-maker and archivist, Germany, resident in Italy

"Why and How I Became Pro-Palestinian"

I cannot keep count of how often I have been asked that question, in a number of different contexts; almost every longer interview I have been asked to give started with "How did you become involved in the issue of Palestine?" Or, particularly in the US, the question asked by members of Jewish communities was: "How could you, as a German, get involved with the Palestinians?" which I used to answer by saying, "Precisely because I am German-born I got involved with the Palestinian people, because of the values I believe in and because of a political and historical responsibility I have felt ever since I embraced these values."

These values were forged at a relatively young age when I joined the Vereinigung der Verfolgten des Nazi regimes (Association of Persecutees of the Nazi Regime/Federation of Antifascists) because of the duty I felt to take a stand against the reappearance of Nazi activities in West Germany. This was at the time of the "Economic Miracle" (*Wirtschaftswunder*), when there was an acceptance of old Nazis in right-wing institutions and a growing denial of the Holocaust along with Germany's responsibilities for the catastrophic events of World War II.

When I speak of "values" (solidarity with those who are weaker, sharing whatever you have with those who do not have, refusal to accept the law of the power of the stronger over the weaker, and over empathy and tolerance), maybe it would be best if I went back to my socialization, the years that formed my character and convictions and which have never changed throughout my adult life, because they are not merely ideological but based on genuine life experiences.

So let me start with my background: I'm the second (middle) child of George, a surgeon, and Erika, a dentist. Our home was bombed and we were displaced to the countryside, to a little village near Munich, where a wonderful and generous farmer gave us refuge in his farm. This offered me the privilege not to go hungry as millions of others were forced to do, and also to learn to admire the work of a farmer, who sees the results of his labour. In fact, when asked as a child what I wanted to become I always answered: a farmer or a ballerina – but the ballerina part comes later.

At the age of five, all of a sudden I could no longer walk. With a high fever and unbearable pain, I was brought to the hospital where I was operated on, not once but five times because of osteomyelitis, an infection of the marrow of the bones. After a year of being imprisoned in a cast, the operated leg was only half the size of the healthy one; the only way not to hobble was to do ballet, which I did in spite of the atrocious pain. Thus I learned that every achievement requires its degree of effort: nothing is for nothing, nothing can be taken for granted. After moving back to the city, I started to paint as a compensation for the years of pain I had gone through, and at some point I applied to take drawing lessons at the Academy of Arts, where I became acquainted with exiles from Franco's Spain, Portugal, and Algeria, which was then under French colonial occupation and in the midst of a national liberation struggle. My acquaintances at this time were from a number of different countries, but they were all united by a common set of principles and values: No to racism and No to colonialism! We shared a belief in Justice and Freedom, and the aim to strive for a society with human dignity for all.

One particular event was key to my future social and political engagement and what I wanted to stand for. During a protest at the university against torture in Algeria by the colonial occupation, we distributed a little book, forbidden in France, entitled "*La Question*" by Henri Alleq. The police immediately intervened, beating and arresting us all. This was my first time in such a situation; it literally hit my head that you cannot stand aside or be "neutral" when it comes to defending life and dignity.

After having finished my studies I started to work as a journalist and film-maker, documenting the harsh living and working conditions of immigrant workers, then cynically called *Gastarbeiter* or "guest workers". I considered them the "Third World" within European capitalist society. At that time the majority of immigrant workers were Italian, Spanish, and later Turkish. Workers from Palestine were fewer in number, but they were the most organized, in the General Union of Palestinian Workers (GUPW), thanks to their outstanding leader, Abdel Jabar Hamad. It was through him that I had the luck and pleasure to get to know a number of Palestinian families and their proverbial hospitality.

During the 1967 War, when Israel occupied the West Bank and Gaza, I experienced the war not through the media, but through the eyes of those families, who were displaced and torn apart, many of them becoming second time refugees. So my empathy with the Palestinians started long before my film work with them began, around 1977. As a convinced internationalist, during the Lebanese Civil War (1975–76) I was involved in working in medical solidarity with the Palestine Red Crescent Society (PRCS), and the PLO's Public Health sector. It was then that I realized the Palestinians were almost exclusively tied to armed struggle for self-determination and their right to statehood as recognized by the international community in the 1947 Partition Plan. It was then, also, that I realized there was hardly any knowledge in the Arab world, not even in the Palestinian diaspora, about the very sophisticated social, medical, and cultural infrastructure of what then was known as the "Palestinian Revolution". Very little was known abroad about the clinics and hospitals that the PRCS had built in and for the refugee camps.

The extremely sophisticated infrastructure of the PRCS, which offered not only medical services but also health education, rehabilitation, and educational services, vocational training and small production sites to combat unemployment, impressed me deeply. I decided to contribute to raising awareness about this "construction of a society of social justice and social change" in which women were also an active and conscious factor. Showing the humanitarian and constructive engagement of Palestinian society became my challenge as a filmmaker, since I was aware that this visual testimony would be an indication of the character of a future Palestinian state. This is what motivated me to live and film in the Palestinian refugee camps in Lebanon from the end of 1977 to the Israeli invasion of 1982 that besieged many of the camps and aimed at destroying all that had been built on the ground and at eliminating any organized presence of the PLO in Lebanon.

A phrase of Dr Said Dajani, a surgeon who after retirement set up several Nursing Schools for the PRCS for boys and girls alike, always echoes in my mind: "We Palestinians are builders, and even if what we build is destroyed, we will continue rebuilding until we go back to our country." Unfortunately, a Jerusalemite, he did not make it back, dying in exile.

Impressed as I was by the PLO's highly developed infrastructure, I wondered why all this was not being sufficiently highlighted, not only to the solidarity committees abroad, but to those who could transform knowledge and solidarity into a concrete contribution to the project of designing the basis for a future Palestinian state, democratic and secular, aimed at social change, justice and full popular participation. And certainly there was no real awareness that many of the Palestinian institutions were in fact models for the whole Arab world. Among these was the Beit Atfal As-Sumoud orphanage for the hundreds of orphans from the Tall-al-Zaatar massacre, established by the General Union of Palestinian Women to help children overcome the trauma they had suffered; and the Ramleh Rehabilitation Centre of the PRCS in which artificial limbs were manufactured by professionally trained persons, many of whom had themselves lost limbs during the continual Israeli raids, which meant that they had a special sensitivity towards patients who needed physiotherapy and/or prosthetics. All of this was free of charge and the only possible means for Palestinians to obtain medical treatment.

In a country that has no public health system, with healthcare inaccessible not only to Palestinians, but also to poor Lebanese, there was a multiple effect: "handicapped" workers continued to be active members of the society, and thus could overcome their trauma and preserve their self-esteem, in spite of their physical situation, while the patients, many of whom were children, could develop a relationship of confidence and trust with their "doctors". Another example of progressive organization was the kindergartens in most workplaces, hospitals, and production units to allow female workers to take care of their kids without giving up their professional activities.

My first documentary shot in this context was "*Palestine Red Crescent*" (1978) on the PRCS, which served among others as an audio-visual statement on the social and medical services of the PLO at the Annual World Health Organization (WHO) Assembly in Geneva. In 1979 – the UN Year of the Child – I made a documentary, "*Children of Palestine*", on how the fundamental rights of Palestinian children (right to life, education, family, healthcare, a home, et cetera) were denied by the constant state of war, occupation, and displacement. This documentary won a number of awards at international film festivals and was distributed in the USA, East and West Germany,

Mexico, and Japan, also touring internationally for a couple of years together with the official UN Film on Children for that year.

While I was filming *"Ashbal: Pulse of Life"* on the activities of this youth organization, on July 17 1981 Israel bombed Fakhani, a densely populated area of Beirut, where many of the institutions noted above were located, killing more than 300 and wounding thousands. It was like a rehearsal for the invasion a year later. I wanted to send a "Telex to the World", an Outcry, against the international silence on this massacre. This became *"Born Out of Death"*, a political poem. About the 1982 war, I made the film *"Why?"* with Abdelrahman Bseisso, head of the Information Department of the PRCS that produced the film, who wrote the Arabic version. *"Why?"* dealt with issues of that war that in my opinion had been given too little media coverage: the fact that the great majority of victims were civilians and civilian institutions and infrastructure such as hospitals, water and electricity plants, and food deposits; the use of weaponry prohibited by international law, such as fragmentation shells, phosphorus bombs, and implosion bombs that buried and carbonized people in shelters. In fact, this last sequence of the film was used as testimony in a US Senate enquiry commission on the violation of the US-Arms Export Act. *"Why?"* was also was widely distributed internationally and created a link with what was then a very strong international peace movement.

As part of the American brokered ceasefire agreement, all staff of PLO institutions and all fighters were forced to leave Lebanon, and became scattered in Tunisia, Algeria, Yemen, Jordan, and Syria. Any form of organized Palestinian presence in Lebanon was forbidden. In 1982, in violation of what was known as the Habib Agreement, the Israelis then invaded Lebanon, besieged West Beirut, looting the Film Archive, the PLO Research Centre, and the Department of Culture. From that time on I felt that the main focus in the Palestinian context should be placed on the situation in Occupied Palestine. So my next film was *"Listen!"*, inspired by the poem of the great Palestinian writer and poet Tawfik Zayyad: "Let them hear, let all the world hear, we may suffer, but we will not kneel. We shall stay here on our land! Listen! Can you hear!" *"Listen!"* is about the daily hardships of life under the Occupation.

By the mid-80s, Palestinian cinematography started to emerge and so grew my conviction that it was more important to help provide a forum for these films to be seen, rather than make films on Palestine myself. Only with the outbreak of the First Intifada, at the end of 1987, did I make one more documentary on the issue – *"Palestine in Flames"* – on the historical and political roots of the Uprising, which I viewed as having started already as a struggle against the colonization of Palestine, even before the Nakba of 1948.

I am still convinced today that the best service that can be provided to the Palestinian cause, in the current phase, is to highlight Palestinian culture as much as possible, especially since the Zionist offensive against Palestine's culture, history, narrative, and identity is growing along with the increase in settler violence. So, for the last twenty years, since 2013, I have been engaged in organizing film screenings, teaching classes as well as curating a monthly Cineforum Palestina at the AAMOD (archive of the working class and democratic movement) in Rome. I also collaborate, as "patron" and head of the Jury of the Al-Ard Film Festival (currently at its 18th edition) as well as Cinema

Senza Diritti (Cinema without Rights) in Venice and Mestre, and with NAZRA, an itinerary Palestinian Short Film Festival.

Another significant effort I have made during these last years has been to digitize all my rushes filmed in the last forty years, thereby making them accessible. As a matter of fact, I often share material for films on Palestine with other filmmakers, such as Mohanad Yacubi, the French Vacarmes Collective, Lina Soualem, Khaled Jarrar, Aude Fourel, Francesca Zonars, Marco Pasquini Gaza Hospital, and for a film portrait "*The Paper Man*" of the great Lebanese journalist Talal Salman.

Furthermore, I deposited many hours of digitized rushes at the Institute for Palestine Studies (IPS) in Beirut, the Arab-American University Library (in Jenin and Ramallah), and the Qattan Foundation in Ramallah, so as to make them accessible to historians, researchers, students, and film-makers. This work has been especially significant since the Palestinian Film Archive was looted in 1982 and all its films have since been "kept captive" in the IDF Archive as Israeli property.

Another of my efforts to safeguard collective Palestinian audio-visual property was to restore and digitize the rushes of the film "Tal al-Zaater" by Mustafa Abu Ali and Jean Chamoun, which was co-produced by AAMOD and the Palestinian Cinema Institution – PLO Unified Information, as well as to restore an Arabic version that had been lost since the '80s, and to screen it in Amman and Beirut in the presence of the protagonists.

My ultimate aim is, together with a group of Palestinian filmmakers (the Archive Team), to create a lobby aimed at demanding the establishment of a Palestinian National Film Archive, with the highest professional standards and within the International Federation of Film Archives (FIAF). It would be a public, independent, and non-profit archive. Finally, after a wait of forty years, this archive would constitute a haven capable of safeguarding the fragmented cinematographic history and heritage of the Palestinian people, their culture, and what is basically their collective memory, which has been and continues to be under attack.

David McDowall

Historian, UK

"Disagreeing with Glubb"

I can remember exactly where I was sitting in the library in March 1963, my last year at school. I was destined for Sandhurst and a career in the army. The book in front of me was John Bagot Glubb, *A Soldier with the Arabs*. It combined my ambition to be a soldier with my fascination with the Middle East, fostered by my late father's photographic collection from his time in the Royal Air Force, flying all over the Middle East. Glubb's account of the Arab-Israeli war of 1948 gripped me, but I remember being troubled by his criticism of the Palestinian Arabs' refusal to compromise with Jewish settlers, their belief in justice though the heavens fall. Why didn't they compromise? I realised that I disagreed with Glubb and agreed with the Palestinians. I simply could not understand how they could or should compromise with a process which was so profoundly unjust, what they correctly saw as the progressive colonization of their country and the wholesale denial of their right to determine their own future as Palestine's indigenous population. In similar circumstances would the British compromise? Like hell they would. Looking out of the library window at the wooded valley beyond, I thought, "This cannot be right."

Yet, because of my traditionalist upbringing I was very reluctant to criticize the British state and so could not at that time bring myself to see the cynical calculations that Britain had actually made, and consequently put the Palestine problem down to an unfortunate conflict of promises. Through Glubb's book I embraced the view that Transjordan's small but gallant Arab Legion had acted on behalf of the Palestinians through its heroic defence of Latrun and Jerusalem. In 1964, as a Sandhurst cadet, I was able to visit Jordan and the West Bank. It was a transformative trip for, apart from a couple of weeks training in Germany, I had never been abroad. Here was a profoundly different land and culture. I fell for the warmth of the people, the beautiful hills, olive groves, and stone villages of the West Bank. I was hooked.

When, in 1966, the army offered to pay my fees should I obtain a place at Oxford, I leapt at the chance. A new course was on offer, Islamic History with Arabic. I struggled with the Arabic but loved the history. I was lucky enough to be taught by the great scholar of Modern Middle East studies, Albert Hourani. Under the influence of his teaching and friendship I turned from a conservative into a liberal. As I moved in my studies through the Crusades, my first lesson in the West's imperialist violence, and eventually to Britain's first exercise in Arab regime change in its occupation of Egypt in 1882, I started to question the fundamentals of British Middle Eastern policy. By the time I read about the Sykes-Picot Agreement, the Balfour Declaration, and Britain's wilful mendacity towards the people of Palestine, I began to see the profound incompatibility between my chosen career and my indignation at my own country's disgraceful, not to say short-sighted, conduct.

In the meantime, the 1967 Six Day War had taken place. There was widespread euphoria in Britain at the triumph of the gallant Jewish democracy over a surrounding sea of Arab tyranny. Across Oxford, and doubtless elsewhere, Arabs went to ground in the humiliation of defeat. I had made no secret of where my sympathies lay, views then considered so perverse that I would find myself routinely challenged, frequently with the implication that I must be an antisemite. The following (autumn) term I ran into a Palestinian student I knew but had not seen since before the war. (There we were, standing just outside our college gate.) I commiserated with him. He was not to be comforted. "They will take everything they want", he said. I still blush to recall my callow remark to him, "Come off it. Don't be so naïve", I said, "Western governments would be totally out of their minds to allow Israeli expansion. It would make the problem insoluble." "My friend", he said, "it is you that is being naïve. They will take everything they want and no one will stop them." And so, of course, it proved to be. By the time of our conversation, the Maghrebi Quarter of Jerusalem had already been razed, on the night of 10/11 June. This first war crime of the Israeli occupation had passed without mention at the United Nations. At least the General Assembly condemned the administrative integration of Occupied East Jerusalem into the Western sector. Yet, the United States abstained in that vote, so Israel knew it had a free hand. But at the time I was unaware of such developments.

A very small number of us students would meet to discuss this second Palestinian catastrophe. We managed to attract a few external speakers, of whom the most notable was the journalist Michael Adams. Following his historic report of Israel's criminal erasure of three villages in the Latrun salient in 1968 – Imwas, Biddu, and Yalu – he was compelled to resign from *The Guardian* newspaper, which was not prepared to jeopardize its advertizing revenue by publishing more of the ugly truth which he so painstakingly uncovered. Adams was unwilling to be silent. His integrity was inspirational to the small but slowly growing band of people who were alarmed by the arrogance of victory.

I returned to the army in 1969 feeling profoundly hostile to what Britain had done in the Near East, not only in Palestine but in Egypt and Iraq also. I no longer trusted my employer, and this was quickly detected. The army graciously let me go, and I returned to Oxford where I studied the 1925 Druze revolt against the French Mandate in Syria. France, of course, was no better than Britain in its mischievous and destructive policies, and I became firmly antagonistic to Great Power interference in the region.

I worked for UNRWA in the years 1977–79, got to know the refugee camps of Lebanon and Palestine and thereafter visited both territories frequently. Initially I was shocked by the impoverished circumstances of life in the camps, but came to admire the resilience of their inhabitants, and in the occupied territory their fortitude in the face of daily humiliations at the hands of soldiers and settlers. British ears were for a long time largely closed to the Palestinian narrative of colonization and oppression, thus hearing not a protest at serious wrongdoing but only a hateful assault on the beleaguered Jewish democracy. When I spoke of the oppression I had seen, my (next-door) neighbour seemed to filter out what did not fit his expectations. "I just don't understand why you have got it in for the Jews", he said.

I was an Oxfam relief worker during Israel's assault on Lebanon in the summer, 1982. Israel deliberately smashed the refugee camps. The largest in Sidon, Ain el-Helweh camp, home to 64,000 refugees, was left with hardly any shelters standing. I saw rightist militiamen, as allies of Israel, given a free hand to drive refugees from the smaller camp of Mieh Mieh. Some refugees sought me out to report next-of-kin abducted, tortured, and killed. I got back to Beirut filled with foreboding. I tried to interest the media in the dangers ahead, but apart from an interview with the BBC, I failed. Newspapers report what is news, not what might happen. I also visited the Maronite Patriarchate where a senior official promised to convey my concerns to militia leaders. I returned to Sidon. When their leader, Bashir Gemayel, was assassinated, the rightist Lebanese Forces imposed a curfew. A Lebanese NGO worker and I were threatened at gunpoint on the street and beat a hasty retreat. A Muslim living in the apartment below us, returning from prayer in the nearby mosque, was less fortunate. He was executed at the roadside.

Then came the Sabra/Shatila massacre. In excess of 20,000 Palestinians and Lebanese perished that summer, three quarters of them civilians. I returned to Britain in a state of shock. The situation cried out for international intervention to ensure the safety of defenceless people now that the PLO had gone, but to Western governments the refugees remained little people of little worth. Eight days after my return, my house caught fire. Four fire engines came quickly to quench the fire, the police to ensure order. In my hand was my insurance policy. The contrast with what I had just witnessed could hardly have been starker.

I stumbled into a writing career. The Minority Rights Group asked me to write an essay on the roots of civil war which had broken out in Lebanon in 1975. It was well received, as was a similar essay on the Kurdish question a couple of years later. In 1987, it asked me to write on the Palestinians. This time, however, all hell broke loose. Zionist luminaries on MRG's Board and Council were outraged. One of these drafted a "balancing" foreword which suggested that my essay lacked balance and one motive might be antisemitism. Following the First Intifada, I was able to write again for MRG, this time unfettered by the pro-Israel lobby, a sign of things changing.

Yet except among the young, the process remains agonizingly slow. It has been inhibited by an apparently deliberate campaign to weaponize antisemitism in order to silence criticism of Israeli lawbreaking. I have recent experience of this when the Liberal Democrat Friends of Palestine (on whose executive committee I then sat) was suspended by the party's Federal Board for supposedly antisemitic Facebook and Twitter posts in 2019. A formal investigation bizarrely declined to consider whether the charges were true. Try as we might, we (two of us being Jewish) could see nothing antisemitic about them and so asked for elucidation, which was not forthcoming. Thus, the accusations remained unresolved. We were admonished and eventually reinstated, but we had also been smeared, not cleared. There was precious little either liberal or democratic about our accusers' conduct. Perhaps they feared the party being targeted, given what had happened to Labour. Terror of denunciation has led to self-censorship on the human rights challenge in Palestine.

Looking back, I see that my initial dismay regarding British policy in Palestine has only deepened. I realize that British official attitudes to Palestine were, and remain, essentially racist. Our political leaders would deny it but to them some peoples are manifestly of less value than others. One sees it in the demeanour of politicians starting with Balfour, who wrote in 1919, "Zionism, be it right or wrong, good or bad, is rooted in age-long traditions, in present needs, in future hopes, of far profounder import than the desires and prejudices of the 700,000 Arabs who now inhabit that ancient land." Throughout its Mandate, Britain's leaders ensured that the Palestinians were denied representative institutions whereby they could democratically halt the Zionist colonization programme. They have consistently favoured Israel ever since. Not a single prime minister has stood up for Palestinian rights. On the contrary all have been at least mildly pro-Israel, with Harold Wilson, Margaret Thatcher, Tony Blair, and Boris Johnson more emphatically so. They habitually decline to recognize the State of Palestine. How, a century after promising the Palestinian people self-determination in 1918, can it still be "the wrong moment" to recognise a Palestinian state? They decline to take those steps necessary to halt Israel's creeping annexation of captured territory in accordance with the tenets of international law. They allow suspected Israeli war criminals to visit Britain under diplomatic cover in blatant defiance of their categoric legal obligations, and currently seek to undermine the International Criminal Court, the creation of which Britain had previously supported, on account of its investigation of alleged Israeli war crimes. (Despite these key failures, they claim to take international law seriously, the claim itself difficult to take seriously.) I doubt that I shall live to see Britain take the steps necessary to remedy even to a small degree its deceitfulness over the past century.

Almost sixty years ago I disagreed with Glubb. Today, the situation is far worse, but I still disagree with him. I believe in the principle of equal rights for all who dwell in the whole territory once known as Mandate Palestine. I insist that the requirements of international humanitarian and human rights law, and also the fundamental rules of the post-1945 international order, must be upheld. Currently, Israel's security claims are allowed to trump these vital instruments, thereby undermining the only road to genuine security for all. The establishment of these principles must come first, come what may. Only then is there any chance of durable peace, regardless of whether it will lead to a two- or one-state solution. With whom do I agree? I agree with those Palestinians and Jews imbued with the steadfastness of purpose necessary for a resolution faithful to these principles.

Philomena McKenna

Anaesthetist, Ireland

"A Compelling Struggle for Justice"

We were not the first in our town to get a television back in 1962. Whether due to embarrassment that her children were obliged to watch it in other people's houses, or because we were never at home at teatime, our mother gave up cigarettes so that she could afford to buy our own TV. And that was when the world entered our house. The television subtly and subconsciously fed our young minds with ideas and images, some of which we carried with us into adulthood. Some images never leave and here I am remembering the black and white screen of trains going to the death camps with their unpronounceable names; the bewildered, fearful faces of men, women, and children whose unimaginable fate, too horrible for words, awaited them. And the agitation I felt because if I had been there, I would surely have told them not to get on the train. The Holocaust and the extermination of six million Jews was something we all knew from the television. No one could explain why this was happening and we were deeply moved. That picture-story was the full extent of my knowledge of Jews. Brought up going to Mass on Sundays, I presume we heard Jews mentioned in the Gospel. But I never once associated the Jews of the Bible with the Jews on the telly. I would love to be able to say I was a well-informed student at university, that I could discuss current affairs, that I got involved in politics; it was 1969 to 1975, the years of "the Troubles" in Northern Ireland. I didn't do any of those things. I did my studies to get through Medicine, went to the Literary and Debating meetings, and generally had a great social life. I was not impressed by anyone until I heard of Bernadette Devlin and Michael Farrell, student leaders of the Civil Rights protests in Northern Ireland. This was something I could truly believe in. Equal rights for all.

I made a well-intentioned effort to learn about the Middle East during my medical internship from 1975–1976, when I was obliged through ignorance to remain dumb while the men surgeons discussed the Arabs and the Israelis. I had a little map of the war zone cut out of the newspaper pinned on the door frame of my room so that I would memorize the relevant names every time I walked through. Not a successful ploy.

Fast forward to summer 1980. I did a locum job in Norway as a favour for a friend who was going to Lebanon for three or four months. Living the summer in Tromso, north of the Arctic Circle was an incredible experience of adventure and beauty. On his return the doctor friend asked if I would be interested in going to Lebanon to work in a Palestinian refugee camp for 3-6 months. It was a humanitarian project, which appealed to me. I asked for a great deal of information to get the picture. It was eerily familiar! Palestinians of the land, dispossessed of home and hearth, banished to exile with nothing more than the meagre necessities they could carry, now struggling with whatever means available to redress a wrong. It was any page of my Irish history book brought real. I insisted that I was not interested in getting involved in the politics. I wished I could have talked to someone from Ireland but, alas, there was no one. Somewhere in the depths of my not knowing anything, I recalled the government of Charles Haughey stating that it recognized the PLO as the "sole legitimate representative of the Palestinian people in their struggle for self-determination". Or something like that. I was given a book to read, *The Palestinians* by Jonathan Dimbleby. An excellent introduction. That Dimbleby felt he had to apologize for writing a book that was only meant to redress the gross imbalance of information available concerning the Palestine-Israeli conflict, but which by his honest reporting presented the Palestinians as hugely interesting, innovative, sincere, and tolerant people, a spectrum from the affluent exiles in the Gulf states to the impoverished refugees in the camps of Lebanon, Palestine, and Syria, from poets and writers to fighters and warriors, from school teachers to furniture makers, from women's groups to trade unions – all revolutionaries – speaks volumes to the deliberate, institutionalized ban that existed on reporting the Palestinians as anything but terrorists. From that book I learned a great deal about the people I had decided to work with; I felt not only the story but the people themselves to be somewhat familiar.

Not everyone felt the same about the Palestinians in the far north of Norway. I had to chew my lip and mumble incoherently when a colleague pointed to the cover photo of Arafat and a young fighter with a gun and round of bullets slung around his shoulder, chided me, saying "this is the terrorist you are going to work for". I didn't think he was correct in his assumption, but didn't have enough knowledge to refute him. I wasn't bothered anyway, I had made up my mind.

Before I departed for Lebanon, I stayed with a Norwegian trade union family in Oslo who introduced me to a priest who had spent years in jail in Israel. I'm not sure now if this man was Hilarion Capucci, the Syrian priest from Aleppo who had been jailed for smuggling weapons to the PLO. I enjoyed many conversations with the priest. I got the impression that my hosts, who were founders of the Norwegian Palestine Solidarity Organisation, were a little disappointed by my lack of personal political affiliation, and I believe they were somewhat anxious about my suitability for the job in solidarity. Even that was a new word in my vocabulary! However, I obviously did pick up enough to satisfy them that I would survive 3–6 months in a refugee camp in South Lebanon, working in a clinic with two Swedish nurses who would know the ropes. They needed a doctor and I was available. And Irish! They liked that.

My colleagues and I settled into a routine in Rashidiyya camp, south Lebanon. We had a house to ourselves, the standard breeze block and zinc roof. I had an interpreter by my side at the clinic; we were invited many evenings to people's houses to hear their stories and partake of their delicious cooking. We stopped on the roads and talked to whoever could communicate with us in English. There was no one following us, censoring our conversations, no restrictions on our movements. We had a van/ambulance for greater mobility. The Swedes were totally fluent in the sometimes-internecine politics of Palestinians, Lebanese, Syrians. Every faction, their left and more left politics, their backers, their enemies. I took it all in. From a distance! The Norwegians sent down David Hirst's *The Gun and The Olive Branch*, a great book that certainly helped me with the historical narrative. By this time, we had chatted to many, many of the women in the camp, usually with their children interpreting. Most of them were widowed and had come traumatized from other refugee camps such as Tel al-Zaater and Qarantina, where massacres had occurred.

Going home to Palestine was the predominant theme; education for their children was the most urgent. UNRWA provided schooling, clinics, and some staple food rations. The PLO provided protein in the form of chickens and a cut of meat delivered weekly to families with no income. The PLO was represented in every walk of life, a diverse well organized body overseeing health care, adult education, cooperatives employing women, factories, social welfare, the arts, chess, media, and politics. It operated openly in a country that wasn't the Palestinians', and which they had no desire to be theirs. It was a light illuminating a better way for the masses of ordinary people throughout the Arab world struggling to participate in something revolutionary, something that resembled a democracy.

Of course we met with the top brass when we visited Beirut, and got a glimpse of how the cogs turned in this juggernaut that spearheaded the Lebanese National Movement. History and politics aside, I learned most of what was important to me in the refugee camps, through the humanity of the people, their warmth, their strength. While we sat on thin foam mattresses on the floor like everyone else, chattering to whoever called to see us, I felt that despite the gap in my knowledge of the history and politics of the region compared to my colleagues, I was the more at ease in our surroundings. It wasn't that with my long legs I found floor-sitting comfortable, but I felt I had much more in common historically and culturally with the Palestinians than my Scandinavian companions.

Three months became six. The next team from Scandinavia arrived. The doctor was David, American, Jewish, communist. David was received with the same generous hospitality that characterizes the Palestinians' welcome everywhere. Their ability to accommodate people from diverse backgrounds, political persuasions, and religious beliefs is striking. They asked only one thing of the volunteers: that we should go back home and tell our peoples what had happened to the Palestinians, the uprooting from their homes, their hallowed land, the keys of their houses still warm in their hands, their dispossession.

I left Lebanon knowing I had awoken from a long slumber. Finally I had a clear appreciation of how the world was divided, and why. I was neither leftist nor rightist but understood that I had just witnessed a revolution in action, a struggle for justice, security, and life against the most powerful country in the world and its ally Israel.

In the summer of 1982, I was working in Ireland when I heard on the news that there had been an attempt on the life of the Israeli ambassador in London. My understanding of politics was so well honed that I recognized that this was it, the pretext that Israel needed to invade Lebanon. Days later the massive might of the Israeli military crossed the UNIFIL peacekeepers' territory into Lebanon where the plan to stop at the Litani river was overturned by Sharon, who ordered the invasion into the heart of Beirut. They met resistance, oh yes they did, and that's when the Israelis used their F16s and shelling from the sea. Thousands of people were burned to death in their shelters. Death roamed everywhere.

I decided I would go back, this time as an anaesthetist even though I was still junior in that field. In the absence of an Irish Red Cross mission, I joined up with my old friends, the Norwegians. People said I was brave to go back but in fact it wasn't bravery. In my mind it was going to be easier to be there with the courageous people I had got to know, who might or might not be dead, whose families might be scattered yet again, and try to do something useful, rather than to stay in Ireland.

I arrived in Beirut from Damascus on the August 12 1982, the day the Israelis dropped an implosion bomb on an apartment block, trying to kill Arafat. Everyone in that building was killed. The underground hospital in the city centre was full of the wounded, amputated, and ill. Water and electricity had been cut. It was airless, hot, and not kind to the nose.

However, worse was to come in the next month when the Israeli-trained Lebanese Phalangist militia, drug and hate fuelled, were given free rein over Shatila camp and the nearby Lebanese suburb of Sabra. Under the eyes of the Israeli commanders, they went from house to house with knives and guns, killing everyone in their path. I was in the local hospital receiving patients with terrible wounds. I wasn't told till later that most admissions went straight to the morgue. When they took us out at gunpoint on the Saturday morning, I guessed something terrible had happened. These militia men were as high as kites. Any slight move, any backchat, anything at all could trigger a shooting spree. The young Palestinian man in a white coat walking with us was simply pulled out and shot against a wall. I was nearly paralyzed with shock, fear, and guilt. The lad had asked me what he should do while we were still inside the hospital, before the militia entered. I told him to put the white coat on, he would be safe with us. The camp was strewn with dead bodies. It was surreal.

In the aftermath of the massacre, I set up a general practice in the middle of Shatila, as much a solidarity presence as a medical service. There I remained until the Lebanese Security considered me and anyone who worked with the Palestinians as undesirable and deported us, one by one.

I am a committed supporter of Palestinians' right to self-determination, and equal human rights in their country, or whatever country they find themselves in. Palestinians are well capable of co-existing and living peacefully with Israelis in the same country, but as long as the world allows Israel to continue its apartheid regime, with the IDF a killing machine, the resistance will continue. Palestinians have no choice. I believe the solution ultimately lies in the US because that is the source of the money and the violent, warped ideologies. Young Palestinian and Jewish Americans are working together in a very tough environment to exert some change in the status quo. And they are winning as attitudes in the US are gradually changing among ordinary people. But there's a long road ahead.

Previous Irish governments have taken strong positions on the diplomatic stage in support of Palestinian self-determination. Ireland refused to establish relations with

Israel until 1975 due to Israel's violations of UN resolutions. In February 1980 Ireland was the first EU country to recognize the PLO and endorsed the recognition of the State of Palestine. As our politicians become more concerned about their careers and less about human rights, they blocked a 2018 Bill which was passed in both Houses, which calls for a ban on Israeli goods made in the Occupied Territories. In May 2021 however, due to huge pressure from the people and committed elected members, in conjunction with massive Israeli bombing of Gaza, the Irish government became the first country in the world to declare Israel's de facto annexation of the West Bank.

Luisa Morgantini

Political activist, Italy

The Palestinians entered my life forcefully only in June 1982, with the Israeli invasion of Lebanon. Until then, I knew very little about the Palestinian "question". Obviously the tragedy of Black September in Jordan in 1970 or Tall al-Zaatar in 1976 in Lebanon had not escaped me, and I too was demonstrating for the *fedayeen* in Italian squares shouting "al Fatah will win". Up until 1982, my internationalist political commitment had been entirely aimed at Latin and Central America, against the military regimes in Argentina, Brazil, Cuba, Nicaragua, El Salvador, the tragedy in Chile, and in support of anti-colonial movements in Africa, Vietnam, and Eritrea, and the anti-apartheid movement in South Africa. My first arrest took place in Bologna in January 1961, for having kicked a policeman and participated in a unauthorized demonstration in protest against the assassination of Patrice Lumumba. For me, a young communist with veins of anarchy, Lumumba was a legendary figure, and embodied the struggle for freedom from colonialism and imperialism.

I had become a communist at the age of eleven, for a strange reason: I loved the cinema but finding the money to go there was hard. That Sunday I had found it, I was happy and eager to see the film several times. In fact, I went in at 2.30pm and came out after the last show. To get to the cinema I had to pass in front of the church. That day, as I passed by, I heard a trumpet strumming a song my mother loved, "Cherry and pink is Spring" – it was an old man begging for alms. I hesitated a lot, I went back and forth: "If I give him the money I can't go to the cinema". But he made me feel very tender, so I made a decision, "Okay, I'll give him the money but I'll become a communist". I had heard that the communists don't do charity but fight so that there won't be any poor people.

I was born in the Ossola Valley, where in 1944 the first Italian Republic was proclaimed, a region liberated from fascism, to a partisan father to whom I looked up with admiration, who always told me that the war was bad wherever it was fought; and to a Catholic but rebellious mother, who nevertheless wanted her daughter to go to church and get married as soon as possible. I, on the other hand, wanted to know the world and know myself; I didn't accept that my destiny was to get married and have children. The mountains of my country made me feel closed in, I wanted to live my life in freedom. I ran away from home when I was still a minor, with my mother following me because she wanted the carabinieri to take me home. But later she accepted my escape and, as she told me later, admired my choice.

It was in my own country and through my curiosity that I started practising internationalism and wanting to be a "citizen of the world". A carter who was almost always drunk had been a volunteer with the International Brigades in Spain, and despite the reproaches of my mother, who considered any contact with him unseemly, I went with him on the cart, and listened raptly as he told me about Dolores Ibarruri, and about his anger against the United States when in 1953, in the period of McCarthyism, Ethel and Julius Rosenberg were accused of espionage for the Soviet Union and executed.

But I don't want to talk too much about myself. This short piece should focus on my encounter with Palestine, and why after almost forty years my actions and thoughts are aimed at Palestine. Since the invasion of Lebanon in 1982 and the massacre of Sabra/Shatila, my commitment has never failed. What I had learned, and then seen, about the daily life of Palestinians under military occupation, Palestinians in Israel, and in the refugee camps was, and sadly remains, one of the greatest injustices and violations of human and social rights in the world.

At that time, I was a union leader of metalworkers in Milan, the centre of workers' struggles in Italy. I listened on the radio – in the deserted offices of the Syndicate Italy seemed crazy for the football championship taking place at the time – to the news of the massacre. I cried with pain and helplessness, and wrote a leaflet in the name of the Syndicate coining a slogan that still exists today: "Life, Land, Freedom for the Palestinian people". Then, with the Milan branch of the General Union of Palestinian Students (GUPS), we prepared a print exhibition on the history of Palestine from Herzl and Balfour up to Sabra/Shatila. We sent it to all the Italian trade union offices. The first pressure from the Jewish community began, condemning a book the Syndicate had published on the invasion of Lebanon edited by Livia Rokach. Unlike today, solidarity with the Palestinians was very strong in Italy where the trade unions, the Communist Party, and the Socialists were all mobilized. In fact, many Palestinians injured in Lebanon were treated in Italy.

In November 1984 I was invited to participate in the Palestinian National Council, held in Amman. It was my first meeting with Arafat and Palestinian leaders like Abu Jihad. I was very naïve, I don't think I understood the complexity of the situation; I remember that I was fascinated by the intelligence and optimism of Nabil Shaath, with whom I did an interview that was published in the union newspaper.

With Amal's war against the camps, the fate of Palestinians and especially of the women, who risked being killed by snipers as they tried to get food from outside the camps, had an enormous impact on the Italian women's movement. We decided to go to Lebanon in solidarity. Despite Syrian and Lebanese control, we entered Sabra/Chatila and I began to learn about the internal divisions, and to know the survivors of the '82 massacre. After this experience, I wanted to see with my own eyes the Palestinians in the West Bank, Gaza, and Israel. A student leader told me about Tawfiq Zayyad, mayor of Nazareth, who organized summer camps as did the University of Birzeit. I contacted the Lelio and Lisli Basso Foundation and organized with them the first of the Italian groups that I accompanied to Palestine. Sixty-five of us left in August 1987 for Taibeh in the "triangle". We were hosted by families; during the day we renovated a kindergarten. Israeli historian Tom Segev became aware of our group and asked me why we Italians, who had so many problems with the Mafia, came to aid the Palestinians. During the camp, I went to the occupied territories to meet people I had references to such as Michel Warshasky and Lea Tsemel. I went to Gaza with the Israeli group "Stop the Occupation", visited Jabalia and Shati camps, and enjoyed my first *maklubeh* in the house of Naila and Jamal Zakout.

I returned to Italy and wrote about Dheisheh camp in Bethlehem, about the fence that surrounded it, about the arrests. Thus began my visits to Palestine, alone, or with delegations. Albert Agazarian, then head of public affairs at Birzeit University, joked that I was not a person but an army. The first Intifadah in December '87 took the world by surprise, but Lea Tsemel had already told me that Gaza would explode. In August '88, with sixty-nine Italian women, we left for Jerusalem with the aim of building relationships between Italian, Palestinian, and Israeli women – not only for solidarity but for building an international women's policy. I went to Palestine several times to try to organize a joint conference between Palestinian and Israeli women's groups, but Sameeha Khalil[1] was adamant: no common assembly with the Israelis. So we opted for separate Israeli and Palestinian assemblies, and a third together with Palestinians participating in a personal capacity. With the Palestinian women we organized a demonstration to reach the Ansar prison in the Negev. The soldiers stopped us in Dhariyeh, but we marched to the prison, where the Israelis received us with tear gas.

The network of women formed then became international, and in 1996 we marched in Jerusalem with the slogan "Two peoples and two states, and Jerusalem as shared capital". The great joy for me was that Sameeha Khalil attended the closing demonstration at the Damascus gate.

Meanwhile, the "Intifadah of stones" continued. In November 1988, while I was leading a delegation of trade unionists, Israeli security denied me entry.

I was desperate. By now my ties with Palestine were deep, I loved the people I knew. While I was on the return plane, I thought about how Palestinians must suffer from being barred from returning home. I continued organizing Italian delegations to Palestine, and Palestinian delegations to Italy. When Israel cut off international telephone communications between the West Bank and Gaza, the National Palace Hotel made a "telephone bridge" so I could still talk to everyone. We proposed a human chain around Jerusalem for December 1990 to be called "Time for Peace" with the slogan "Two Peoples and Two States". It was painful not to be there physically but I was there by phone, organizing meetings of the more than 1,300 Italians. During the demonstration, more than 30,000 Palestinians, Israelis, and Italians held hands around Jerusalem.

In October '91 came the Madrid negotiations, led by Haider Abdel Shafi. Zahira Kamal told me to come, I flew. It was a moment of great hope. Then the Oslo Accords. Ilan Halevi convinced me that Rabin was thinking about returning the territories, but Haider and others understood that they had been caught in the trap. In 1994, the five years of my denied entry expired and I returned to Palestine, finding loved friends, smells, and colours. In 1996 I was an election observer in Gaza, and followed Sameeha Khalil's campaign for the presidency. Arafat won.

---

[1] Sameeha Khalil [1923–1999] was a prominent Palestinian activist, founder of the NGO Inash al-Usra.

The Oslo accords were crumbling. Rabin was killed by a Jewish settler; Hamas began its suicide bombings; settlements and apartheid grew; Palestinian mobility was increasingly restricted by checkpoints; fragmentation of the territory in which the Palestinian state should have existed increased.

In 1999, I was elected to the European Parliament as an independent on the Communist Refoundation list and became responsible for relations with the Palestinian parliament. The European Parliament became a hotbed of initiatives, exhibitions on Palestinian culture, hearings with representatives of Palestinian civil society, with Israelis from refusniks to "Breaking the Silence", and with parliamentary delegations. With the left-wing group Gue, we financed the stay in Brussels of a Palestinian and an Israeli woman active in the Jerusalem link, and later the presence of Palestinian and Israeli representatives of the Popular Committees for Nonviolent Resistance, Against the Wall, and the Occupation. But the European Commission was deaf to our request to act against Israel. There were denunciations of Israel's expansionist politics and human rights violations. They donated to UNRWA, to Palestinian and Israeli NGOs for the defense of human rights, to the Palestinian Authority, but, as the Israelis argued, the Europeans were payers not players. Whenever it was proposed to suspend the association agreements with Israel, given that they were in breach of article 2 of agreements about human rights, the answer was No, because as Xavier Solana said, for Israel to consider the EU an honest broker we have to give them carrots and more carrots, and not suspend the association agreement. Thus, instead of making Israel pay the price for colonialism and military occupation, the European Union and other donors became accomplices, violating the Geneva Convention, which claims that the occupying country must provide welfare to the occupied population.

Netanyahu's victory, Sharon's provocation at the Temple Mount, Israeli army repression, Hamas suicide bombings in the second Intifada, Israeli propaganda claiming that Israel had to defend itself against terrorism, created division within institutions and civil society. Yet between 2001 and 2002 we brought delegations to Palestine, and acted as human shields in front of Israeli soldiers at checkpoints in Gaza and the West Bank, brought support to Arafat besieged in the Muqata'a, and to hospitals and ambulances.

By 2006, Hamas had decided to end the terrorist actions that mainly harmed the Palestinians, and unexpectedly won the elections. The Europe that had supported the democratic nature of the elections responded by banning the Hamas government; Israel arrested almost half of those elected to the Palestinian Legislative Council. In the EU parliament we organized a protest and decided not to accept the boycott of a freely elected government. We met Ismail Haniyeh in Gaza, even after the coup in 2007, and during the "Cast Lead" operation, I organized a parliamentary delegation to Gaza. Today the European parliament has changed a lot, the right-wing forces are stronger, and the Palestinian question is no longer considered central.

After leaving the EU Parliament I continued my commitment to Palestine and Italy by founding the AssopacePalestina association, bringing every year more than 200 people to Palestine to see with their own eyes, and bringing to Italy representatives of the popular committees for nonviolent resistance, formed to respond to the construction of the Separation Wall and the settlements, and above all to make

Palestinian culture known, as well as the younger generations who, through art, cinema, and theatre are manifesting their right to freedom.

Sometimes I think about giving up Palestine and the Palestinians, because I am ashamed that we haven't been able to stop Israel and the settlers. But I will never do it. As long as there is a Palestinian who resists even through breathing I will be next to him. As long as I have life I will fight for the freedom of every single Palestinian prisoner, for Palestinian self-determination, with the hope that one day Palestine will be free, democratic, and secular. Yet the responsibility for the injustice suffered by the Palestinians lies with the entire international community, which is complicit with the politics of Israeli occupation and the colonization of Palestine.

Birgitte Rahbek

Cultural sociologist, Denmark

"I Had No Choice."

I landed in Lebanon in the hot late summer of 1968, shortly after the Soviet invasion of Czechoslovakia. I told a young Lebanese acquaintance that I was very worried about the whole situation in Europe. "You should rather worry about our refugees", he said. "Who are they?" I asked. Well, since then hardly a day has passed without me thinking of those refugees.

My visit to Lebanon was not rooted in any deep knowledge of or interest in the Middle East (ME), but motivated solely by the fact that as an airhostess I got almost free plane tickets to get here and on top of that I got to stay at a beach resort at a very low cost. So what was not to like about it for me and my Norwegian colleague?

Until then I had not been very interested in politics apart from being against war in general and the war in Vietnam in particular, and also being strongly anti-racist. I knew nothing about Palestine and Israel, so I was neither for nor against either party, but since my childhood I had a predisposition for siding with the underdog and a very strong sense of justice.

I grew up in a provincial part of Denmark where – unlike for instance people from Copenhagen – I had not known anybody who went to a kibbutz, so I first got to know Israel when I landed on the side where their bombs fell.

Two years later, in Fall 1970, I had the good fortune to attend a semester of classes at The American University in Beirut (AUB). I was only auditing, meaning that I did not have to submit assignments or pass any exams so I had the opportunity to fully open up and take in all the wisdom presented to me by professors like Walid Khalidi in Palestinian history or Hisham Sharabi in political science. Hisham Sharabi, who also became a friend, was a slender and soft-spoken teacher who, no matter the subject, ended all his classes by cursing American imperialism in front of many bewildered American students.

AUB at that time was a progressive and lively university with a speakers' corner and evening talks where Palestinian resistance figures were invited to speak. I learned more in this one semester at AUB than anywhere else, including my many years at various universities in Denmark.

Besides attending classes, I met Anni Kanafani and her husband Ghassan, who took the time to introduce me further to the Palestinian cause. Add to that meeting a fellow classmate in anthropology, Rosemary Sayigh, who became and remains a cherished friend.

Upon my return to Denmark I felt that my newly acquired knowledge of the ME conflict obliged me to pass it on, i.e. to spread the message in the naïve hope and conception that if people only knew, then they would surely change their attitude. Little did I then know what powers I was up against. So I contacted and joined a small rather extremist solidarity group in Denmark. Later on, I cofounded another group with the central aim of publishing a magazine called *Palæstina Orientering* that existed until a few years ago. The other founder was Professor Svend Holm-Nielsen, who was one of the first Danes to support the Palestinians and who until his death remained a staunch critic of the Zionist enterprise. Besides that, I wrote articles for a leftist magazine called *Politisk Revy (Political Review)*, and later on for the communist daily, *Land og Folk (Land and People)*.

I became publicly known to the extent that the Danish Broadcasting Corporation, DR, now and then interviewed me about the Palestinian issue, as a kind of hostage to my sex and my political opinions: a woman who supported the PLO.

In 1971, I visited Chile and fell in love with that country and its hospitable people; I have often thought that I might just as well have committed myself to the solidarity movement for Chile after the disastrous coup in 1973. I also partly did that, but I think that the reason I have spent so much energy and so many feelings in the struggle for justice for the Palestinian people is the glaring hypocrisy surrounding this issue.

I returned to Lebanon in 1973 during the October War between Israel and the neighbouring Arab countries (except Lebanon) and already on board the plane, I sensed the optimistic atmosphere among Palestinian passengers, so much so that when my Palestinian friend picked me up at the airport he said "I think we'll get our own state now". This optimism among Palestinians was quashed shortly after, when the war ended with yet another defeat for the Arabs. I still remember the feeling of a dark cloud descending on and silencing Beirut.

In many ways the 1970s was an optimistic decade with the liberation of Vietnam, the fall of the Portuguese dictatorship, and the liberation of various African colonies. But nothing of this translated into any more freedom for the Palestinians. One of the reasons was that most Danish, and I guess Western, papers and news channels covering the Middle East were controlled by friends of Israel. Thus, they also controlled the narrative, which up until now claims it is a conflict between two peoples/religions fighting over the same piece of land, with one being smarter than the other. For many years, the Middle East conflict has been the most widely covered conflict in the world, but unfortunately also the least understood due mainly to this narrative.

Also in the 1970s, I was introduced to the Israeli left and visited Moshé Machover in London and learned about his uncompromising stance against Israel and Zionism, which was so rare among Israelis at that time. Later on, I met some Israeli communists in Denmark, and I remember thinking how much they reminded me of Palestinians, and what a wonderful country they could build together. They were mainly Arab Jews and recounted the discrimination that they suffered from in Israel where everything Arab – language, food, music et cetera – was despised.

During the civil war in Lebanon, which erupted in 1975, I was not able to visit the country, but followed the war closely from Denmark. Then came 1982 and the Israeli invasion of Lebanon, where I spent the summer crying over the bombardment of Beirut and the defeat of the PLO. As atrocious as the Sabra and Shatila massacre was, I was sure that this would be the turning point; that everybody would clearly see the mentality and methods of the Israeli army and its fascist allies. But alas, how many turning points we have since passed without the world really reacting.

In 1984, I started working at the Danish Broadcasting Corporation (DR), which also gave me the opportunity occasionally to make programs about the Middle East, where I tried especially to introduce to the Danish public new voices such as Edward Said, Ilan Pappe, Norman Finkelstein, and many others. Anybody producing public content on the ME in the Western world, who does not share the mainstream Zionist narrative, knows all too well how much restraint – i.e. self-censorship – you have to put on yourself. One of the first times I was interviewed at DR, the topic of discussion was poisoned Jaffa-oranges, and I had said that people should just refrain from buying Israeli oranges. "I can't broadcast that!" the interviewer told me in spite of being pro-Palestinian herself.

Later on I got my own radio show, a kind of social science program dealing with all sorts of issues. I remember that Norman Finkelstein was very impressed that I was able to air the interview with him on Danish public radio, telling him, "No problem". But later on, the bourgeois daily *Berlingske Tidende,* whose opinion editor at the time was extremely reactionary and ultra-Zionist, started a campaign against me, and when I told Finkelstein about it, he responded, "Of course you have to pay a price for telling the truth, otherwise everybody would do it."

The same opinion editor and another ultra-Zionist kept putting pressure on my bosses at DR to have me fired. In the end and after the coming to power of a very reactionary and Islamophobic Danish government after 9/11, my program was closed and I was sidelined and prevented from making programs on the Middle East.

But let me go a little back in history. For many years I only knew about Palestine and Israel from TV programs, books, articles, and friends. Because of my Palestinian friends in Lebanon, many of whom were active in the resistance, I dared not travel to Israel, especially after a Danish woman was arrested there on the accusation of having smuggled money into the country hidden in some cheese. But then came the Oslo Accords. In the beginning I channeled my hopes into that agreement. I noticed that all the Palestinians that I looked up to, first amongst them Edward Said, were against the agreement. But as someone who for many years had done solidarity work with the Palestinians, I just needed some hope, some straw to cling on to, so I forced myself to give it a chance.

At least it gave me a chance to visit Palestine under the auspices of the UN. The Danish Ministry of Foreign Affairs asked me to be the Danish representative in a UNDP delegation with the purpose of making an Assessment of Women's Needs. It felt strange that suddenly "official Denmark" would summon the work and support of a former political outcast such as myself.

Although I did not like the approach and project design of the UNDP delegation, it was a fantastic experience to see with my own eyes what I until then had only studied and looked at from the outside. I was shocked by the settlements, their location and architecture being like a fascist fist in the face of the Palestinian people. It also struck me how these and all their bypass roads had destroyed the old biblical landscape, and I always wondered why the Evangelical Zionists of the world never complained about that. Included in this vandalism was the constant uprooting of thousands of old olive trees in the West Bank, and this combined with the perpetual campaign, "Plant a tree in Israel" is another example of the roaring hypocrisy of Zionism.

Much like the rest of the international donor community, we stayed at the American Colony in East Jerusalem. This place inspired me to return to and gather material for several radio programs including the montage "*The American Hotel*" and thereafter my book, "*Tro og skæbne I Jerusalem*", which was coauthored with my husband, Mogens Bähncke, and translated but never published as "Faith and Fate in Jerusalem". The book is about the reality behind Selma Lagerlöf's novel *Jerusalem*, a wonderful story that also showed the shared and peaceful life of Muslims, Christians, and Jews in Palestine before the advent of Zionism.

This first trip to Palestine was followed by many others, where I met several of the outstanding Palestinians that I had until then only read about and from, for example Mustafa Barghouthi and Rita Giacaman. On several occasions, I also interviewed my long-time hero (from decades of reading Le Monde Diplomatique) Amnon Kapeliouk, and Jeff Halper, who was my first tour guide to the settlements.

Later on in Denmark, I met Ilan Pappe, whose book "*The Ethnic Cleansing of Palestine*" I had the honour of translating into Danish. Ilan became a dear friend of mine and it is difficult to overestimate the importance of my acquaintance with the many such anti-Zionist (or at least non-Zionist) Israelis.

In the meantime, I had written my own book about the conflict, *En stat for enhver pris (A State at any Cost)*. Funnily enough, it is also the title of the recent (2019) biography of David Ben-Gurion written by Tom Segev. My book was published in September 2000 after the failed Camp David talks, but I had actually chosen the title to refer to both sides of the conflict, as I had expected Yasser Arafat to give in to American and Israeli pressure. During my research for the book, I read many Israeli books, including by Benny Morris, Ilan Pappe, and Tom Segev, whose book *The Seventh Million*, about how Holocaust survivors were treated by the Zionist establishment in Palestine at the time, was very shocking. That book is very important to keep in mind when confronted with Israel's flagrant exploitation of the tragedy of the European Jews. I also read almost all available material about the Oslo Accords, which showed me that once again, the Palestinians were caught between their own lack of professionalism and the Norwegians' and Israelis' dishonesty bordering on scoundrelism.

For some years in the last decade, I was a board member of the Danish House in Palestine (DHIP), which "promotes cooperation and collaboration between Danes and Palestinians through cultural and vocational exchange". It is a wonderful project, supported by the Danish Ministry of Foreign Affairs, that brings Palestinians and Danes together in various initiatives, for example circus shows, publishing children's books, concerts, olive picking, and much more.

One of the first projects of DHIP, before we had a physical space, was a cooperation between our most famous Danish chef, Rasmus Kofoed (at that time only famous in

Denmark) and a Jerusalamite Palestinian chef, Youssef, who cooked together for a week and served up many delicious dishes for a broader public in Ramallah. I recorded them for an alternative radio station and that might have been one of my easiest and most joyous tasks as a pro-Palestinian.

Thinking back on my more than fifty years of engagement with the Middle East and especially with Palestinians, I find it incredible how much it has marked my whole life. I have been enriched with very dear friends and wonderful memories, with one's political position toward this conflict becoming a kind of a litmus test of people's attitudes for me, in the sense that, "Don't tell me that you are a peacenik if you support Israeli occupation and wars."

Was it worth all the troubles, the harassment, the disappointments? I don't know, I had no choice, savoir oblige, though it must indeed be fun to support a winner.

Leena Saraste

Photographer, Finland

For the media, people in crisis areas and especially refugees do not have identities, only destinies as victims or potential terrorists. Refugees are news when massacred or when condemned as criminals.

No passport = no identity.

Before my first journey to Beirut in 1980 I had been analyzing the press coverage of the Middle East for years, but it did not prepare me for anything I met there. How could it? Journalists stay a week or two and carry on to another war. Newspapers publish just one picture a day delivered by photo agencies: a big media event or suffering faces. During war times in Lebanon journalists were taken around by the Israeli army, and they had to submit their pictures to censors, who took away negatives they disliked – or wanted to use themselves.

The image of Palestinians for me was Arafat and his *fedayyeen*, with *kuffiyehs* and klashnikovs.

I tried to understand how continuous political crisis and conflict affect people. But where to publish photos of the effects of war instead of actions only? And how to mediate the warmth and pride of the old ladies, young girls, and ardent revolutionaries I met, who always invited us into their hospitable homes? Is it possible to make pictures tell about the feeling of being at home with these great women? Instead of giving statistics it is important to tell their stories, show their faces.

In the 1980s everybody in the refugee camps wanted to be photographed, preferably showing the V-sign and guns. The departure of the Palestinian fighters from Beirut in 1982 was almost a victory. They were told they had not been defeated, and there was hope of returning to their home country. Today the majority of the refugees are still in the camps, forgotten, and not willing to be photographed in their misery. Identities have changed. First "*From peasants to revolutionaries*". Now to what? The squalid houses in the camps grow ever higher, always a new room above the original hut. Hope vanishes. No photographs, please! Photographic art and journalism have also changed, rejecting classical black and white "humanistic documentary".

In 2005, going back after twenty years of absence, everything looked different. Beside misery I saw stunning wall paintings, artistic, political graffiti. And I found some people whom I had photographed in 1982, a short time before the massacre. Before, the biggest daily in Finland had eagerly published photos of them, hinting they were dead. In 2005 the same paper did not want to publish the story of their survival.

Lex Takkenberg

Legal scholar, Netherlands

"It Did Not Happen by Design."

In 1982, as part of my studies in international law at the University of Amsterdam, I was introduced to the issue of forced displacement and refugee law through my participation in the Philip J. Jessup International Law Moot Court Competition. Our team did not win, but the experience nevertheless triggered a curiosity in me that would last a lifetime, and that made me enroll later that year in a three-week summer course in International Refugee Law at the University of Thessaloniki in Greece. This in turn was instrumental in my international law professor urging me, several months later, to apply for a position as Legal Officer at the Dutch Refugee Council. I had not yet finished my studies, still had to write my thesis and was in no rush to graduate, but who was I to challenge the ever formal and stern Professor Herman Meijers, who was both my professional and academic supervisor and, as I later found out, a member of the Advisory Council of the Dutch Refugee Council.

To my surprise and somewhat to my dismay, I was selected and, in early 1983, started in the newly established position. What followed was a fascinating introduction to the field of refugee work, including legal aid and protection, capacity building, advocacy, networking, and research. After about four years with the Council, I had reached the conclusion that this was the professional field in which I wanted to continue. As several friends from the European networks, of which the Dutch Refugee Council was a member organization, had recently moved to the UNHCR I became keen to follow a similar path and expand my horizon beyond the Netherlands. A friend who had recently joined the UNHCR informed me that UNRWA, the UN agency for Palestinian refugees in the Near East, was looking for professionals with a refugee protection background. As I could not find any vacancy announcement, I sent an open application with my CV.

Several months later – it was spring 1988 – I received a phone call from an UNRWA recruitment officer, who told me that the agency was interested in my profile, and inquired whether I would be available to start a protection job in Gaza at short notice – literally the next week. I responded that I was very flattered and interested but was about to go on leave and that upon my return there would be some projects I had to complete with my current employer. To make a long story short, I joined UNRWA in early 1989 on an initial five-month contract, for which I gave up my permanent job at the Refugee Council.

Five months became nearly thirty-one years, working for and with Palestinian refugees throughout the Eastern Mediterranean. During the first decade with UNRWA, I enrolled in a remote Ph.D. programme at the University of Nijmegen, also in the Netherlands, writing a dissertation on the status of Palestinian refugees in international law, subsequently published by Oxford University Press in English, and by the Institute for Palestine Studies in Arabic. A second edition of the book, entitled *Palestinian Refugees in International Law*, co-authored with Francesca P. Albanese, was published by Oxford University Press, in 2020. I retired from UNRWA at the end of 2019 but continued to remain active in numerous ways with respect to the Palestinian refugee question and the unresolved Israeli-Palestinian conflict.

My first assignment with UNRWA took me to the West Bank, where I worked as a Refugee Affairs Officer (RAO) in a new protection programme – the first in the agency's history – introduced in response to the first *Intifadah*, the popular uprising that had commenced in late 1987. I remember vividly my first tours of the West Bank, with fellow RAOs who had arrived several months earlier. It was February, the almond trees were blooming, and the scenery was pristine --an anti-climax since, naively, I was expecting burning tires wherever I went. We went from camp to camp, where we were warmly welcomed by Camp Services Officers and Health Centre staff who provided us with updates on casualties and arrests that had taken place during daily skirmishes with the Israeli army. Despite the occasionally tense environment, I remember that my first encounters with my new Palestinian colleagues felt like being covered in a warm blanket. For them, our bearing witness to what they had been experiencing – since 1948 and then following 1967, and most recently since the start of the Intifada – was of critical importance. Being the eyes and ears of the international community was indeed the most important feature of the RAO programme, established at a time when – very different from today – the UN Security Council was actively engaged with respect to the human rights situation in the occupied Palestinian territory.

In terms of the Israeli-Palestinian "conflict" I was a novice, so much so that my colleagues at the Dutch Refugee Council took it upon themselves to provide me with some training to prepare me for the things I was likely to encounter. I turned out to be a quick learner though, especially when Professor Guy Goodwin-Gill, then editor of the *International Journal of Refugee Law*, invited me to contribute an article on UNRWA's inroads into the field of refugee protection for a special volume of the journal on the 1951 Refugee Convention's 40th anniversary. When researching the article, I realized that although lots of literature existed on the Palestine-Israel situation, including legal studies, there was virtually nothing on the legal aspects of the Palestinian refugee question.

By that time, I had taken up a new position with UNRWA in the Gaza Strip, coordinating food and financial assistance as part of an emergency programme that was developed in response to the *Intifadah*. As Gaza was designated then, and still is today, a "non-family duty station", my family stayed behind in Jerusalem and accordingly I had time to engage in projects beyond work. It gradually dawned on me that the legal aspects of the Palestinian refugee question would make an excellent subject for a Ph.D.

The Netherlands academic system provides for so-called external Ph.D. students, and through my previous contacts with the Dutch Refugee Council, it did not take me long to identify two excellent and motivated Ph.D. supervisors. Looking back at it, more than twenty-five years later, I realize that the "dual track" of working with and for Palestinians during the day, and then engaging on my Ph.D. research at night, provided a unique immersion into the "question of Palestine". As I wrote in the preface to the dissertation, I would not have been able to write the same book had it not been for living and working alongside my Palestinian colleagues and the Palestinians aided by UNRWA.

I wrote the book in a most tumultuous era in recent Palestinian history. I started writing during the tail end of the first *Intifadah*, and was transferred to Syria in the summer of 1993, literally weeks before the news of the Oslo breakthrough. Naïve as so many of us were at the time, I was angry for not being in Palestine as history was unfolding there. A year later I was able to return to Gaza. I arrived in Gaza on 1 July 1994 from the Erez crossing point in the north of the Strip, literally an hour or so before Yasser Arafat entered Gaza to take up residency from the Rafah border crossing in the south. I dropped my suitcases and rushed to one of the central squares in Gaza where Arafat was due to address the excited crowd. The subsequent years were fascinating and hopeful, to the point that I was – once again naively – getting worried that my book might be redundant before I finished it. But gradually it dawned on me that Edward Said and Haider Abdel Shafi had been right in their criticism of Oslo. I continued working on the dissertation, which was finally completed in the autumn of 1996, with the public defense in early 1997. I was honoured that Professor Camille Mansour, who at the time was setting up the Bir Zeit Law Centre, agreed to join the committee tasked to judge the dissertation, along with Professor Goodwin-Gill, *the* expert at the time on general international refugee law. It was Goodwin-Gill who was also instrumental in getting the book published by Oxford University Press. Due to the good offices of Professors Salim Tamari and Elia Zureik, the book was subsequently published in Arabic by the Institute of Palestine Studies.

It was during my Gaza years that I really became invested in the Palestinian cause. Not just through my research, but first and foremost through the friendships I was able to develop, and the support and camaraderie I experienced during my work at UNRWA. I had fallen in love with Gaza almost from my first arrival. The overwhelming hospitality of the Gazans, as well as their inspiring and unprecedented resilience; the delicious Gaza cuisine; the flamboyant flame trees; the beach and the sea that became fully accessible after the Israeli withdrawal from Gaza in 1994. Professionally, my near decade in Gaza, initially heading UNRWA's Relief and Social Services Programme and then as Deputy Field Director, was the most memorable of my career. In early 1999, my then wife and I had the opportunity to adopt a Palestinian baby girl from the Crèche in Bethlehem, another life changing experience. A year later, I was transferred for the second time to Syria, for what became another fascinating and equally rewarding experience. My experience in Gaza has however remained the most profound in my three decades in the region, so much so that I have been proudly identifying myself as a *nus Ghazawi*, "half Gazan", ever since.

Despite its failure, the Camp David summit in 1999 represented an important turning point in that through former US President Clinton's initiative, the so-called permanent status issues continuing to divide Israelis and Palestinians were demystified. This included, importantly, the resolution of the Palestinian refugee question and the right of return. This paved the way for the emergence of what became known as the Right of Return Movement, led in important ways by the Badil Resource Centre in the West Bank. Having become an expert on the status of Palestinian refugees in international law, I started to informally advise and otherwise support Badil and Ai'doun, its counterpart in Lebanon and Syria. Lifelong friendships with Mohamad and Ingrid Jaradat, Terry Rempel, Susan Akram, Jaber Suleiman, Raja Deeb, and many others were forged over time. It was also the time that Chatham House – the Royal Institute of International Affairs – initiated a decade-long programme, led by Rosemary Hollis and Nadim Shehadeh, on the Regional Aspects of the Palestinian Refugee Question. I had the privilege to be a regular participant in workshops organized as part of the programme, which introduced me to a range of other experts on the subject.

My thinking on Israel-Palestine evolved in a gradual manner over the years. In the lead-up to joining UNRWA, the first *Intifadah* was still regular frontpage news in the Netherlands and elsewhere in the Western world and, combined with the publication of the first edition of Benny Morris's *The Birth of the Palestinian Refugee Question*, the narrative on the conflict gradually began to shift. From what initially seemed like a black and white situation of the good guys – the Palestinian stone throwers – and the bad guys – the Israeli occupation army, through my doctoral research and lived experience, I rapidly discovered that the situation was – or seemed to be at the time – much more complex. I realized that as a child of parents who had lived through the Second World War, I was raised with the prevalent sympathies vis-à-vis Jews and the state of Israel. Scattering those preconceptions was at times confusing. In 2008, after having visited Yad Vashem, the official Israeli Holocaust memorial in Jerusalem, half a dozen times I discovered that one of my uncles (who was close to sixty when I was born) had been honoured as one of the so-called Righteous Among Gentiles for having rescued several Dutch Jews during the War. It was an emotional encounter, especially after I was able to access the survivors' testimonials that had underpinned the inscription and had the opportunity to speak to one of them.

I first began to realize that the Holocaust and the Nakba are intimately connected after I read Robert Fisk's *Pity the Nation*. Primarily directed at the Jewish people, and precisely for this reason – to use the words of Gideon Levy, one of Israel's most courageous journalists – "one must not ignore the conduct of its victims towards the secondary victims of the Jews' Holocaust, the Palestinian people. Without the Holocaust they would not have lost their land and would not be imprisoned today in a gigantic concentration camp in Gaza or living under a brutal military occupation in the West Bank." In a groundbreaking book, leading Arab and Jewish intellectuals examine how and why the Holocaust and the Nakba are interlinked without blurring fundamental differences between them.[1] The book made me realize that only when the parties and the world at large are committed to fully confronting both foundational tragedies will

[1] *The Holocaust and the Nakba – A New Grammar of Trauma and History*, edited by Bashir Bashir and Amos Goldberg, Chichester and New York, Columbia University Press, 2018.

it be possible for power to shift and a world of justice and equality to be created between the two peoples.

During my final decade at UNRWA, it gradually dawned on me that it would be important to update my book on the legal status of Palestinian refugees. As I dreaded having to embark on another protracted period of seclusion, I decided to look for a co-author and found former UNRWA colleague Francesca Albanese not only ready to be my partner in crime but to lead the writing of what became a new and largely expanded book. *Palestinian Refugees in International Law* was published in the summer of 2020, once again by Oxford University Press. It not only provides a state-of-the-art overview of the legal aspects of the Palestinian refugee question but is at the same time a manifest for using the law as a tool for enhanced protection of the refugees and, ultimately, Palestinian liberation. We were fortunate to find in Samar Muhareb, the visionary Jordanian-Palestinian founder of the Jordanian NGO "Arab Renaissance for Democracy and Development", an institutional home to pursue our desire to move beyond the academic into concrete action to advance Palestinian rights: a future that sees the dismantlement of the very foundations of Apartheid – decolonization, liberation, justice, and dignity.

Toine van Teeffelen

Scholar and educational advisor, Netherlands, lives
in Bethlehem/Beit Lahem

"Sumud and Solidarity"

Growing up during the late 1960s as a teenager in the Netherlands I absorbed the influence of both the Third World Movement and the peace movement. An anti-authoritarian atmosphere left its mark on university students like me. I took part in preparing issues of a progressive pacifist-religious magazine and compared armed tactics by liberation movements in the Vietnamese and Palestinian contexts.

My studies kindled a theoretical interest. At the end of an MA study in anthropology I went to Jerusalem to meet some thirty-nine anthropologists working on Israel – both Jewish and Arab. My thesis concluded that story structures like romance and tragedy are implicitly used to understand the organization and interpretation of anthropological data. I concluded that Palestinians studied by Israeli-oriented anthropologists are often put in a "tragic" frame, showing incapacity to overcome societal conflicts. Oriental (Mizrahim) Jews coming from Arab countries tend to be shown in the opposite "romantic" frame. The research stimulated my interest in narratives representing social and national communities.

At the time, Palestine increasingly became part of the discussions within the Dutch Third World Movement. During the 1967 June war, support for Israel's interpretation of events had been extremely high in the Netherlands, even compared to other European countries. Palestinians were entirely left out of the public debate. The new Netherlands Palestine Committee, a lone voice in the wilderness, started in 1969 to bring out a less romantic interpretation, calling for solidarity with the thousands of Palestinian refugees. The Committee was a small group, primarily consisting of university students, teachers, and activists. It also included Piet Nak, formerly one of the organizers of the February Strike in 1941 in Amsterdam in support of the Dutch Jews. In 1978, I and some others had the opportunity to work on the Committee due to the financial support that came from hundreds of individual sympathizers. My work there continued for twelve years.

The work of the Committee's staff and core group was to bring out the Palestinian political story, among other things by publishing a bimonthly newsletter, as well as pamphlets and publications about the PLO at a time when the movement was publicly identified with terrorism. The newsletter dealt with political developments, human rights, and Palestinian culture. The Committee's public meetings provided a political commentary on ongoing events. Guest speakers included progressive personalities within the mainstream PLO, as well as members of Matzpen, a small anti-Zionist group of Jewish intellectuals analyzing Israel as a colonial project rather than in nationalist terms.

Looking back, I remember a strange conversation. A Dutch film-maker/producer once came to the Committee's office to ask me for a couple of slides of a Palestinian refugee camp in Lebanon. Why did he need them? It was for a film about Jewish identity and the trauma of the Holocaust. Instead of illustrating Palestinian suffering, the film would present the pictures as part of a pro-Palestinian discourse that was fashionable among the left. I asked him, if this was the case why did he come to the Palestine Committee? He replied that he had heard from a PLO representative in Europe that any publicity for the Palestinians – good or bad – was helpful for the cause, and that he assumed that Palestine Committee members followed the PLO's "orders"!

The issue of how far solidarity should go was actually quite alive in the Committee. Faithful to my background, my own voice leaned towards non-violent tendencies within the Palestinian and solidarity movement, taking distance from certain armed PLO actions in Israel. Around 1981 I became active in the Dutch section of the peace movement Pax Christi and its Middle Eastern group, representing a pro-Palestinian stream in a politically more heterogeneous organization.

During the 1980s, Dutch public opinion and political parties moved toward a recognition of Palestinian national rights, especially after the 1980 Venice Declaration of the European Community (later the European Union), in which the EC expressed the need for a Palestinian state for the first time. At that time, Dutch public opinion was dealing with an increasingly strong ideological tension on the issue of Israel/Palestine. On the one hand, many Dutch politicians and intellectuals took the application of international law as the cornerstone of international relations. For many it was not a coincidence that The Hague is the location of the International Court of Justice. Also, the Dutch anti-apartheid movement, basing itself on international law along with many Third World committees, was active and strong compared to other countries.

Yet a great many Dutch also felt a collective guilt over the fate of the Dutch Jews in the Second World War, of whom no less than 90% had been transported to the Nazi concentration camps. Also, many identified with the "young" and "pioneering" western-oriented Israeli state. During the 1960s and '70s the kibbutz was a most popular destination for backtracking youths looking for new experiences.

The ideological tension was somewhat neutralized by those who advocated for a symmetrical approach to Palestine/Israel. Opinion makers on the left frequently coupled solidarity with Palestinians to solidarity with Israel. Under the influence of Israeli intellectuals like Amos Oz, the conflict was portrayed as a "tragic" confrontation between the equal rights of two national movements, in opposition to the view of Israel as a colonial settler state. In the Dutch context at the time, two states as a solution to the conflict was perhaps a step forwards. However, it also took eyes away from the ongoing Israeli colonization of occupied Palestine.

In 1980, echoing the symmetrical approach, the Dutch Minister of Development Affairs gave public advice to the Palestine Committee to link its work to that of "critical Zionists" – whoever these were – as a condition for becoming eligible for the government subsidies which other solidarity committees received at the time.

The Palestine Committee didn't only work on the political level, but also took up humanitarian and social causes. During the '70s and '80s, the Dutch Medical Committee for Palestine organized material support, and sent out medical volunteers to the camps in Lebanon, deeply affected by the "War of the Camps" during the Lebanese civil war.

I myself became active in setting up new links with occupied Palestine. Partly inspired by the "peace twinnings" between cities in West and East Europe, members of the Committee worked, often through the intermediary of new platforms, on exchanges between Palestinian and Dutch labour unions, women, and universities.

Here there were some concrete results. During the 1980s the University of Amsterdam and the Delft University of Technology set up academic agreements with Birzeit University in the occupied West Bank. Mutual visits were key. Personal meetings and friendships, along with the "magic of Palestine" that visitors experienced when meeting welcoming Palestinians, gave life and blood to a sometimes abstract cause. A group of articulate workers and intellectuals at Birzeit University – male and female – inspired me and others in the solidarity movement. They helped us keep going in what sometimes looked like an endless, defensive struggle.

In September 1982 the Palestine Committee held its largest demonstrations ever against the mass murder of refugees in Sabra and Shatila by the Lebanese Phalangists, protected by the Israeli army. During the main demonstration the Committee's office in Amsterdam was set on fire by unknown persons. The polemics around anti-Zionism and anti-Semitism reached a peak. Committee members were invited by the main left weekly, *De Groene Amsterdammer*, to articulate our positions next to those of left-wing Zionists.

At a personal level I became increasingly interested in the Palestinian concept of *sumud* (steadfastness) as described by Raja Shehadeh in *The Third Way*. According to him, *sumud* was a way of active civil resistance, in opposition to passive resignation on the one hand, and getting stuck in a vicious cycle of violence on the other. *Sumud* resonated with values of active nonviolence developed in the peace movement. I wrote a Dutch-language book about the concept, which was based on my visits to the West Bank and Gaza; it was published in 1985 in cooperation with Pax Christi.

In the second half of the 1980s, I started a Ph.D. at the University of Amsterdam on the representation of Palestinians and Israel in bestselling western novels published after the Second World War. Inspired by Edward Said's statement that Palestinians needed "permission to narrate", I looked at dozens of pre-9/11 terrorist thrillers and Israel-centered "birth of the nation" stories like Uris' *Exodus*. Not surprisingly, Palestine was systematically de-narrativized or appropriated into others' narratives. Moreover, the Palestinian voice, when represented at all, was usually put in a negative and threatening context, even when quite reasonable things were said by the Palestinian characters.

At the end of the study and thesis, in 1933, I had the opportunity to make use of the cooperation agreement between the University of Amsterdam and Birzeit University, to get a European scholarship for giving workshops on "discourse and Palestine" in and out of Birzeit University. The objective was to foster a critical understanding of how language, narrative, and the manipulation of voice shaped textual representations of Palestine, and how Palestinian students could develop ways to counter this.

In 1995 I married Mary Morcos of Bethlehem, and we decided to establish ourselves in the city. Since then I have stayed, like so many other foreigners married to Palestinian ID holders, on a 2B tourist visa. For about ten years I travelled every three months in and out of the country to be able to renew short-term visas without the need to travel. Yet the visa application was never without hurdles. Once during an interrogation at Tel Aviv airport I was asked by security whether I had "right-wing or left-wing or radical left-wing" sympathies, and – introduced by the warning that this was a "very important question" – whether I had "any contacts with the International Solidarity Movement (ISM)." Membership in ISM was a reason not to be allowed into the country. Nowadays the same applies to vocal supporters of BDS.

I also experienced the hurdles of life in Palestine while learning Arabic. Over the years learning the language has remained a frustration and source of embarrassment, especially for someone with a professional background in language like me.

Mary and I had children. To our first one, Jara, I wrote a letter before she was born, wishing her to combine the warmth of Palestinians with the levelheadedness of the Dutch, and not to be "closed up by the closures". The second, Tamer, was born just days before the Israeli army entered Bethlehem in April 2002, during the second Intifada. His first three weeks of life were under curfew.

As for work, I shifted from university to school education, working on school- or community-based projects in the Bethlehem area, aiming to strengthen the communication of Palestine in different extracurricular subjects. I helped to raise funding, set up projects, write reports, teacher manuals, and evaluations, mostly for the Arab Educational Institute (AEI), a partner of Pax Christi that had signed up to the 2005 BDS call. I followed a guiding course to better inform Dutch groups visiting Bethlehem and Palestine. However, the Second Intifada (2000–2004) brought tourism to a standstill.

For over a year I locally coordinated United Civilians for Peace (UCP), an initiative of several Dutch development organizations, to have a group of civilian observers on the ground in the West Bank and Gaza. Later on, UCP was integrated into the Ecumenical Accompaniers of the World Council of Churches, which are conducting observer tasks to this day.

During the Second Intifada I also started to write a diary or "letter from Bethlehem", mainly to keep Dutch and international audiences in the peace and solidarity movement informed. It was circulated through the *Electronic Intifada* website, among other channels.

In one case, I worked together with a teacher from St Joseph School in Bethlehem on a diary project for girls aged between sixteen and seventeen years. The English-language diaries were a way to communicate Palestine's "abnormal normal" daily life, especially during the Second Intifada. As preparation, the young women read girls' diaries from different countries and periods, including Anne Frank's diary. The teacher said that the girls first rolled their eyes when hearing about the very different context of the Second World War, but when reading the diary they made parallels between Anne's imprisonment and the curfews which Palestinians experienced. As others could not enter Jerusalem, I brought copies of Anne Frank's *Diary* from Steimatzky's Jerusalem bookshop. (A related memory: When going to work at the Palestine Committee in the center of Amsterdam, I used to pass rows of visitors waiting in front of the Anne Frank House.)

In spring 2002, during the Israeli military siege of Bethlehem's Nativity Church, where some hundreds of Palestinian militants had taken refuge, one of the diary writers lived in an apartment which was taken over by the Israeli army. Her family was forced to stay in one room. To go to the bathroom, permission was needed from a soldier. One morning, the girl asked the soldier, "Do you know the Diary of Anne Frank?" The soldier, "Sure, would you like to read it?" The girl, "No, I want *you* to read it!"

Later on I started working with the *sumud* concept at AEI's Sumud Story House, located in the north of Bethlehem near the Wall circling Rachel's Tomb. AEI staff encouraged, especially among women and youth groups, the telling and documentation of stories of *sumud*. Many such stories were put on display on hundreds of weather-resistant, thin-metal posters glued to the Wall. Together they formed a statement that the narrative goes on and crosses walls despite people's imprisonment. Supporters of the "Wall Museum" paid for the posters, which over the last ten years have been viewed and read by thousands of visitors.

The next challenge is to integrate *sumud* into Palestinian education. The concept represents an interesting educational angle as it combines the large, national story of steadfastness on the land with the multitude of persevering "small stories" from daily life that can be collected, told, analyzed, and dramatized by school students. In interviews about *sumud* organized by AEI, it turns out that heads of NGOs, intellectuals, and Muslim and Christian religious leaders consider the concept a fruitful angle to tell the story of Palestine educationally, particularly at a time when Palestinians more than ever need to preserve dignity, morale, community, and links connecting them across borders of all kinds.

Note

Thanks to Robert Soeterik and Rosemary Sayigh for helpful comments.

Klaudia Wieser

Ph.D. student/activist, Austria

In August 2021, I met Anni Kanafani during the worsening of multiple crises in Beirut. I had researched the history of the Palestine Research Center founded by the PLO in the 1960s/1970s, and wanted to know more about her engagement with that institution. What started with my interest in Anni's work turned into a conversation about her lifelong engagement with a people's cause. And something about our encounter still affects me: her deeply felt relationship with Palestine.

"The Personal is Political"

Equipped with a flashlight, Anni Kanafani welcomed me and a friend outside her apartment building and navigated the stairways in the dark due to the recurring electricity cuts. We entered a beautiful, welcoming living room. While Anni was preparing tea, we felt her husband Ghassan Kanafani's spirit strikingly present: the black and white picture of *Umm Sa'ad* at the small table next to the couch, the bookshelf filled with revolutionary writings, and his artwork decorating the walls. After a while, sitting down under the original painting of *Antara*,[1] she started to recall the 1960s, in particular the story of a trip to Damascus to learn more about the Palestinian struggle.

> I come from a very leftist family. My father was a worker but a very intellectual person. He worked in the resistance movement against Nazi Germany, and he was always very political and my older brother the same. My younger brother was not, and I was in between. But we were on the left, all of us. And that is how I got in contact with Palestinian students. I met some of them in Dubrovnik in Yugoslavia. It was in 1960 and then they started to talk about what had happened in Palestine. And I was very much shocked because I didn't know anything. I came from a leftist family, and yet it wasn't talked about.

---

[1] *Anatara*, painted by Ghassan Kanafani in 1967, was printed as posters circa 1980, by the Ghassan Kanafani Cultural Foundation. This and other Palestinian posters can be viewed in the Palestine Poster Project Archives: https://www.palestineposterproject.org/poster/antar-kanafani.

The following year I came to Damascus, and I met with some of the students I had met before from the Palestinian student union. I wanted to go to Egypt, but I got stuck in Lebanon. It's a long story.[2]

In Beirut, Anni Høver got introduced to Ghassan Kanafani. Eager to know more about the Palestinian people, she wanted to visit the camps. But Ghassan made clear that "Palestinians are not like animals in the zoo"[3] and that she had to engage with history first. Anni learned fast and became involved in the transnational struggle for the liberation of Palestine.

> From the very beginning after I came to Lebanon, I started to correspond with a lot of people, friends mainly in Scandinavia. And I remember one very good friend, she was a leftist; when I came here and started to tell her in my letters about the situation of the Palestinians, she did not really react. And I was very disappointed. Then Ghassan wrote *Men in the Sun*, and it was translated into Swedish quite early. And I sent it to her, and I got a letter from her saying, "Now I understand".[4]

The practice of amplifying Palestinian voices, building connections, and engaging in translating the cause is a skill and a political act that Anni Kanafani has mastered. During our meeting, the charismatic woman didn't speak much about herself. She mentioned that her children are always asking her to write about her own story. But – as she stated – "it needs a lot of time". Anni Kanafani is busy: managing the Ghassan Kanafani Foundation during a pandemic and economic collapse in Lebanon takes a lot of effort.

The Pink Booklet

During our visit, Anni Kanafani put a small pink booklet on the table. Edited by Mahmoud Darwish, *Ghassan Kanafani* by Anni Kanafani was (re)published by the Palestine Research Center in 1973. The design is presented in white and pink, featuring pictures and memories of the family archive of the Kanafanis. The publication opens with the personal narrative about the moment when Ghassan and his niece Lamees – who was visiting with her family from Kuwait – left the house to go downtown. The day before, the extended family took a trip to the beach together, but on Saturday it was only Ghassan and Lamees. The two never arrived at their destination. The explosion of a Mossad car bomb targeting the militant intellectual took their lives right outside their home.

The intimate portrait of her "love and teacher" is unquestionably a treasure of people's history, as well as a remarkable historical document. From the photograph of

---

[2] Interview by the author, August 2021.
[3] Anni Kanafani, *Ghassan Kanafani*, Beirut, Palestine Research Center [PRC], 1973.
[4] Interview with Anni Kanafani by the author, August 2021.

the house of the Kanafanis in Acre, Palestine – at the time of publishing the book this had been taken over by Zionist settlers – to the young student sitting between a pile of books in Damascus, and then Ghassan the political activist being interviewed by Danish TV in his office, Anni Kanafani invokes scenes of the revolutionary author's life. Nevertheless, the booklet is as much about Anni Kanafani as it is about her husband:

> I came to Lebanon more than ten years ago to "study" the Palestinian problem. In you I found Palestine – the land and its people – and through our marriage I became a part of Palestine, and the mother of our two Palestinian children, Fayez and Laila.
>
> For Fayez, Leila, and me, you were not only a wonderful father and husband, but you were also a teacher and comrade too.[5]

That Anni Kanafani became part of the Palestinian community in Lebanon is beautifully captured in a condolence letter by George Habash, founder of the Popular Front for the Liberation of Palestine, which is also published in the booklet:

> Anni – I know very well what Ghassan's loss means to you, but please remember that you have Fayez, Laila, and thousands of brothers and sisters who are members of the PFLP, and above all you have the cause Ghassan was fighting for.
>
> Anni – we need your courage. Your courage at this crucial moment means a lot to me, and to all comrades and fighters of the PFLP. What hurts me most, at this moment, is that Hilda and I cannot be beside you. The reasons are well known to you, I suppose. It is a deep pain to me not to see Ghassan and talk to him before his burial.
>
> What I must repeat: we need your courage and your feeling that you are not and never will be alone. Waiting for the first opportunity to see you, Hilda and I remain your sincerest sister and brother.[6]

Anni Kanafani did continue the fight. Nearly five decades later, back at her apartment, we laughed about the two-lira price of the booklet when it was first printed by the Palestine Research Center. Like the many other political leaflets and transnational communication materials printed during the Palestinian revolution in Beirut, the timeless document represents a precious tool to steer curiosity about the history of the Palestinian revolution, and to advocate for the Palestinian cause. Next to a picture of Ghassan and his parents, Anni Kanafani writes in the pink booklet: "I did my best to join Ghassan in his struggle; I made contacts with people in the West interested in knowing the truth about the Palestinian struggle."[7]

5   Anni Kanafani, *Ghassan Kanafani*, Beirut, PRC, 1973.
6   In Anni Kanafani, *Ghassan Kanafani*, Beirut, PRC, 1973.
7   Anni Kanafani, *Ghassan Kanafani*, Beirut, PRC, 1973.

The Lillehammer Affair

In 1973, Mossad agents mistakenly killed Ahmed Bouchiki, a Moroccan immigrant to Norway, thinking that he was Ali Hassan Salameh, the prominent security adviser to Yasser Arafat, and member of the militant group *Black September*. The case became known as the *Lillehammer Affair* – named after the small village in Norway, where Bouchiki worked as a waiter – and made one of the biggest scandals for the Israeli intelligence network in Europe.

A process report published by Anni Kanafani in *Shu'un Falastiniyya* (1974),[8] the monthly magazine of the Palestine Research Center, sheds light on the details of the Mossad killing mission. Discussing her article more than five decades later, the author remembers that she put a lot of work into translation and communication with contacts in Scandinavia. She walks the reader through the court case, assembling press reports and summaries published by the Norwegian communist newspaper and police statements. There is no doubt that Anni was not only writing about Bouchikhi's killers but also investigating her husband's murderers. This report shows that writing was not only a personal endeavour to commemorate her husband, but an act of support for the Palestinian cause as such. There is much power in relating the personal to the collective, and Anni Kanafani's message in the report is explicit. The tactics, traces, and support structures of the assassins of Ahmed Bouchiki display striking similarities to the killing of Palestinian intellectuals and militants such as Wael Zuaiter in Rome, Basil al-Kubaissi in London, and Kamal Adwan, Kamal Nasir, and Abu Yousef al-Najjar in Beirut. The likely involvement of the assassins on trial with these operations becomes visible and – as Kanafani ends – "therefore, we can also assume that they are responsible, or at least partly, for the murder of my husband."[9]

Making Palestine Present

The *Lillehammer Affair* is not the only contribution dealing with assassinations of Palestinian political figures one finds when skimming though the many pages of the revolutionary journal. Indeed, the case of Ali Hassan Salameh was brought up again five years later. In a commentary titled *The Lover*,[10] the editorial board of *Shu'un Falastiniyya* commemorated Salameh, who was targeted by Mossad in Beirut and killed by a car bomb. The farewell letter concludes that Salameh and his martyrdom contributed to "the presence of Palestine in the world". Through making Palestine present – the contributors argue – Israel becomes absent.

My encounter with Anni Kanafani taught me many things. The most important might be that as much as I tried to direct our conversation towards her personal story, she steered it back to a collective perspective of struggle, making Palestine present. For

[8] Anni Kanafani, "The Case of Ahmed Bouchiki", *Shu'un Falastiniyya* 33, 1973, 156–165.
[9] Ibid.
[10] Editorial team of Shu'un Falastiniyya. 1979. "The Lover", *Shu'un Falastiniyya* 86, 206–207.

me, this practice represents the essence of pro-Palestinian writing and activism. And after more than a decade of working on the question of Palestine, I became conscious of the fact that there is power in extending this action to our own localities. As I work and write from Vienna, making Palestine present in the light of politically motivated smear campaigns[11] and the criminalization of Palestinian colleagues and pro-Palestine activists also means fighting anti-Muslim and anti-Palestinian racism at home.

Who is Yasser Arafat?

On 9 November 2020, I woke up to news of brutal raids that took place across Austria in the early morning carried out by the government under the name of Operation Luxor. Based on one and a half years of investigations and surveillance, these unlawful actions targeted Muslim-led institutions, charity organizations, renowned scholars and social media activists.

It took days until those targeted could report some of the horrors they had experienced, while the Austrian Interior Minister, Karl Nehammer, exploited the raids to cover up another scandal. Nearly a week before, a terror attack in Vienna killed four people and injured twenty-three. As serious allegations against state authorities – "the government was reportedly too focussed on preparing for Operation Luxor to deal with intelligence about this actual attack"[12] – became public, anti-Muslim hate was at its peak and public media outlets uncritically reproduced Islamophobic and xenophobic discourses of the state in the aftermath of the raids.

Though seventy households were raided, up to now none of those affected have been arrested and charged. The unlawful operation against Muslims in Austria was closely coordinated with Egyptian and Israeli security apparatuses trying to crack down on communities and individuals allegedly associated with the Muslim Brotherhood or Hamas.

Testimonies by those affected started to appear, mostly on social media. A Facebook post by an Arab-Palestinian association provided the first detailed list of questions posed by the police during interrogations; shedding light on the bizarre reality of Austria's engagement with the European strategy of targeting Muslim communities:

- What are your thoughts on establishing a caliphate?
- Are you in favour of conducting and supporting the dialogue and peace negotiations with Israel?
- How do you see a marriage of "underage" girls, e.g. from the age of 9?
- How do you feel about female circumcision and what is the aim behind it?
- Should Austrian children or those who grew up in Austria be raised to be martyrs?
- Do you want an Islamic caliphate and the establishment of Sharia law?
- Who is Yahya Ayyash?

[11] https://elsc.support/news/austrian-advocates-facing-lawsuit-for-a-post
[12] https://www.cage.ngo/operation-luxor-report

- Do you think it's right that a member of the terrorist organization Hamas is given a stage on Facebook?
- Are you familiar with the Protocols of the Elders of Zion?
- Do you know Yasser Arafat?

For the authorities, Yasser Arafat symbolized the face of terror. The same stereotype was used some days before the raids, when local broadcasting stations complemented their live reports on the attack in the city centre of Vienna, remembering the so-called "first terrorist attacks" in Austria dating back to a Palestinian operation in the 1980s.

The inclusion of allegedly Hamas-affiliated organizations and individuals in this unlawful raid represents a new chapter in Austria of targeting Palestinians through anti-terror legislation. Operation Luxor sent a message to pro-Palestinian and Muslim civil society that simply knowing who Yasser Arafat is represents a threat to Austrian national security, and qualifies one as a potential terror suspect. Considering these developments, the act of making Palestine present through our networks, writings, and actions symbolizes not only pro-Palestinian solidarity but a constant practice against the erasure of the history, present, and future of Palestine liberation.

AUSTRALIA, NEW ZEALAND

Stuart Rees

Founder of the Sydney Peace Foundation, co-founder of the Centre for
Peace and Conflict Studies at the University of Sydney, Australia

"Outrage on Behalf of All Palestinians"

Through childhood, school, and university, I have been excited by the goals of universal human rights, and have been an activist for civil liberties in several countries. To have ignored human rights-based values by not acting for justice for Palestinians would have placed me in an intellectual and emotional corner from which there was no escape.

Outrage grew in response to a range of controversial issues, from support of Hanan al-Ashrawi for the international Sydney Peace Prize to advocacy of the BDS movement; from friendships developed in visits to Gaza and the West Bank to opposition to the Israeli lobby's campaign to have the IHRA definition of antisemitism, which even Israeli critics regarded as confusing, adopted by an Australian government.

My social work career in Britain, Canada, the US, and in *Save the Children* projects in Sri Lanka prompted me to take stands on human rights issues. By 1978, as Professor of Social Work and Social Policy in Sydney University, I had responsibilities to research, teach, write, and take action on matters of social justice, domestic, or international.

One of those issues concerned the troubles in Northern Ireland, which I had stereotyped as an unending struggle between Catholics and Protestants, hence my putting that topic in the "too hard" basket. Stereotyping had also made me ignorant of Israel's policies towards the Palestinians: one side had allegedly made the desert bloom, the other, under the leadership of Yasser Arafat, blew up airliners in the desert. Mainstream media in the UK, the US, and Australia promoted these stereotypes. The deceit in the 1917 Balfour Declaration that a homeland for the Jewish people could be created without affecting the indigenous people of Palestine was not acknowledged.

The word "indigenous" struck a chord in me. As a member of my state's committee for reconciliation with Aboriginal citizens, I examined records of the murder and dispossession of the original inhabitants of Australia. That examination began with events in 1788, which marked the arrival of English invaders, whose colonial perspectives justified the claim that Australia was an empty land, easily possessed for the English crown.

The comparable date for the indigenous people of Palestine was 1948, when Zionist/ Israeli forces claimed that Palestine was a land without a people for a people without a land. Colonial perspectives once again weaponized the pretense that indigenous people did not exist, or if they did, they were of such little consequence that their homes could be destroyed, their land stolen, and thousands killed with no-one held accountable.

The common grounds of 1788 and 1948 underlined injustice and fed my dismay.

My first visit to Israel/Palestine occurred in the mid-'90s at an international social welfare conference in Jerusalem, in which Shimon Peres was the keynote speaker. He described Israel as a miraculous nation but said nothing about the Palestinians.

I needed to hear other accounts. On the last day of the conference, an Israeli academic from the Hebrew University walked with me on the West Bank. Pointing out new houses on a hillside, he explained, "These are the homes of settler arrivals from the Bronx. I suspect they were a menace in their homeland, they'll be an even bigger menace here." This was my introduction to the arrogance and aggression of Israeli settlers.

On return to Australia I participated in a workshop on the objectives and strategies of the BDS movement, an experience which highlighted the Geneva Convention rationale for the basic rights of self-determination of any people. Prompted by the Australian-based Israeli lobby's accusations that the BDS campaign was antisemitic and aimed to eradicate the state of Israel, I realized the widespread and toxic influence of this lobby.

That controversy raised questions about the Australian media's one-sided accounts of the Israeli-Palestinian conflict. The virtues of Israel were dramatized, while Palestinians were treated as synonymous with a supposedly untrustworthy Yasser Arafat, and with the alleged terrorist organization Hamas.

Influenced by views about the need for balanced reporting, Australian mainstream media insisted on parrying accounts of Palestine with Israeli views. But if one country commanded all the military, economic, and diplomatic resources, and the people they opposed had no resources, claims about balanced reporting seemed obscene.

An event of dramatic impact did most to solidify my commitment to the rights of Palestinians, and gave me direct experience of the malicious and cunning influence of the Israeli lobby. In late 2002, I sat on the jury which selected the recipient of Australia's only international award for peace, the prestigious Sydney Peace Prize.

At the Madrid peace talks in 1991, I had watched the impressive Palestinian spokesperson Dr Hanan Ashrawi, had admired her courage, and subsequently investigated her career. I proposed Ashrawi as one of the candidates for the Sydney Peace Prize to be awarded in November 2003.

The jury selected Ashrawi, and early in 2003, before the winner was formally announced, I travelled to Ramallah, met Hanan, and discussed her subsequent travel from Ramallah via London to Sydney.

In Australia, when the formal announcement of the recipient of the 2003 Sydney Peace Prize was made public in early August, all hell let loose. Objection to the selection of a Palestinian came in floods of letters to newspapers, in weeks of protest on commercial talkback radio, in headlines in the Murdoch News Corporation, and from members of the Israeli lobby intent on having the choice of Ashrawi cancelled.

In the furore, this distinguished, principled Palestinian was called a terrorist, a threat to the women and children of Australia, and even, in the Australian Jewish News, a Holocaust denier, though that accusation was withdrawn twenty-four hours after it was made. The idea that mud sticks had been followed.

The chairwoman of the Foundation which arranged the prize phoned me several times to say that she was under extreme pressure to withdraw Ashrawi's candidacy, and that on condition that I agreed, the very substantial sums awarded to the Foundation by corporate sponsors could be retained. Otherwise, hundreds of thousands of dollars would be lost. I rejected her demands saying, "Even if we only have one cent left, I intend to stand by the choice of this brave Palestinian. If we surrender on this issue, we will stand for nothing."

In this specific controversy, I did not and could not act alone. In addition to colleagues and students who were appalled by the vitriol thrown at this Palestinian woman, I was aided by two important figures: the influential Labor Premier of New South Wales, Bob Carr, had agreed to present the prize at the ceremony to honour Dr Ashrawi. In spite of being attacked for supporting her, and for saying he would welcome her to the country, Premier Carr stood firm.

My second significant ally was the late Alan Ramsey, a highly influential political journalist with the *Sydney Morning Herald*. Ramsey not only reported the controversy, he exposed and damned the injustice. I sent him a recording of the telephone conversation when the chair of the Foundation, at the behest of the Israeli lobby, asked me to renounce Ashrawi. I thought that Ramsey might at some future point use material from this recorded conversation. Instead, in a full page spread the following weekend, he published the whole recording including my comment, "I don't care if we only have one cent left."

This publicity opened public debate about injustices to Palestinians. In this groundbreaking experience, several issues stood out. Hanan Ashrawi's presence in Sydney enabled the public to witness a courageous, sophisticated Palestinian, and thereby remove the derisive stereotypes used by the Israeli lobby. Saying what we stood for and that we would not be overawed by bullies, crafted that sense of identity which told the Israeli lobby, "On issues of basic justice, we are not about to compromise."

The Ashrawi controversy taught me a final lesson: bullies perceive being placated as a sign of weakness which only encourages them to continue their abusive conduct.

In the years that followed, I travelled several times to the West Bank, to Israel, and to diverse refugee camps in Jordan, Lebanon, Gaza, and to bedouins' tented homes. Meetings with beautiful, generous human beings in the wretched conditions of refugee camps underlined the cruelties imposed on them.

After a generous lunch in the Beirut camp, Bourj al-Barajneh, Hosni Abu Taha, chairman of the camp committee and a former farmer from Galilee, told me, "We want to live our lives in freedom, as we did before 1948. We deserve the chance to prove we are human beings."

I followed these visits with projects to enable students to escape Gaza to study and settle in Australia. Once the students arrived, they had no means of returning to visit their families in Gaza, at least not until they might achieve Australian citizenship, so I agreed to visit their families, and used those occasions to participate in seminars with young Gazans on the means of promoting the BDS campaign.

Hospitality from families living under siege emphasized their generosity in the face of cruelty, their dignity despite oppression. During a long lunch on a Gazan beach, I was challenged to swim in the polluted sea, or to risk taking a trip on a Gazan fishing boat at risk of Israeli gun boats. Ironic laughter could not obscure the cruelty.

Following the Israeli invasions of 2009 – "Operation Cast Lead" – and in 2014 "Operation Protective Edge" – my outrage at the cruelties inherent in the siege of Gaza turned to disbelief. The casualties were horrendous. In the 2009 conflict, 1,398 Palestinians were killed, including 455 women and children. Four Israelis lost their lives, a Palestinian/Israeli death ratio of 366:1. With no evident military purpose, over 3,500 homes and 268 factories were destroyed.

In the 2014 Israeli "Operation Protective Edge", the Israeli human rights organization B'Tselem recorded 2,200 Palestinians killed including 526 children, a quarter of all those who died in the operation. Sixty-six Israeli military were killed and seven Israeli civilians. Eighteen thousand Palestinian homes were destroyed and an estimated 108,000 people made homeless. In a war crimes act of collective punishment against a whole population, Gaza's only power plant was knocked out, together with water treatment and sewage plants, wells, pipelines, and reservoirs. Fifteen thousand tons of liquid waste leaked into the streets of Gaza.

Each Israeli operation was called a war but in retrospect looks more like organized slaughter.

In spite of the killing and destruction, Israel tried to deflect attention from their actions and justify them. Hamas as a US designated terrorist organization fired rockets into Israel, so automatic references to "a terrorist organization" could explain the deaths of thousands of innocents. I do not justify Hamas' authoritarian rule of Gaza, but I was there for the 2006 election, which elected that party and did so in a vote conducted openly and fairly.

Beyond belief claims that Israel has the most humane army in the world are compounded by western powers suggesting that even in the destruction of schools, hospitals, water, and sewage plants, let alone the slaughter of whole families, Israel showed restraint. That moral cop-out came with the usual US policy narrative that Israel is entitled to defend itself, hence the massive US arms sales to Israel and their demonizing any party that Washington could label terrorist.

Assumptions that Israel was exceptional lay at the heart of cruelties which the Israeli military thought would impress a stigmatized people. Israel's view of their country as the world's victim meant that when destroying Palestinians' lives and prospects, Israel could act with impunity and should never be held accountable.

In the amoral playbook of international relations, criticism of Israel could be stifled with the accusation that critics must be antisemitic. In common with any ingrained prejudice, including anti-Palestinianism, I take antisemitism seriously, but charges of antisemitism are too often used to suppress free speech and to insist that Israel must remain an exception to the rule.

I am an enthusiastic supporter of the BDS campaign, but not for one minute does this make me antisemitic. I have watched the Israeli lobby's campaign to have governments adopt the International Holocaust Remembrance Association's definition of antisemitism, a document decried by many Israelis as confusing, slovenly, and ineffective, concerned more with preventing criticism of Israel than with antisemitism.

My explanation of support for the human rights of all Palestinians finishes with a reference to the influence of the late French diplomat Stéphane Hessel, who had been a contributor to the crafting of the Universal Declaration of Human Rights. My conversations with him about his life and work followed the publication of his best-selling book "Indignez vous", or in English, "Be Outraged".

Stéphane was Jewish. As a French resistance fighter he had been captured by the Nazis, and imprisoned in Buchenwald concentration camp, from which he eventually escaped. In that last book, he explained that in his long life he had been outraged by three particular developments. The first was the cavalier attitude affecting governments' and corporations' destructive treatment of planet earth. The second was the uncritical reliance on neoliberal, free market economic policies, and consequent worldwide social and economic inequalities. But as a Jew, Hessel said he had been most outraged by the continuous, unimaginable cruelty of Israeli governments towards the people of Palestine.

That judgement echoed my reasons for commitment to the universal human rights of all Palestinians. Decades of encounters with "Israel right or wrong" supporters has solidified my sense of disbelief and outrage at the cruelties imposed upon a stigmatized, dispossessed, and persecuted people.

Janfrie Wakim

Educator/activist, New Zealand

"My Awakening to the Colonization of Palestine and Aotearoa-New Zealand"

I was born in Wellington, New Zealand, in 1945, just months after my father's only sibling was killed in World War 2. I grew up hearing the stories of war and of the grim times that so many families suffered. Both my parents were born just prior to World War 1 and, having lost relations in that war too, I also learned through them of the aftermath of war. As a child, I heard stories of Japanese and German atrocities, especially the Holocaust, and Anne Frank's diary haunted me. Places in the "Holy Land » became familiar through Sunday school colouring-in maps. As a teenager I read Leon Uris's novel *Exodus*, and was moved by the film (especially by Paul Newman!), and I accepted that account of the State of Israel's founding as factual. At high school I was aware of Jewish students who were exempt from attending Christian-centred assemblies but had no understanding of the political events taking place in the Middle East. I studied science, so had had no introduction to the colonization of Palestine at college or university; besides, the war in Vietnam claimed my interest and I was only vaguely aware of the 1967 Six Day War.

However, like many young New Zealanders in the '60s and '70s, I travelled overseas and the hijacking of airplanes became a source of concern and bewilderment. The PLO began to enter my consciousness. I was in England at the time of the 1972 Munich Olympic Games and was appalled by the hostage-taking. Almost exactly a year later, in September 1973, the same month as the Yom Kippur war, I took up a position as a student counsellor in West London, after working in Canada and studying at Exeter University.

I joined a community flat in Wimbledon and met David Wakim, who was working as a pharmacist nearby.

David was born in Sydney, Australia. His father had emigrated from Lebanon as a young man in 1934; his mother was a second-generation Lebanese who grew up speaking little Arabic but was immersed in the Sydney Lebanese community. En route to the UK, David spent time in Lebanon meeting his grandmother and numerous aunts, uncles, and cousins for the first time. He was very excited to be connecting with his Lebanese Christian Maronite family, soaked up all the stories, and delved vigorously into the country's history.

We talked about the different ways we had each arrived in the UK, and among his many stories he described touring around Beirut, noticing the refugee camps and enquiring about them. He was told they were occupied by Palestinians who arrived when the state of Israel was created and had caused trouble ever since. That piqued his curiosity and he explored their history. When we met, our conversations rekindled my recall of events in Munich and reverberated with the events of September 1973.

Subsequently, we fell in love. After we'd travelled in Europe together, David returned to Australia via America and I embarked on a (mostly) overland journey from London through to Indonesia, finally arriving in Sydney six months later. We married in Auckland, New Zealand in 1975, had four children in quick succession, and bought a pharmacy serving a very diverse community. The previous owner was Jewish and many customers thought David was too, but a resident Lebanese recognized the Wakim name and welcomed us into the local Lebanese society.

For us, a turning point occurred when Israel invaded Lebanon in the late '70s. By this time we had learned something of the 1947 partition of Palestine by the UN, the 1948 Nakba, and the formation of the PLO. We knew that the expulsion of mostly Muslim Palestinians from Jordan to Lebanon had threatened to upset the population balance between Lebanon's Christians and Muslims. Israeli incursions into South Lebanon in attempts to drive out the PLO resulted in more refugees and civilian deaths. In 1981, Israel bombed PLO targets in Lebanon, and in June the following year it launched its *Operation Peace for Galilee* and invaded Lebanon up to the outskirts of Beirut. The Lebanese community in Auckland, which up until then had had more of a social and cultural focus, mobilized politically to express its outrage, with newspaper advertisements, letters to editors, and meetings with politicians and community and church leaders.

We discovered that a group had been formed in 1975 called *The Friends of Palestine,* mostly comprising immigrants from Arab countries, but also including New Zealanders who understood that "Palestine is the issue" because they had visited or worked in the Middle East. It also included people who had served in the New Zealand military in Palestine, Egypt, and Libya during WW2 and were well informed about the history of the region.

David became very active in what was to become the Palestine Human Rights Campaign (PHRC), networking with the other groups established around the country. The support from prominent anti-apartheid activists, opponents of the 1981 Springbok rugby tour of New Zealand, was immensely helpful as we grew more aware of other liberation struggles. Locally, beginning in the mid '70s, there were significant challenges by Māori to Pākehā (Europeans) to re-examine our nation's history of British colonization, and the consequences of cultural alienation and land dispossession. By the 1980s, our government had accepted that these issues needed to be resolved. There were abundant parallels between our history and the colonization of Palestine by the Zionists and their allies, and the PHRC welcomed the solidarity of Māori activists themselves.

The '80s was also a decade of great political change nationally, with the arrival of the fourth Labour government and a new Prime Minister, David Lange. My husband and I were active in our local Labour Party branch agitating for nuclear-free legislation and other progressive changes. David and others tried hard within the Party to secure recognition for the PLO as the legitimate voice of the Palestinian people, only to have every move sabotaged by Zionist elements.

As it happened, it was the conservative National Party which first gave recognition to the PLO when Foreign Minister Warren Cooper met with PLO representative Ali Kazak in 1982. This was the first meeting of a western foreign minister with the PLO. David was present for another significant meeting, that between the National Party Prime Minister Robert Muldoon and visiting Professor Ibrahim Abu-Lughod. Muldoon had served with the NZ Army in WW2 and, like many returned servicemen, had sympathy for Palestinians who, he observed, had paid the price for European antisemitism.

Inspired by the precedent set by the anti-apartheid movement, the PHRC mounted protests whenever sporting contacts with Israel took place. One of the most notable events took place in March 1988 when the Israeli soccer team played New Zealand at the renowned rugby ground, Eden Park, in Auckland. (At Eden Park in 1981, protestors had worn helmets and body armour while battling heavy police action, deployed to ensure the rugby game between apartheid-era South Africa and New Zealand went ahead.) The match attracted television coverage in Israel and we were elated that our banner stating in Arabic, "Our hearts are with the Palestinians", was seen on screen.

Prominent overseas speakers came to New Zealand to speak at various PHRC meetings and conferences, but the forces seeking to suppress debate were ever present. At Auckland University's Continuing Education Department, a 1986 seminar on "Zionism and the Palestine Question" was well attended but prompted objections from the Auckland Zionist community. Subsequent events were blocked and, without a formal university academic freedom committee to appeal to at that time, it was twenty years before a similar event was hosted by a department at the university.

Constant misinformation emanated from the Israeli Embassy and local Zionist supporters, and their impact was exacerbated by the general public's poor understanding of the genesis of the conflict. This was especially marked at the time of the first intifada. PHRC worked hard to raise awareness, to lobby politicians, and to challenge the media's inaccurate presentations of Palestinian/Israeli issues. The bias was so evident in the coverage in the newspapers, radio, and television that complaints were made to the Press Council and the Broadcasting Standards Authority, many of which were successful.

Notable among the overseas speakers over the decades have been Sami Hadawi, a prominent Palestinian writer; the erudite Palestinian-American professor Ibrahim Abu-Lughod; Mysoon Saath and the Jewish activist Manfred Ropschitz (April 1989); Islah Abdel-Jawed and the Jewish Al Haq lawyer Marty Rosenbluth (May 1990); and Sami Musallam from the PLO (February 1993). The Palestinian journalist Leila Deeb, Dr Fathi Arafat (Yasser's brother), and Ali Kazak, the representative of the General Palestinian Delegation to Australia, New Zealand, and the Pacific, have also toured Aotearoa/New Zealand.

More recently, there have been lectures, tours, conferences with Dr Izzeldin Abuelaish, Ramzy Baroud, Ali Abunimah (editor of *Electronic Intifada*), Emad Burnat,

Huwaida Arraf, Samah Sadawi, Dr Salman Abu Sitta, as well as sympathetic Israeli Jews: Jeff Halper, Gideon Levy, Amira Haas, and Miko Peled.

Palestine supporters keep up a constant flow of letters to the press, while others use talkback radio and even a dedicated community radio programme to educate people on Palestine and promote relevant movies. The campaign provides speakers for schools and public and private meetings and there have been successful cultural displays in libraries, halls, and churches. One significant project was to provide updated text on the Palestine/Israel situation for senior students studying in New Zealand secondary schools.

We often encountered objections to some of these initiatives but pressed on, undeterred, and even enjoyed strengthened support from some who witnessed the opposition in action.

We have held numerous dinners on Palestine National Day, and at other times to raise funds to support the Union of Palestinian Medical Relief Committees in Palestine. For a time, these funds were subsidized by the New Zealand government. We met so many wonderful people who feel deeply about the gross injustices that Palestinians have had to endure, as well as the plight of refugees, their dispossession from their land, the brutal occupation of the West Bank and siege of Gaza, on top of the fatalities and injuries inflicted by the military might of Israel and its sponsor, the United States. Combatting the deliberate lies, propaganda, and media bias requires constant effort, inspired by the "*sumud*" (steadfastness) of the Palestinians themselves. Significant and enduring relationships have grown, nationally and globally, with others who advocate for a free Palestine.

In 1995, just after the Oslo accords, David and I visited Palestine with our children and witnessed first-hand the appalling treatment of the Palestinians. This was evident at the border and checkpoints and from the obscene development of settlement colonies in the West Bank. We were horrified when visiting Hebron that while we were free to explore an historical site of interest, armed soldiers prevented our Palestinian hosts from entering. This blatant discrimination, denying our friends their humanity, left a deep and lasting impression of disgust. David and I visited refugee camps in Gaza and witnessed the humiliation of the people processed at the Beit Hanoun/Erez crossing, surrounded by electronic fencing and a caged passageway resembling a cattle run.

We lobbied for the closure of the Israeli embassy in New Zealand. It did close in 2002, but has since reopened. However, Prime Minister Helen Clark suspended high-level diplomatic relations between Israel and New Zealand in 2004, when two Mossad agents were caught and jailed for illegally trying to obtain New Zealand passports.

Soon after the Al-Aqsa Intifada in September 2000, a monthly rally was instituted in downtown Auckland to support Palestine. It continues today; we distribute pamphlets, recruit allies, and promote the Boycott, Divestment and Sanctions campaign launched in 2005. Protest marches in the city centre have occurred with each of Israel's deadly wars, in 2006, 2008–09, 2012, and 2014.

In 2010 I was arrested on several charges after taking part in a protest action against the inclusion of Israeli tennis player Shahar Pe'er in an international tournament held annually in Auckland. Thanks to outstanding lawyers, I was discharged without conviction, and Pe'er never returned to the tournament. It was always a given that we would get lots of publicity for protesting at the Jerusalem Quartet concert tours. We responded to our critics by saying that the Quartet relied on the support of Zionist institutions.

In 2005, David and I embarked on travel in Africa, where he challenged any Israeli he encountered about the treatment of Palestinians, the occupation, the right of return, and BDS. He died suddenly of a heart attack while in Namibia and I returned to New Zealand shattered by this devastating turn of events. As David's prime support in his indefatigable efforts to seek justice for Palestinians, I knew I had to continue the work with the assured support of our children. And so it has unfolded in the years since he died.

Perhaps the most significant action I have taken occurred in the year after David's death. Former Israeli General and War Minister Moshe Ya'alon, who feared charges in the UK of war crimes committed in Lebanon, visited New Zealand on a fundraising mission. Acting on a tip-off, in accordance with the principle of universal jurisdiction, and with help from a variety of legal experts, I successfully sought a private prosecution for his arrest and was delighted when a District Court judge agreed to issue an arrest warrant. Unfortunately, the Attorney General at the time, Michael Cullen, quashed the warrant and allowed Ya'alon to leave the country. It was a crushing disappointment.

The campaign advocating justice for Palestine has grown significantly in recent years and the Palestine Solidarity Network Aotearoa (PSNA) now incorporates nationwide groups that work locally and internationally to free Palestine. The presence of Kiwi activists on the flotillas to Gaza gained media attention. A highlight was when Marama Davidson, a Maori Green Member of Parliament, joined the 2016 Women's Boat to Gaza, which was intercepted by the Israeli Navy. Lorde, the Kiwi singer/songwriter, attracted international attention when she cancelled her planned concert in Jerusalem in 2017, citing an "overwhelming number of messages and letters" she had received urging her to re-think her plans.

This year, 2021, marks the 40th anniversary of the 1981 Springbok rugby tour of New Zealand, when protests reverberated around the world. Though hampered by Covid-19, John Minto, National Organiser for HART (Halt all Racist Tours) in 1981, and now Chair of PSNA, organized a country-wide tour acknowledging the demise of apartheid in South Africa, and mobilizing support for the campaign against apartheid in Israel and the BDS movement.

The struggle for justice in Palestine continues . . .

LATIN AMERICA

Bianca Marcossi, Coletivo Vozes Judaicas por Libertação[1]

Educational/militant group, Brazil

"Displacing Ourselves: Jews Becoming Pro-Palestinian"

On the morning of August 6, 2014, a group of approximately twelve young Jews gathered in front of the building where the Israeli Consulate in São Paulo is located, wearing *keffyehs* and holding up posters with slogans reading "As Jews we Refuse to Occupy", "There is no Peace Without Justice", and "Against Israeli Oppression". At that time, Israel had carried out one of the most destructive and lethal attacks on the Gaza Strip, impacting the lives of more than two million Palestinians confined under the Israeli blockade. Standing on the sidewalk, photographed by the main media outlets in São Paulo, and receiving looks of disapproval from the security guards and other Jews who were present, we called out the name and age of each Palestinian victim. This event gave rise to our collective: Vozes Judaicas por Libertação (Jewish Voices for Liberation).

The persecution of communist movements, to which anti-Zionist Jews were linked during the military dictatorship (1964–1985); the socioeconomic rise of the Brazilian Jewish community, which no longer belonged mainly to the working class; and the hegemony of the liberal peace paradigm of the 1990s, erased Jewish groups critical of Zionism from the political and social scene. The 2014 act, though somewhat improvised, meant the encounter of trajectories of rupture with Zionism – founded, among other policies, on the dispossession of Palestinians in 1948, the appropriation of land in 1967, the ongoing confiscation of Palestinian land through settler colonialism and the denial of the Palestinian Right of Return – and initiated a search for a new space where we could publicly express our solidarity with the Palestinian struggle and, at the same time, affirm an anti-racist, anti-colonial and anti-apartheid Jewry, a non-Zionist Jewry.

---

[1] Coletivo Vozes Judaicas por Libertação seeks to confront the hegemony of Zionism over the Jewish community and identity in Brazil, as well as to be a vehicle for a radical solidarity with the Palestinians and other subalternized peoples from Palestine to Brazil. Its members include Bianca Neumann Marcossi, Shajar Goldwaser, Juliana Esquenazi Muniz, Bruno Huberman, and Yuri Haasz.

In the last eight years, with the rise of the Jair Bolsonaro administration and the consequent strengthening of Brazil-Israel relations, there have been several transformations and disputes within and outside the Jewish community in relation to Israel-Palestine: we see both a strengthening of a Zionist right explicitly aligned with Bolsonarism and manifestations that reincarnate old paradigms and beliefs such as "Two States for Two Peoples". Against this "left-wing Zionism" (which tries to reincarnate Oslo and talks about Palestine and Palestinians without talking about rights, reparation, justice, and equality), and without repudiating fascist Zionism, we find ourselves without a place in the Jewish community. And, along with this displacement – this *strangeness* – we are faced with the task of building a different Jewishness from the one in which Israel speaks on behalf of, and which, refusing an exclusionary framework, is founded on an ethics and politics centered around subalternity, whether in Palestine, or in Brazil.

The following testimony brings together the experiences of the members of this collective, who – although leading different paths – have undergone experiences that we see as common on this road toward "becoming pro-Palestinian". Thus, this is a fiction of collective testimony, the narrative form that we have found to share stories of rupture with an inner and outer place, in which Zionism, even that of the "left," organized our reality as "Jews of the diaspora" and our relationship with Palestine and the Palestinians, until the arrival of an active place of solidarity with the Palestinian resistance to state violence. The present text is inserted within this context of searching for this new place, from this point of no return, the result of the encounter with *Palestinianess* and its subaltern condition.

Becoming Jewish-Zionist

Families certainly hold a privileged space in the process of developing Jewishness. They are the ones who bring the blood, cultural, and ethnic ties that ensure Jewishness between generations, as well as festive and affective traditions. As Brazilian Jews, we inherit from families stories of displacement and refuge, both from European antisemitism and from poverty in Turkey, and also from the pride of being diasporic Jews. Some of us, in our family trajectories of exile, ended up having Israel as our birthplace, but Brazil as our territory of creation.

However, despite the centrality of the family in this development, we perceive Jewish-Zionist institutions, both formal and informal, as the main spaces for the construction of Zionist subjectivity. This includes, above all, schools, clubs, and youth movements. It was in these places that we learned to identify with Israel, understanding it as a fundamental space for our survival. There, an inseparable bond was built between Judaism, this abstract and diverse category, and the almost physical feeling of belonging to a place. The Israeli flag was always next to the Brazilian flag; and we sang *Hatikva*, the Israeli anthem, with greater passion than the Brazilian. Even in a Brazilian Jewish school, what really mattered was the Israeli symbols and historical landmarks, especially Yom Hatzmaut ("Independence Day") and Yom Hazicarón ("Day of Remembrance of the Dead Soldiers of Israel and Victims of Terrorism").

The Zionist education limited our ability to build a true sense of belonging to the Brazilian territory and nation. Through learning Hebrew and about Israeli landmarks, and through projects such as sponsored trips to Israel, we built a separate ethnic-national identity. The idea of a prior belonging prevailed, something deeper and more relevant. *Jewish-Brazilian*, and never the other way around. Our Jewish-Zionist education was meant to remind us that we are a Community in Exile, that is, we have, even if indefinitely, a place of origin and a date of return – a right guaranteed by Israeli law.

Alongside pride, there was the infliction of the fear of persecution against us Jews – something that we did not feel directly as middle-class whites in large urban centres in Brazil, where the oppressed are black, peripheral, and indigenous populations. We learned in Jewish history classes that "antisemitism" was an irrational and unfounded hatred of the "Jewish people", whose origins went back to the biblical people of Amalek, and extended to all those who, in the present and in the future, will always "hate us" – from the ancient Persians to Hitler and, in a more contemporary version, "the Palestinians", "the terrorists", the "Arabs", and the "neo-Nazis", confusing labels that produced fear. It seemed to us a duty, on behalf of our grandparents and our future children, to defend the threatened state of Israel, an extension of our family and ancestry.

This fear was not only taught, but was also experienced and reinforced in the youth movement summer camps through games that, for example, simulated kidnappings of children at night, or through functions like guarding the Israeli flag overnight while waiting for an alleged attack, or simulations of military training by Tzahal, Israel's "defense" army. Above all, we had to learn to defend ourselves.

Becoming Outsiders: Encounters with Palestinianess

It was precisely in the encounter with the Palestinian "Other" that we accessed the contradictions that this Zionist education had raised in us. This encounter was a choice, and for it to happen, a certain distance from the Jewish community was needed. The encounter with alterity presupposes leaving our comfort zone, moving, taking risks, looking critically at ourselves and those around us.

We had to look at ourselves objectively and question our own position in the society in which we live, belonging to the white middle-class in Brazil, and also as Zionist Jews in the face of the Palestine/Israel issue. This work signified the heartfelt recognition that 1) our Jewish identity had been hijacked by Zionism; 2) in this Brazil-Palestine context, we were not the oppressed, but the oppressors; and 3) in our name, "antisemitism" was being used to silence and produce a subaltern Palestine.

An initial shift took place at the university: the words our professors used to talk about the state of Israel were a shock. Terms like "ethnic cleansing", "racism", "apartheid", "annexation", and "colonization" operated as cracks in our mindset. In reading new Israeli historians such as Ilan Pappé, as well as Palestinian historians such as Rashid Khalidi, we came closer to Palestinian narratives about the events of 1948, the Nakba, and the expulsion of the Palestinians. This historical reconsideration, in addition to contemporary Israeli crimes in the occupation of the Palestinian territories of the West Bank and Gaza Strip, disrupted foundational myths in our own identities as victims and heroes, even leading to physical pain and states of deep depression and anger. The lies we had been told, believed, and propagated were so many! It was necessary to decide whether we would experience these layers of deconstruction and face the task of looking for a new place of belonging that was more coherent with our values, or whether we would deny everything that Israel represented in our lives, including our Jewishness.

Once the decision to fight for a new place was made, came the desire to address this anguish through mobilizations before a state that spoke on our behalf. Spaces formed by left-wing Zionist Jews who criticized the Occupation, but supported Israel's established foundations – such as the denial of the Jewish state's responsibility for the 1948 ethnic cleansing – lost their meaning

An important space for building a possible non-Zionist Jewry was the FFIPP – International Network for Human Rights in Palestine/Israel – whose branch in Brazil served as a meeting place for Jews in the process of contesting Zionism. The FFIPP allowed us to travel to Palestine/Israel to personally see the reality experienced not only by subjugated Palestinians, but also the contradictions of the Israeli society that promotes this oppression. Another space was EAPPI – Ecumenical Accompaniment Program in Palestine and Israel, a program created in 2002 by the World Council of Churches in response to the call of Palestinian churches for a protective international presence in those years of escalating violence.

In this displacement, we witnessed a restricted territory divided by electric fences, walls, and checkpoints, the ruins of houses and mosques demolished by Israel as a policy of discrimination, military incursions into schools and the imprisonment of children, a legal system that grants privileges based on religion and ethnicity and uses the law to restrict access to land, water, and basic services, and humiliates, expels, and imprisons stateless people.

When we met the Palestinians, we understood that what we believed to be our land and our culture really was not. We were welcomed by several Palestinian families in their homes in Nablus, Jenin, Ramallah, Bethlehem, and Bardala, who, even though we were Jews, knew that we were not the same as the soldiers, or even the settlers spread throughout the West Bank.

For talking about or simply having had these experiences in Palestine, some of us were rejected by Jewish institutions, insulted by friends and relatives, and even fired from our jobs for posting pictures of the Palestinian reality on social media.

We came to understand that it was not about a "conflict" between "two peoples", neither could we accept the pacifying words of "two states for two peoples" as envisioned by "pro-Palestinian" colleagues who, without moving towards the "Other" and putting their ideas to the test, insist on believing in a possible "left-wing Zionism", sustained as this idea is by the materiality of laws, borders, territory, and military forces that govern lives in the territory. Radical solidarity with the Palestinians we knew was essential for their liberation, and Zionism would not allow that.

In Brazil, another complementary path in this road toward becoming pro-Palestinian was the work alongside Brazilian social movements, in particular the movement of mothers and family members who have been victims of state violence and who deeply criticize racism and state terrorism in Brazil. At Julho Negro (Black July), an event that discusses racism, militarization, and apartheid at an international level in Rio de Janeiro, we saw the Palestinians side by side with the movements from the *favelas*, the Mães de Maio, and the Rede de Movimentos e Comunidades Contra a Violência (Network of Movements and Communities Against Violence).We listened to the Palestinian Movement, the Mapuche, the Bolivian indigenous peoples, members of Mexican and South African social movements, and we asked ourselves: what do they all have in common?

We began to discuss the processes of militarization at the international level, gradually understanding the role that the state of Israel played in this. The colonialist and racist logic in which Zionism and Israel operated in the world became increasingly evident, naturalizing extremely violent mechanisms for silencing the native populations not only in Palestine, but in different parts of the globe, through funding and investment in Israeli military strength and apparatus. These apparatuses were tested and improved on the same Palestinian bodies and lives that had welcomed us in the West Bank.

Anti-Zionist Jewry and Radical Solidarity with Palestinians

Since the 2014 act, it has been a challenge for us to build an ethical Jewry, not separate or exclusivist, centered on the values of equality, justice, and freedom, and, therefore, disconnected from Zionism. Even so, we see this challenge as fundamental. Giving up this Jewishness would be accepting Israel's monopoly over the memory of our grandparents and ancestors, victims of state violence, and assuming that racism and apartheid are the legitimate answer to fascism and Nazism. We do not condone it. As part of this effort, we founded the Coletivo Vozes Judaicas por Libertação (Collective Jewish Voices for Liberation) as a way to confront the hegemony of Zionism over the Jewish community and identity in Brazil, and also as a vehicle to build radical solidarity with the Palestinians and other subaltern peoples.

Inspired by Angela Davis, who says that "it is not enough to be non-racist, we must be anti-racist", the way left and right Zionists are pro-Palestine maintains Jewish exclusivity over the land, privileges based on ethnicity and religion, and silences debates that raise, for example, the systematic racial discrimination experienced by Palestinians who have acquired Israeli citizenship and who live within exclusively Jewish areas, but in a marginalized way. For them, racial hierarchy, apartheid, and colonialism remain. For us, it is not enough to say we are pro-Palestine, we must have an anti-racist and anti-colonialist discourse and practice, to destroy the structures that subjugate and plunder the Palestinians.

This kind of action reveals how Zionism will always be incapable of building what Judith Butler calls in "Parting Ways: Jewishness and the Critique of Zionism" an ethics of *cohabitation*, for Zionism is a particularly exclusive type of colonialism over the land, as Patrick Wolfe notes in "Settler Colonialism and the Elimination of the Native". As a collective, our effort is in the construction of an anti-Zionist Jewry from Brazil, based on the Jewish diasporic experience, coexistence and radical co-responsibility for the "Other". It is also in the militancy alongside other subaltern peoples who find themselves involved in the anti-racist and anti-colonial struggle for the construction of a world that can be inhabited by all.

For us, becoming pro-Palestinian was first about becoming anti-Zionist and breaking with many paradigms and ways of interpreting our family histories. Returning to a place where one is "Jewish" in spite of the world, or even against the world, is no longer possible for us. To be Jewish is to be in the world, for the world.

From the painful stories of our grandparents and ancestors, we learned the lesson that the "Other" is simply us and that, therefore, the radical co-responsibility with whom we share the world is what guides our actions. It is necessary to reinterpret the sense of Jewishness that we wanted to recover, to *invent* a habitable place in the sense of invention proposed by Edward Said, when remembering his home in Talbieh, in an interview with Ari Shavit:

> [...] I realized that the world I grew up in, the world of my parents, of Cairo and Beirut and pre-1948 Talbieh, was a made-up world. It wasn't a real world. It didn't have the kind of objective solidity that I wanted it to have. For many years, I mourned the loss of this world. I truly mourned it. But now I discovered the possibility of reinterpreting it. [...] I understood that my role was to tell and retell a story of loss where the notion of repatriation, of a return to a home, is basically impossible.
>
> Said, 2002, p. 453

For this collective, the Jews must be the ones who celebrate their eternal diaspora by showing that nations are modern barriers. Borders have never defined us, nor prevented us from flourishing. What has always allowed this is diversity, and the possibility of feeling at home anywhere, and being able to call anyone, from any people, ethnicity, or religion, a brother or sister. The struggle must be local to be global. Decolonization is a movement that crosses from Brazil to Palestine.

Reference

Said, Edward, "My Right of Return (interview to Ari Shavit)", in Viswanathan, Gauri (ed.), Power, Politics and Culture – Interviews with Edward Said, New York, Vintage Books, 2002, pp. 443–458.

O. Hugo Benavides

Ph.D. faculty/activist, Ecuador, currently at Fordham University, US

"Julia and I: How I Became Aware of the Palestinian Struggle"

You think your pain and your heartbreak are unprecedented in the history of the world, but then you read. [...] the things that tormented me most were the very things that connected me with all the people who were alive, who had ever been alive.

James Baldwin[1]

Surprisingly, it is not that hard to remember when the Palestinian cause initially became present or an important part of my life. Perhaps what might seem most contradictory, at least on the surface of things, is that both the Palestinian struggle and the plight of the Holocaust of World War 2 were jointly embedded in my young mind. Indeed, it was toward the end of the 1970s, when I was around ten years old, that both historical events became intimately intertwined in my political imagination. This intermingled reality was singularly linked through the film "*Julia*", and through the two main female characters' portrayal played by activist actors, Vanessa Redgrave and Jane Fonda.

The film itself, "*Julia*", is an adaptation of one of Lillian Hellman's memoirs, where she recounts the story of her best childhood friend, Julia, hence the title. The film is a poignant portrayal of Julia's plight, first as a child of an aristocratic albeit quite loveless family, later as a resistance fighter against the Nazis. In the initial flashbacks of the young women's friendship, we see a brave and outgoing Julia egging Lillian on to be courageous, but above all telling her to pace herself and keep true to who she is. This will serve as the central element of the film when as an adult Julia reaches out to Lillian, now a famed American author, to smuggle money through Germany to the resistance in Europe. The smuggled money will be used to fight against the Nazis during the height of WW2, Julia tells her in what would be, unbeknownst to Lillian, their final meeting.

The film received recognition and many international accolades, including an Oscar nomination and an award for Vanessa Redgrave, who played Julia, for best female

---

[1]   LIFE Magazine, 24 May, 1963, p. 82.

supporting role. The film served to sensitize an immigrant child from Ecuador living in New York City to the plight of the Jews who, with other groups, were slaughtered in the Nazi Holocaust of WW2. However, it was Vanessa's acceptance speech during the Oscars that also became embedded in my young immigrant mind, and that provided in a very clear way the basis for my recognition of the Palestinian struggle, and the linkage of all struggles for social justice, dignity, and global human rights.

What I heard in Redgrave's words that night, amidst enormous applause and boos, was how the Palestinians' on-going fight for their territory, identity, and livelihood was not separate at all from my parents' immigrant struggle, or even from the focus of the film, i.e. fighting against racism and fascism. What I was less prepared to understand is how that short speech, just a couple of minutes long at the most, against racism, antisemitism, and fascism would be misinterpreted and used repeatedly to boycott Redgrave and Fonda, and almost destroy their artistic careers.

Perhaps it has taken this long, almost half a century, to realize that what seems obvious to a child's eye is not so readily apparent to adults, and even less to the hungry hounds of capitalism. I was delighted when I recently read Redgrave's (2018) comments about her 1978 Oscar acceptance speech, when she was given a lifetime achievement award by the Venice Film Festival: "I didn't realize that pledging to fight antisemitism and fascism was controversial. I'm learning that it is." And perhaps even harder than remembering when my understanding of the Palestinian struggle began has been realizing, during these past four decades, how hard it is for far too many of us to make the global linkage in the fight for equality and social justice.

What solidified when I heard Redgrave's simple words, and the bombastic fascist response to her support for the struggle for universal human rights, is the fact that the Holocaust and the Palestinian struggles were not the only ones already linked in my young life. In a way, that acceptance speech was one of many texts and accounts that enabled me to translate and make sense of the unequal world in which I had been born, and that was part of my own existence. Soon after that it would be Rodolfo "Corky" Gonzales' text (1967), "I am Joaquín/Yo Soy Joaquín", that would connect my experience and the Palestinian struggle to the plight of millions of undocumented Mexicans who tirelessly worked the land and formed a human migrant chain from the shores of California to Chicago's urban setting.

It was also learning in those years the story of the "Trail of Tears" that narrated the uprooting of millions of Native Americans from their homes to satisfy the hungry beast of colonialism and capitalism. And understanding how it was those same alienating forces that had centuries later made my family leave their home in Ecuador, including their land and language (my parents never learned English) to work and survive in the cold streets of Nueva York. And finally, it was that same immigrant plight, this time enacted by Irish immigrants who were treated worse than animals as they looked to make a home away from their distant shores, that entered my focus. All of these experiences made their way very early into my adolescent political framework, when I would talk until my early thirties about a geographical triangle that united Palestine, Latin America, and Ireland in the same struggle for dignity and justice.

This initial reckoning would only be further amplified when my parents moved us back to Ecuador, where I would see in the plight of the indigenous people the same oppression and repression that I had experienced as a Latino kid in New York City. And of course it was the same Ecuadorians who had suffered abuse at the hands of the colonizing North who turned around, almost naturally, and dealt out the same oppressive treatment to their national brethren without any visible remorse. This once again impressed upon my adolescent mind the equally problematic erasure that enabled them not to see the linkages that were unbearably obvious to me, both in my own experience and in the exploited labour of my immigrant parents.

However, this would be tempered by an ever growing left-leaning political movement that was sweeping through Latin America, one that would come to power towards the last decades of the twentieth century. This movement would lead to the end of the fascist dictatorships of the Southern cone, allowing progressive politics to be enacted in defense of workers and Indigenous communities throughout the Andes and Brazil, and that has ultimately provided a coherent cultural frame of artistic and musical revival in what is now known as the Nueva Trova Cubana, Música Protesta, and Música Popular Brasileira (MPB), in artists such as Mercedes Sosa, Inti Illimani, Caetano Veloso, Oswaldo Guayasamín, and Pedro Lemebel, among many others.

It was this same progressive Latin American political movement that would see in the Palestinian struggle what I had seen a couple of decades before: a struggle for justice and equality, but above all for human dignity. In this manner, it echoed what Mahatma Gandhi had claimed against the British almost a century ago: "We only wanted what you have and is our right, to be treated as you expect to be treated, as equal human beings." It was this welcome recognition that others in Latin America easily saw, that had impressed me so strongly as a child, and that had very much tempered my education, career, and life choices.

At seventeen I went against my parents' desires for me to study law because they thought it would provide me with financial stability. Instead, I opted to study anthropology in a burgeoning School of Archaeology at the ESPOL (Escuela Superior Politécnica del Litoral) in Guayaquil, that still exists today. In this choice I expressed my desire to contribute to the progressive politics that seemed right and just at that time, as they do now, and that allowed me in many ways to embody that struggle for equality, human rights, and dignity that had enlightened my imagination at such an early age. My hope was that through a lifetime of scholarship and research I would contribute and be able to give back to my Indigenous ancestors what my other ancestors, the European colonizers, had taken away from them (and from me and my family as well).

What has been harder to see, and of course hindsight is 20/20, is what that first consciousness of the Palestinian struggle and the backlash that standing for what you believe in would have in me: How seeing "*Julia*" and Redgrave's acceptance speech, and the corresponding fascist outrage, as a young ten-year-old would stay with me for the rest of my life. How it would fuel a desire to be part of that struggle and make amends for what decades, and at a time centuries, of exploitation had caused. I think very much that it was that inkling of the Palestinian cause at such an early age that contributed to many things that now are an essential part of who I am, becoming an anthropologist, coming out as a gay man, and above all always attempting to stand with myself and by my fellow brethren, whatever the cause.

"I had to do my bit", Redgrave says in her recent interview, "Everybody has to do their bit, to try and change things for the better. To advocate for what's right and not be dismayed if immediately you don't see results." I firmly believe that this is what learning about the Palestinian struggle afforded me so early in my life and continues to provide for me until this day. A reality I would find echoed in Adorno's and Horkheimer's (1944) phrase decades ago: "Only the conscious horror of destruction creates the correct relationship with the dead; unity with them because we, like them, are victims of the same condition and the same disappointed hope."

Helena de Morais Manfrinato Othman

Ph.D. student/activist, Brazil

"Engaging Myself 'Body and Soul' in the Question of Palestine: Militancy and Anthropology"

Like many Latin American people, I first learned about the Middle East from television, the news, foreign films, and soap operas. We tend to see this part of the world as a space and time distinct from the West (which we inadvertently feel part of) that is characterized by war, exoticism, veiled women, and petroleum. Prior to September 11, narratives discrediting Shi'ite Islam were commonly found in the Brazilian press, synonymous with "religious radicalism" resulting from a long-standing geopolitical interest in this subject. Naturally, after September 11 the narratives shifted to the Gulf, and Sunni Islam came to be described as a threat to Western civilization. The "Palestinian question" occasionally appeared on the radar, in newspapers or in study guides for college entrance exams in the area of geopolitics.

My own knowledge was entirely framed by the Orientalist attitudes present in television and printed media. At the same time, I was born and raised in inland São Paulo state, where there are next to no Muslims, and I only met descendants of Christian Arab families (originally from Lebanon or Syria) whose surnames like "Chalita" or "Haddad" stood out among the Italian names where I lived. Some had lost the language of their ancestors, along with contact with their country; others kept this relationship with their ancestral identity alive through cuisine and connections with local "Syrian-Lebanese" organizations.

I first visited a mosque during my undergraduate studies (also in inland São Paulo state) in social sciences in 2010, after an exploratory field trip in the city of São Paulo. This came about after a man helped my mother manoeuvre her car into a tight parking spot; he turned out to be a Libyan interpreter hired by Mesquita Brasil, Brazil's oldest mosque, who was accompanying a *sheikh* on a visit to the region. When I mentioned my research interest, Hadi told me he was willing to talk. He scribbled his email on a pamphlet about "Human Rights in Islam" that included the addresses of two Sunni entities in São Paulo. We made plans to meet near the 25 de Março shopping region, which is full of shops run by Arabs, mostly Lebanese who migrated to Brazil during the Civil War. In a café between the shopping street and what used to be a Benedictine monastery in the heart of old São Paulo, I asked my first clumsy research questions.

234 *Becoming Pro-Palestinian*

What attracted me at the time was the idea of a "fundamental antagonism" that marked media narratives on Islam and Muslim populations in contrast to the "West". This was when I encountered Edward Said's work and his critiques of Orientalism, while my ethnographic incursions demonstrated that the September 11 attacks and especially the narrative of a threat to the "Christian West" generated waves of Islamophobic and xenophobic attacks on Brazil's Muslim communities. From there, I decided to analyze the impact of these discourses on local Muslim communities and how an institutional response to violent religion-associated narratives was organized.

Sunni organizations responded to this narrative by promoting *dawa* (spreading information about Islam) to combat "mistaken" notions about Islam. Some also offered legal and psychological aid, as many members of the communities (particularly women) suffered Islamophobic attacks. The institutional responses to this problem were the focus of my undergraduate and later my Master's degrees, more specifically how three organizations mobilized strategies involving positive visibility to disassociate the image of Islam – and Muslims – from violence, mainly using the narrative of human rights.

While doing my undergraduate research and writing my thesis, I was able to visit one of these organizations, the União de Entidades Islâmicas (Union of Islamic Entities) (UNI), where I was received by two journalists responsible for the communications division, Samara and Dalila.[1] Both were leftist, and incorporated their critical perspectives into the organization's communications work. Without previous ties to the community, they arrived at UNI via Abbas,[2] a left-wing Brazilian-Palestinian activist for the "Palestinian cause" whom they met while writing their undergraduate thesis. Their project described the experiences of Palestinian refugees who migrated to Brazil via a solidarity resettlement program in Mogi das Cruzes,[3] in the greater São Paulo area. During this research they met Abbas, the founder and leader of the Movimento Palestina para Tod@s (Palestine for Everyone Movement, MOP@T), and when they completed their thesis they joined the organization.

During my Master's program, I moved to São Paulo to carry out my research. I contacted Samara via Facebook and she invited me to a MOP@T meeting.

As a newcomer to São Paulo, I was eager to expand my contacts in a field I only knew from afar. The little I had absorbed through interviews and reading on the Palestinian issue had stirred an intellectual and political affinity. My incursion into MOP@T helped me gain access to the networks of Muslims in São Paulo, the Palestinian cause, and leftist activities in the capital, contributing to my research relationships during this time. This period was marked by debates, trainings, street demonstrations, and projects. MOP@T was working to link the Palestinian question to Brazil's political

---

[1] Pseudonyms.
[2] Pseudonym.
[3] After the fall of Saddam Hussein and the American invasion, the Sunni Palestinian population was persecuted in Iraq and sought refuge outside the country in refugee camps. One camp, Al Ruwaished, was on Jordan's border in the wilderness; its occupants were gradually relocated to countries in Europe and the Americas, and Brazil received its last 100 refugees. In 2007, just over 100 Palestinian refugees came to Brazil, where they settled in several Brazilian cities including Mogi das Cruzes, in greater São Paulo.

struggles, since connections to local agendas seemed the obvious way to generate more supporters.

In June 2013, São Paulo was rocked by massive street demonstrations against new increases in public transport fares, placing urban reform at the centre of many leftist political coalitions. MOP@T participated in the protests, and connections made during the protests brought it together with collective housing movements such as Terra Livre (Free Land). In broad terms, a housing movement is based on access to decent housing for low-income families, residents in areas of risk, as well as to land reform, urban reform, and access to the city centre, where urban resources such as health, work, education, and leisure are concentrated. One means of political action by these housing movements is to occupy legally and physically abandoned buildings and land in an activity called *ocupação urbana*.

At the same time, the collective learned that Palestinian refugee families from the Syrian conflict were living in the city in precarious boarding houses. Palestinian refugees from Syria have been arriving in Brazil since 2014, as refugee camps such as Sbeineh and Yarmouk were bombed. The idea of bringing them to live at one of the Terra Livre buildings[4] came about in this context. It did not take much time for the news to spread, and two months later there were sixty Palestinians living on four continuous floors, while Brazilian families lived on the other four.

This composition of residents came about through a partnership between the Terra Livre housing movement and MOP@T. During an assembly marking the foundation of the settlement, one Terra Livre activist proposed it be named as a tribute to the Palestinian militant Leila Khaled, which was approved by the group as a whole. Initially, we all (to various degrees) tried to meet the immediate needs related to getting the families housed and internal organization. One of the first of these activities was organizing an event to generate political support and donations, with debates on housing, the war in Syria, and Palestinian refugees.

The event, called Jornadas de Yarmouk, coincided with a series of news stories about the refugees fleeing to Europe, which included a photo of a drowned Syrian toddler named Aylan Kurdi. The image had widespread percussions that eventually impacted the event, bringing several hundred participants: not only those connected to the social movements and the NGOs, but neighbours and Brazilians expressing solidarity.

The donations, visits, and interviews continued for another two months, shaping the relationships established between the Palestinians, activists, and Brazilian residents. External demands initially overburdened the activists and drew attention away from the internal construction of the planned occupation. Discomfort then spread among the Brazilian residents, who were almost always excluded from the acts of solidarity and journalistic interest. Finally, the constant interviews, with invasive questions about war-related losses, began to become troublesome for the refugees.

---

[4] The movement generally seeks out empty, derelict, abandoned buildings that are decades overdue on property taxes. They often belong to failed companies, and are auctioned along with other properties to pay off old debts. The abandoned building in question belongs to TELESP, a private Brazilian company that is now defunct.

Political expectations in the movements were still high at that time. Meetings were held to organize trainings about the respective forms of action and struggle, and to organize workshops and classes for the residents. Most residents were not politically militant in any way, which is normal in occupations. The aim of the movement was to bring the residents into the struggle, explaining its operations and expanding the ranks of activists, as well as engaging them in the long, drawn-out struggle for the building. In the case of the *ocupação* Leila Khaled, there was an additional objective: to raise awareness among the Brazilian families about the refugees and the war that brought them to Brazil. Meanwhile, MOP@T's goal was to engage the Palestinians in the collective and rearticulate the agenda related to the refugees' right of return, which was established in UN Resolution 194 but never achieved after they were driven off their lands in 1948.

Up to this time, I was very excited about these developments, but it hadn't occurred to me to do research there. I was about to conclude my master's degree and was working on a doctorate project that was an extension of my thesis, and almost entirely unrelated to my work as activist. My eventual doctoral research began when I saw the enormous impact of war-related photography (namely the photo of Aylan Kurdi) that brought broader attention and sympathy from the Brazilian public.

But most of the donations went toward the refugees, who were also the focus of interviews and solidarity efforts. This selective humanitarian aid transformed the *ocupação* Leila Khaled into an extremely volatile environment, causing mistrust and conflicts to emerge among the residents.

Another challenge was communication. Even though we did not speak Arabic, I and other MOP@T activists helped communicate with the press, organize the Portuguese course, with efforts related to health, school enrollment, and collecting the proposals for work and donations that were offered on the occupation's official website. The political aspirations of the plan were abandoned to deal instead with conflicts and misunderstandings, with the Brazilian residents, as well as a lack of Palestinian engagement in the housing movement's activities.

My relationship with the Palestinians was limited because of my position in MOP@T and my near-total ignorance of their language. The younger people's English was limited (as was mine) and the older people were inaccessible because I did not speak Arabic. I was also concerned that I might be seen as just one more of the countless students, researchers, and journalists who were at their doors every day asking questions.

Something that was quickly made clear to me (and which I had ignored until this time) was the vast distance between the left and the Palestinians' reality. There was an idealized perception of the Palestinian people as in line with leftist political ideals, aesthetically as well as politically. The image of a fighter wearing a *keffiyeh* scarf (exemplified by Leila Khaled or Yasser Arafat) aligned with the political imagination about conflicts occurring elsewhere. The Palestinians in this popular imagery did not have their own cultural or religious sensibilities, nor did they question governments that the Brazilian left believed to be "anti-imperial"; the "ideal Palestinian" was in line with the agendas of the left and its international solidarity.

The Palestinians in Sao Paulo often resisted this type of classification, which in turn was interpreted as hostile or misinformed behaviour by the activists, who zealously upheld their ideals of right and wrong. I noticed a certain distance between the revolutionary icons of the Brazilian left and the Palestinians, who had a sharply critical perception of political movements and humanitarian organizations based on their own experiences in the refugee camps in Syria. This critical perception gradually undermined my activist certainties and shifted my position as a researcher.

Around May 2016, the situation changed. With some friends from MOP@T and four Palestinians I joined the staff of a Palestinian bar/restaurant created by Abbas. Even though they did not speak a lot of Portuguese, and I spoke even less Arabic, we managed to establish a relationship by working together every day. In this environment, our broken dialogues allowed me to better understand their experiences. It was the first time I heard directly from them that they did not like the expressions of pity they received from the Brazilians, or how exposed they felt when portrayed as refugees in Brazil.

Now, as I finally began to build a relationship with them, I realized that using any conventional scientifically objective approach for research would be useless. Borrowing their critiques of the images that objectified them, I cast a critical eye at the social movements and journalists whom I considered to be creating their own "platforms" and "political agendas". I could not help but talk about "selective solidarity", which turned the Palestinians into precarious and vulnerable bodies worthy of compassion, while making the Brazilians in the occupation invisible.

I needed to give up my former elaborate ideas of the Terra Livre (Free Land) and MOP@T in creating a certain notion of political and cohesive collectivity while we developed our hybrid relations and broken and imperfect communication. I accepted that before we could communicate in Portuguese or Arabic, we would use the political languages of the left, of work, and of food.

While my Master's research experience had opened the door to my engagement with the Palestinian question, my doctorate allowed me to be part of the world and life of the Palestinians. Although all knowledge is embodied and politicized, I took on the unique requirements of this research, which involved a series of ethical and political commitments to my interlocutors, and incorporation of their critiques of the objectifying practices of researchers, journalists, and activists (Asad, 1973).[5] My "becoming pro-Palestinian" began with media imagery and ignorance of the research topic, and later involved activism in an international solidarity movement.

As an activist, I participated in the *ocupação* Leila Khaled and met Palestinian refugee families, where I decided to conduct my doctoral research. This intensive experience and especially the Palestinian people I met challenged the parameters of international leftist activism, as well as the limits of anthropological practice itself.

---

[5]   Asad, Talal (ed.), *Introduction. Anthropology and the Colonial Encounter*, New York, Humanities Press, 1973.

Natalia Revale

Visual artist/teacher/activist, Argentina

Being able to feel any injustice against anyone, anywhere in the world, that is the quality of a revolutionary.

Perhaps this phrase written by Che Guevara can in some way illustrate the reason for feeling part of a just cause, in this case, the Palestinian struggle.

I am of Jewish origin, and that somehow resonated with me historically, the family discussions, the tensions, the binarisms. I understood as a young woman that I could feel empathy with the Palestinian people, and not for that reason renounce my roots, but rather the opposite. There is a land that unites us, and from Latin America and Argentina we could somehow make visible a conflict that erased the existence of a people from the map.

In that sense, artistic practices were the place from which I could express this idea.

Murals for Palestine was an initiative that I proposed to the culture section of the Embassy of Palestine. The project consisted of proposing to muralist groups to carry out murals for Palestine on public roads in the different provinces of the country. It was articulated with neighbourhood cultural spaces and neighbours who wanted to join the initiative so that I would also have local support. The embassy helped by providing paint to make the murals.

In 2016, I organized the exhibition "Palestinian Position" in the cultural space of Radio La Tribu, which has a bar where we organize exhibitions. Artists from all over the country converged there. The exhibition was accompanied by a Palestinian cinema cycle and various talks.

In a part of the graphic campaign called "We Want Ourselves Alive", we made an engraving where three women were represented, one Palestinian, one from the Mapuche people, and another from Kurdistan. Art can articulate, unite, bring together what is most complicated in everyday life.

Graphics, murals, poetry put in images and words, symbols of struggle, that in their insistence on naming and multiplying naming form an exercise of active memory for a people that exists and resists.

Name Palestine!

Pronounce the word. Assimilate its resonance.

To think of Palestine, to dream of it, as those do who think of returning to their land.

To feel Palestine, deep down, like any other injustice.

Living Palestine, going through the bodies.

Paint Palestine, flame red, olive green.

Draw Palestine, outline a new horizon.

Record Palestine, footprints on the ground.

The Palestinian position: inhabit it.

Contributors

Allen, Lori is an anthropologist at SOAS University of London, writer, and editor. She is author of *The Rise and Fall of Human Rights: Cynicism and Politics in Occupied Palestine* and *A History of False Hope: Investigative Commissions in Palestine*, Stanford, Stanford University Press, 2013, 2020.

Ang, Dr Swee Chai is the first woman orthopaedic surgeon appointed to St Bartholomew's, London, in its 1,123-year history. In 1982 she was head of trauma and orthopaedic service in Gaza Hospital during the Sabra Shatila Massacre and wrote about it in her book *From Beirut to Jerusalem* (2007). She co-founded Medical Aid for Palestinians, which continues to serve the Palestinians in Exile and Occupation.

Baumgarten, Helga was born in Stuttgart (Germany) in 1947 and is a political scientist at Birzeit University in Occupied Palestine. Her last book, *No Peace for Palestine: The Long War Against Gaza, Occupation and Resistance*, was published by Promedia in Vienna.

Benevides, O. Hugo was born in Guayaquil, Ecuador, and grew up as an immigrant in the United States. He is currently an anthropology professor at Fordham University, and lives in Brooklyn with his partner of thirty years and two adorable felines.

Borhani, Hadi is Assistant Professor at University of Tehran. He holds a Ph.D. from the European Center for Palestine Studies (ECPS) in the University of Exeter, United Kingdom. His book, *Textbooks on Israel-Palestine*, has been published by Bloomsbury Academic.

Coletivo Vozes Judaicas por Libercatao:i) **Shajar Goldwaser** is a Jerusalemite with Jewish citizenship, raised between Buenos Aires and São Paulo, who actively participates in youth Zionist educational activities inside the Jewish community. He has a degree in International Relations from PUC-SP, and is a member of the SEDQ International Network. ii) **Bianca Neumann Marcossi** holds a Bachelor's degree in History (USP) and a Master's degree in Social Anthropology at Museu Nacional/UFRJ. Her research focused on the process of producing the belief in a "left-wing Zionism", investigating its discourses, troubles, and limitations in the Brazilian progressive scene. iii) **Juliana Esquenazi Muniz** is from Rio de Janeiro and works in the film and audiovisual sectors. She directed the short film "I Prefer Not to Be Identified" (2018), along with the movements of mothers and families of victims of state violence. Currently, she is a Master's student at Universidade de São Paulo (USP), studying audiovisual culture in the Zapatista context. iv) **Bruno Huberman** is a Professor of International Relations at the Pontifical Catholic University of São Paulo (PUC-SP), Brazil. He earned his Ph.D. in International Relations from the San Tiago Dantas Program (UNESP/UNICAMP/PUC-SP), Brazil, and was a Visiting Research Student in the Department of Development Studies at SOAS, University of London, between 2018 and 2019. His research focuses on the political economy of Israeli settler colonialism in Jerusalem. v) **Yuri Haasz**, born in Haifa and raised near Tel Aviv, moved to Brazil at fifteen. He holds an MA in IR from ICU (Tokyo) and an MA in Social Sciences from the University of Chicago (US). Founder of FFIPP Brazil (2012) and founding member of SEDQ International Network, he works with dialogic facilitation methods of difficult conversations involving identity, culture, and power asymmetries.

Dadoo, Suraya is a South African writer and author. She is a regular contributor and commentator on Palestine in South African media, and presents educational workshops on the Israeli occupation of Palestine. She is the co-author of a comprehensive reference book called *Why Israel? The Anatomy of Zionist Apartheid: A South African Perspective* (Porcupine Press, 2013), and is currently working on a youth guide to understanding the Israeli occupation of Palestine.

Deeg, Sophia grew up in Bonn in the 1950s and '60s, and studied literature, philosophy, and literary translation at Munich's Ludwig Maximilian Universität. She has worked as a teacher, and later as a translator, editor, and journalist. She is nowadays retired, though not from activism. She lives in France.

Donini, Elisabetta did research in Elementary Particles Theory. The 1968 turmoil led her to privilege studies about science and society relations according to a Marxian approach during the '70s. She then committed herself to feminist critiques of science from the '80s until now.

Esack, Farid is Professor and Senior Researcher at the Johannesburg Institute for Advanced Studies. He has taught at Harvard, Amsterdam, Hamburg, and Gadjah Mada universities. He is a former President of the International Qur'anic Studies Association and Chairperson of Boycott Divestment and Sanctions-South Africa.

Frere, Jane is an artist, born in Scotland, educated at the Slade School of Fine Art, University College London. She has exhibited in galleries, private collections, and permanent displays. Her "Return of the Soul" installation, created in Palestinian refugee camps, was shown in East Jerusalem, Lebanon, Jordan, and Scotland.

Giannou, Christos was born in Canada in 1949, the son of Greek immigrants. From 1980–90, he was a surgeon with the Palestine Red Crescent Society in Lebanon. He went on to work for the International Committee of the Red Cross, becoming Head Surgeon from 1998 to 2005. He was awarded the Star of Palestine by the

Executive Committee of the PLO in 1987 and as inducted a Member of the Order of Canada in 1990 for his humanitarian work in the Palestinian refugee camps of Lebanon.

Grorud, Mats was born in 1976 and is a Norwegian animation filmmaker. He premiered with his feature "The Tower" in 2018, a film based on his experiences living for a year in the Palestinian camp Bourj El Barajneh in Beirut in the early 2000s. His films are social and political in content.

Hass, Amira has been reporter for *Haaretz* on Israeli occupation in the West Bank and Gaza since the early '90s. She lived in Gaza between 1993 and 1997; since then in El-Bireh. She is author of *Drinking the Sea at Gaza* and of two compilations of articles for *Haaretz* and the Italian weekly *Internazionale*. Born in Jerusalem in 1956, she studied History in Jerusalem and Tel Aviv universities. She was already active in left-wing groups in high school.

Heacock, Roger and his wife, Laura Wick, lived in Palestine for thirty-five years, where they raised their three children, until deported by the Occupation. Roger was and continues to be a Professor of History at Birzeit University, teaching in the Ph.D. program in the social sciences.

Hendriks, Bertus is a journalist specializing in the Middle East, was Senior Middle East Editor at Radio Netherlands Worldwide and Head of its Arabic Service, and also a regular analyst of Middle Eastern Affairs for Dutch Public Radio and TV Home Service stations. From 2008 to 2021 he was an Associate Fellow at the Netherlands Institute of International Relations, Clingendael.

Hussain, Ilias M. is Professor at the School of Gandhian Thought and Development Studies and Dean of the Faculty of Social Sciences, Mahatma Gandhi University, Kerala. Prior to Joining MGU, he was Professor at the Centre for Contemporary Middle East Studies, Southern Denmark University and Professor and Director at India-Arab Cultural Centre, Jamia Millia Islamia, New Delhi. Areas of his research interest include Gandhian Philosophy, the Palestine Question, Islam in South Asia, Religion and Visual Culture, Government and Politics in the Arab World, and South Asian Diaspora in the GCC Countries.

Jeenah, Na'eem is Executive Director of the Afro-Middle East Centre; Advisory Board member of the Centre for Africa-China Studies; Deputy Chair of the Southern African Catholic Bishops' Conference's Denis Hurley Peace Institute; and Board member of the Tambo-Dadoo Palestine Legal Fund. His publications include *Pretending Democracy: Israel, an Ethnocratic State*.

Johnson, Penny worked at Birzeit University from 1982 for the University's Human Rights Committee and was a founding member of the University's Institute of Women's Studies. She is currently on the editorial committee of the *Jerusalem Quarterly*. With

Raja Shehadeh, she edited and contributed to *Seeking Palestine: New Palestinian Writing on Exile and Home* (Interlink, 2013) which won the 2013 Palestine Book Award and *Shifting Sands: The Unraveling of the Old Order in the Middle East* (Profile, 2015). Her latest book is *Companions in Conflict: Animals in Occupied Palestine* (Melville House, New York, 2019).

Kanafani, Anni was born in Denmark in 1935, graduated in Early Childhood Education from Copenhagen Teacher Training College in 1956, worked as a kindergarten teacher in Denmark and Norway. She travelled to Syria and Lebanon in 1961 to "discover" the Palestinian people's tragedy and struggle. Was introduced to Ghassan Kanafani, worked in a kindergarten in Beirut, and subsequently married Ghassan. After his assassination in 1972 she and friends established the Ghassan Kanafani Cultural Foundation in his memory. She runs kindergartens, libraries, and art centres in six Palestinian refugee camps in Lebanon.

Lascaris, Dmitri is a human rights and class actions lawyer based in Montreal. He has been recognized professionally as one of the top 25 lawyers in Canada.

Manfrinato, Helena de Morais Othman is a Brazilian anthropologist and activist, mostly in two local organizations in São Paulo (2013–2017 and 2017–2020). She is currently finishing her thesis at São Paulo University about a housing movement, Palestinian refugees from Syria, and humanitarian solidarity. She is a member of the Center for Latin American Palestinian Studies, Middle East Studies Center (UFF), and Religions in the Contemporary World (USP/CEBRAP).

Maurer, Monica was born in Munich, Germany, studied Journalism and Sociology, and worked for German newspapers and the US magazine *Ramparts*. In 1967 she started to write and direct features for television, and since 1972 has been an independent filmmaker and producer, who has worked with the Palestine Red Crescent Society and the Palestinian Cinema Institution (Beirut), and made ten documentaries on Palestine. She lives in Rome and continues to lecture and work as consultant and curator for festivals promoting Palestinian cinematography. She is a member of the Audiovisual Archive of the Working Class and Democratic movement and curates the monthly *CINEFORUM PALESTINA*.

McDowall, David is author of *Lebanon: A Conflict of Minorities* (Minority Rights Group, 1983); *The Kurds* (MRG, 1985); *The Palestinians* (MRG, 1987); *Palestine and Israel: The Uprising and Beyond* (I. B. Tauris, 1989); *The Kurds: A Nation Denied* (Minority Rights Publications, 1992); *The Palestinians: The Road to Nationhood* (Minority Rights Publications, 1994); "Clarity or Ambiguity? The Withdrawal Clause of Resolution 242", *International Affairs*, 90:6, November 2014; and *A Modern History of the Kurds* (I.B. Tauris, 1st edition 1996, 4th edition 2021).

McKenna, Dr Philomena is an Irish physician who has worked as a general practitioner in Rashidiya refugee camp, as an anaesthetist in Beirut, and a general practitioner in

Shatila in 1982. Returning to anaesthetic training in London, she joined the board of MAP. She is currently a member of the IPSC.

Morgantini, Luisa was born 1940 in Italy. She is a lifelong defender of human rights, a trade unionist for over thirty years, the first woman elected to leadership in a male dominated union, the Federation of Metalworkers and was in charge of the Union's International department from 1985–1999. She is committed to the liberation movements of South-Africa, Angola, Mozambique, Algeria, Vietnam, Argentina, Brazil, Chile, Salvador, and Nicaragua, and is spokesperson of the Italian Peace Association. She is a founder of the Women in Black movement against war and violence. Elected to the EU parliament in 1999, she chaired the EUP delegation to Palestine, and was elected EU Vice President. She has been committed to Palestine since the Sabra and Chatila massacre. After retirement she founded AssoPacePalestina, a nationally-based organization.

Naramoto, Eisuke was born in Japan in 1941. He has taught modern and contemporary history of the Middle East at Hosei University and Dokkyo University near Tokyo, after working as a news correspondent for the *Mainichi Shinbun*.

Öztürk, Sanem was born in Ankara, Turkey in 1979. She is a sociologist/activist based in İstanbul, received her sociology degree from Middle East Technical University and Master's degree from Mimar Sinan Fine Arts University. She taught at Marmara University Fine Arts Faculty, writing a Master's thesis on "Internet as a Trans-Border Space of Communication and Palestinian Refugees' Construction of Social Identity" (2009). She is currently a Ph.D. candidate at Marmara University, Institute Research of Middle East and Islamic Countries. She volunteered for Women's Solidarity Foundation (KADAV) in 2011 and worked for the foundation on projects related to gender-based violence, conducting workshops on gender for Turkish and refugee women.

Pappe, Ilan is Director of the European Center for Palestine Studies at the University of Exeter. He has published twenty books so far, among them *The Ethnic Cleansing of Palestine* and *On Palestine* (with Noam Chomsky). His two most recent books are *Our Vision for Liberation* (with Ramzy Baroud) and the *Palestine Historical Dictionary* (with Jonny Mansour).

Prashad, Vijay is director of Tricontinental Institute for Social Research and Chief Correspondent for Globetrotter. His most recent book, with Noam Chomsky, is *The Withdrawal*. He is Non-Resident Senior Fellow of Chongyang Institute for Financial Studies Renmin University of China.

Rahbek, Birgitte has a BA in French, Magister in Cultural Sociology, and a Ph.D. in Education, and is author of several books and numerous articles, as well as editor at the Danish Broadcasting Corporation, translator of books from English and French into Danish, and conflict mediator for the Danish police.

Rajan, Zahid is a publisher by profession and coordinator of Kenyans for Palestine. He is a Kenyan by nationality and Executive Editor of AwaaZ www.awaazmagazine.com, director of Zand Graphics Ltd www.zandgraphics.com, and Festival director of the Samosa Festival www.samosafestival.com.

Rees, Stuart is former Professor of Social Work & Social Policy at the University of Sydney, a human rights activist in several countries, co-founder of Sydney University's Centre for Peace & Conflict Studies, and founder/director of the Sydney Peace Foundation. He received an honorary doctorate from Soka University, Japan (1998) and their "award of highest honor" for service to world peace; also the Order of Australia for service to international relations (2005); and the Jerusalem (Al Quds) Peace Prize (2019).

Revale, Natalia is a visual artist, professor, and activist. Her artistic practices are framed in public spaces and areas; she is linked through informal education and social work to projects around memory and human rights. She is also a founding member of the collectives Arde! Collective Action Art (2002–2006 and 2011–2014), Popular Sculpture (2006–2009), Muralismo NómadeNómade en Resistencia (2014–current), and Graphic campaign Vivas nos quemos (We Want Ourselves Alive) (2015–current).

Ryantori is an Associate Professor of International Relations at Prof. Dr. Moestopo (Beragama) University, Jakarta. A native Indonesian, he was born in Jakarta. He is also the Executive Director of the Indonesian Society for Middle East Studies (ISMES). He graduated from Padjadjaran University, Bandung in 2018 with a Doctoral Degree in International Relations.

Saraste, Leena born in Finland, is an independent photojournalist, artist and researcher with a Ph.D. in Art History. She taught in universities from the early 1970s, and served as head of the Department of Photography at the University of Art and Design (now Aalto University). She has published several books on photography and photographic volumes, and exhibited widely, including "Beirut – a Farewell in August" in 1983; her retrospective exhibition was shown in 2015 in The Finnish Museum of Photography. She has been twice awarded the State Prize of Finnish Photography.

Sayigh, Rosemary is an oral historian and anthropologist, with a Ph.D. from Hull University in 1979. She is author of *Palestinians: From Peasants to Revolutionaries* (Zed Books, 1979); *Too Many Enemies: The Palestinian Experience in Lebanon* (1st ed Zed Books, 1994), and the eBook *Voices: Palestinian Women Narrate Displacement* (2007). She is Retired Visiting Lecturer at CAMES, the American University of Beirut.

Silver, Rafi was born in the United States and migrated to Israel in 1971, where he was a member of a kibbutz, served in the army, and after his military service became a social worker. A long time peace activist and community organizer, Silver was involved with the Israeli Committee Against House Demolition as well as Amnesty International. He left Israel in 2001 and moved to Montreal, Canada, where he now resides.

Suzuki, Hiroyuki is a Project Associate Professor at the University of Tokyo Centre for Middle Eastern Studies (UTCMES) and Sultan Qaboos Chair in Middle Eastern Studies. He has volunteered with several civil groups, and he has assisted in organizing public seminars and open lectures regarding Middle Eastern issues.

Takkenberg, Lex is Senior Advisor on the Question of Palestine at ARDD, and non-resident Professor of Humanitarian Affairs at Fordham University. From 1989 to 2019, he worked with UNRWA, most recently at its Amman headquarters as the agency's first Chief Ethics Officer, previously as UNRWA's General Counsel, Director of Operations, and (Deputy) Field Director in Gaza and Syria. He obtained a Doctorate in International Law from the University of Nijmegen in 1997 after defending his doctoral dissertation on *The Status of Palestinian Refugees in International Law*, later published by Oxford University Press. A new version of the book, co-authored with Francesca Albanese, was published by OUP in 2020.

Van Teeffelen, Toine is an anthropologist with a Ph.D. in discourse analysis from the University of Amsterdam. Besides guiding visiting groups, he works as an educator and project developer at the Arab Educational Institute in Bethlehem, where he lives with his wife Mary Morcos.

Wallace, Naomi: "I don't believe I learned anything in high school about Palestine and the Middle East. In the 1970s in Kentucky even to say the word 'Palestine' meant that you were some left-wing nut sympathetic to terrorists. I learned about Palestine mostly from my mother, and then from my own studies. And through the Palestinian struggle, I learned more about racism, colonialism, and war. In the '90s I organized a trip to Palestine with a group of US playwrights to connect with our colleagues in the Occupied Territories. I have written a play, 'The Fever Chart: Three Visons of the Middle East'; two of the plays are about Palestine. With Lisa Schlesinger and Abdel Fattah Abu-Srour I wrote 'Twenty One Positions: A Cartographic Dream of the Middle East' but the Guthrie Theatre's dramaturg accused us of 'supporting terrorism' and they declined to publish it."

Wakim, Janfrie is a mother of four and grandmother to eleven *mokopuna* (grandchildren); a science graduate, she shared ownership of community pharmacies with her late husband. She is now retired from work in education. Since her student days she has been active in social justice organizations, and was a founding member of the Child Poverty Action Group NZ. She revels in the company of her *whānau* (family), and currently lives in Tāmaki Makaurau, Auckland.

Wieser, Klaudia is a Ph.D. candidate at the Department of Social and Cultural Anthropology, University of Vienna. The working title of her dissertation is *Epistemologies of Liberation: Palestinian Affairs in Revolutionary Beirut*. She is currently a project member of *Know War – Knowledge Production in Times of Flight and War: Developing Common Grounds for Research in/on Syria* (https://www.know-war.net) and a volunteer at Dokustelle – a documentation and counselling center combatting anti-Muslim racism and Islamophobia in Austria (https://dokustelle.at).

Further reading

Abdel Jawad, Saleh (2007), "Zionist Massacres: The Creation of the Palestinian Refugee Problem in the 1948 War", in *Israel and the Palestinian Refugees*, eds Eyal Benvenisti, Chaim Gans, and Sari Hanafi, Berlin, Springer.

Abdo, Nahla (2014) *Captive Revolution: Palestinian Women's Anti-Colonial Struggle Within the Israeli Prison System*, London, Pluto Press.

Abdo, Nahla and Nur Masalha, eds (2018), *An Oral History of the Palestinian Nakba*, London, Zed Books.

Abulhawa, Susan (2010), *Mornings in Jenin*, London, Bloomsbury.

Abu-Saad, Ismael (2008) "Present Absentees: The Arab School Curriculum in Israel as a Tool for De-Educating Indigenous Palestinians", *Holy Land Studies* 7:1, May.

Abu Sitta, Salman (2017), *Mapping My Return: A Palestinian Memoir*, Cairo, New York, American University of Cairo Press.

Alareer, Refaat, ed. (2014), *Gaza Writes Back: Short Stories from Young Writers in Gaza, Palestine*, Charlottesville, Just World Publishing.

Albinese, Francesca and Lex Takkenberg (2020), *Palestinian Refugees in International Law*, Oxford, Oxford University Press.

Al-Hardan, Anaheed (2016), *Palestinians in Syria: Nakba Memories of Shattered Communities*, New York, Columbia University Press.

Allan, Diana (2014), *Refugees of the Revolution: Experiences of Palestinian Exile*, Stanford, Stanford University Press.

Allan, Diana, ed. (2021), *Voices of the Nakba: A Living History of Palestine*, London, Pluto Press.

Allen, Lori (2021), *A History of False Hope: Investigative Commissions in Palestine*, Stanford, Stanford University Press.

Anziska, Seth, (2018), *Preventing Palestine: A Political History from Camp David to Oslo*, Princeton and Oxford, Princeton University Press.

Aouragh, Miriyam (2011), *Palestine Online: Transnationalism, the Internet and the Construction of Identity*, London and New York, I. B. Tauris.

Benvenisti, Meron (2000), *Sacred Landscape: The Buried Landscape of the Holy Land Since 1948*, Berkeley, University of California Press.

Blumenthal, Max (2013), *Goliath: Life and Loathing in Gaza*, New York, Nation Books.

Blumenthal, Max (2015), *The 51 Day War: Ruin and Resistance in Gaza*, London and New York, Verso Books.

Brenner, Lenni (1984), *The Iron Wall: Zionist Revisionism from Jabotinsky to Shamir*, London, Zed Books.

Brynen, Rex (1990), *Sanctuary and Survival: The PLO in Lebanon*, Boulder, Westview and London, Pinter Publishers.

Dunsky, Marda (2008), *Pens and Swords: How the American Mainstream Media Reports the Israeli-Palestinian Conflict*, New York, Columbia University Press.

Feldman, Keith (2015), *A Shadow Over Palestine: The Imperial Life of Race in America*, Minneapolis, University of Minnesota Press.

Finkelstein, Norman (2000), *The Holocaust Industry: Reflections on the Exploitation of Jewish Suffering*, London, New York, Verso.

Graham-Brown, Sarah (1980), *Palestinians and Their Society, 1880–1946: A Photographic Essay*, London, New York, Quartet Books.

Gresh, Alain (1985), *The PLO: The Struggle Within*, London, Zed Books.

Haugbolle, Sune and Pelle Valetin Olsen (2023), "Emergence of Palestine as a Global Cause", *Middle East Critique* 32:1, pp. 129–148.

Hughes, Matthew (2019), *Britain's Pacification of Palestine: The British Army, the Colonial State, and the Arab Revolt 1936–1939*, Cambridge, Cambridge University Press.

Irfan, Ann (2019), "Educating Palestinian Refugees: The Origins of UNRWA's Unique School System", *Journal of Refugee Studies* 34:3.

Jegic, Denijal (2019), *Trans/Intifada: The Politics and Poetics of Intersectional Resistance*, Heidelberg, Universitatslag WINTER.

Khalili, Laleh (2007), *Heroes and Martyrs of Palestine: The Politics of National Commemoration*, Cambridge, New York, Cambridge University Press.

Masalha, Nur (1992), *Expulsion of the Palestinians: The Concept of "Transfer" in Zionist Political Thought, 1882–1948*, Beirut, Institute for Palestine Studies.

Masalha, Nur (2018), *Palestine: A Four Thousand Year History*, London, Zed Books.

McDowall, David (1975), *The Palestinians*, London, The Minority Rights Group.

Pappe, Ilan (2006), *The Ethnic Cleansing of Palestine*, London, Oneworld.

Sa'di, Ahmad H. and Lila Abu-Lughod, eds (2007), *Nakba: Palestine, 1948, and the Claims of Memory*, New York, Columbia University Press.

Sayigh, Rosemary (1979), *The Palestinians: From Peasants to Revolutionaries*, London, Zed Books.

Sayigh, Yezid (1997), *Armed Struggle and the Search for State: The Palestinian National Movement 1949–1993*, Washington, Institute for Palestine Studies/Oxford, Clarendon Press.

Schiocchet, Leonardo (2022), *Living in Refuge: Ritualization and Religiosity in a Christian and a Muslim Palestinian Refugee Camp in Lebanon*, transcript Verlag ielefeld.

Sharif, Regina (1983), *Non-Jewish Zionism: Its Roots in Western History*, London, Zed Press.

Shehadeh, Raja (2020), *When the Bulbul Stopped Singing: Life in Palestine During an Israeli Siege*, Hanover, Steerforth Press.

Smith, Barbara (1993), *The Roots of Separatism in Palestine: British Economic Policy 1920–1929*, New York and London, I. B. Tauris.

Suleiman, Yasir ed. (2016), *Being Palestinian: Personal Reflections on Palestinian Identity in the Diaspora*, Edinburgh, Edinburgh University Press.

Tamari, Salim (2011), *Year of the Locust: A Soldier's Diary and the Erasure of Palestine's Ottoman Past*, Berkeley, University of California Press.

Turki, Fawaz (1972), *The Disinherited: Journal of a Palestinian Exile*, New York, Monthly Review Press.

Zureik, Elia, David Lyon, and Yasmeen Abu-Laban, eds (2010), *Surveillance and Control in Israel/Palestine: Population, Territory and Power*, New York, Routledge.